GLOBAL TYRANNY
...STEP BY STEP

GLOBAL TYRANNY
...STEP BY STEP

The United Nations and the Emerging New World Order

by
William F. Jasper

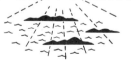

WESTERN ISLANDS

PUBLISHERS
APPLETON, WISCONSIN

First Printing .... December 1992
Second Printing .... March 1993

Published by
Western Islands
Post Office Box 8040
Appleton, Wisconsin 54913
(414) 749-3786

Printed in the United States of America
Library of Congress Catalog Card Number: 92-081764
ISBN: 0-88279-135-4

To Carmen,
Jonathan and Christopher,
and my father and mother,
with love and gratitude

Contents

Introduction

America and the world stand on the brink of one of the most perilous epochs in this planet's history. According to the purveyors of conventional wisdom, communism is dead, the Cold War is over, and the greatest threats to world peace and security are rampant nationalism, inequitable wealth distribution, overpopulation, and environmental degradation. Yet the threat to a just world peace and comity among nations and peoples comes not from political fragmentation, ozone holes, greenhouse gases, an over-abundance of people, a shortage of natural resources, or even from the frequently offered scenarios of "rogue" elements in the former USSR acquiring control of nuclear weapons.

The true, imminent danger to America and to all nations seeking peace and good will stems from widespread acceptance of the monstrous falsehood that in order to live in an "interdependent" world, all nation-states must yield their sovereignty to the United Nations. This lie is given dignity by other lies, chief of which is that Soviet totalitarianism has been buried forever.[1] A too wide acceptance of these dangerous falsehoods is resulting in: 1) a massive transfer of wealth from the taxpayers in the West to the still-socialist governments of the East that remain under the control of "former" communists; 2) the gradual but accelerating merger or "convergence" of the U.S. and Russia through increasing economic, political, social, and military agreements and arrangements; and 3) the rapidly escalating transfer of power — military, regulatory, and taxing — to the UN. Unless the fiction underlying these developments is exposed, national suicide and global rule by an all-powerful world government are inevitable.

"The Bush Administration," *Time* magazine noted on September 17, 1990, "would like to make the U.N. a cornerstone of its plans to construct a New World Order."[2] That observation merely stated the obvious. In his speech to the nation and the world on September 11, 1990, Mr. Bush stated: "Out of these troubled times, our fifth objective — a new world order — can emerge...." He proceeded to an-

ix

nounce his hopes for "a United Nations that performs as envisioned by its founders."[3] It became abundantly clear to veteran students of "world order" politics that a major new push for world government had begun. Only a few years ago, any such attempt would have flopped miserably. During the 1970s and 80s, the UN's record as an enclave of spies, a sinkhole of corrupt spendthrifts, and an anti-American propaganda forum for terrorists, Third World dictators, and Communist totalitarians, had thoroughly tarnished its carefully manufactured image as mankind's "last best hope for peace."

From 1959, when the UN could boast an 87 percent approval rating, the annual Gallup Poll showed a continuous decline in popularity for the organization. By 1971, a Gallup survey reported that only 35 percent of the American people thought the UN was doing a good job. By 1976, Gallup claimed that the support had dropped to 33 percent. In 1980, it declined further to an all-time low of 31 percent. "At no point since [1945]," said Dr. Gallup referring to his latest figures, "has satisfaction with the overall performance of the world organization been as low as it is today."[4] The John Birch Society's long and frequently lonely billboard, bumper sticker, petition, letter-writing, and pamphleteering educational campaigns to "Get US out! of the United Nations" had made good sense to many Americans.

In the early years of the Reagan Administration, UN-bashing became positively respectable, even fashionable. U.S. Ambassador to the UN Jeane Kirkpatrick could be seen and heard almost daily denouncing the world body's anti-Americanism, tyranny promotion, and fiscal profligacy. Editorials opposing UN actions and the organization itself began appearing with frequency in local and regional newspapers, and occasionally even in major national news organs.

Anti-UN sentiment had already reached the point in 1981 that veteran UN-watcher Robert W. Lee could report in his book, *The United Nations Conspiracy*: "Today the UN is increasingly regarded not as a sacred cow, but rather as a troika composed of a white elephant, a Trojan horse, and a Judas goat."[5] The supermarket tabloid *Star*, while not exactly a consistently reliable heavyweight in the news and analysis category, expressed the sentiments of a large and growing segment of the American people with a November 3, 1981 article by Steve Dunleavy entitled, "Rip Down This Shocking

Tower of Shame."

In March of 1982, syndicated columnist Andrew Tully authored a piece headlined: "[Mayor] Koch Should Chase UN Out of Town."[6] Many similar articles and editorials could be cited, but perhaps one of the most surprising was the August 24, 1987 cover story by Charles Krauthammer for *The New Republic*, entitled "Let It Sink: The Overdue Demise of the United Nations."

But the advent of Mikhail Gorbachev's "new thinking" in the late 1980s coincided with the beginning of a remarkable rehabilitation in the public's image of the UN. First Gorbachev, and then Boris Yeltsin, won plaudits for reversing the traditional Soviet (or Soviet surrogate) practice of using the UN as a venue for strident anti-American diatribes. Yassir Arafat and his PLO terrorists dropped their regular anti-Israel philippics. And the UN's "peacekeepers" won a Nobel Prize and worldwide praise for their roles as mediators in Afghanistan, Cambodia, Central America, Southern Africa, and the Middle East.

Then came Operation Desert Storm, the holy war against the aggression of Saddam Hussein. And *mirabile dictu*, the United Nations was once again the world's "last best hope for peace." Suddenly UN "peacekeepers" began to appear almost everywhere — with more than 40,000 troops in the field in Africa, Asia, Europe, Central America, and the Middle East[7] — and every new day now brings new appeals for the world body's intervention and "expertise."

On United Nations Day 1990, a new Gallup Poll indicated that "American support for the United Nations ... is higher than it has been in over 20 years." According to the national polling organization, "Fifty-four percent of Americans now think the United Nations has done a good job of solving the problems it has had to face...." The poll cited the "rapprochement between the U.S.S.R. and the U.S., and the dissolution of the Iron Curtain," as well as the developing Persian Gulf situation, as major factors contributing to the enhancement of the UN's image.[8]

Gallup reported that "almost six out of ten Americans think that the U.N. has been effective in helping deal with the current [Iraq-Kuwait] crisis, with only 8% saying that the U.N. has not been at all effective." Even more disturbing, if accurate, is the poll finding that 61 percent of those surveyed thought it a good idea to build up the United Nations emergency force to "a size great enough to deal with 'brush fire' or small wars throughout the world."[9]

The euphoria following the Persian Gulf hostilities temporarily boosted George Bush's approval rating to an all-time high for any president. Rude economic realities and an accumulating number of political problems then caused his star to plummet just as rapidly as it had risen. The UN's gains, however, appear to have been more durable. As reported by Richard Morin ("U.N. Real Winner After Gulf War," *Salt Lake Tribune*, January 24, 1992), a survey by the Americans Talk Issues Foundation "found that approval for the United Nations actually increased from 66 percent in June to 78 percent in November [1991], a period when other measures of war-induced euphoria were sinking fast."

The *Tribune* reported:

[H]alf of those questioned — 51 percent — agreed that "the U.S. should abide by all World Court decisions, even when they go against us, because this sets an example for all nations to follow." That was up from 42 percent in May.

More than half also would support increasing the amount of dues that the United States pays to the U.N. to "help pay for a U.N. space satellite system to detect and monitor such problems as arms movements, crop failures, refugee settlements and global pollution."

And, remarkably, 38 percent of those questioned said United Nations resolutions "should rule over the actions and laws of individual countries, where necessary to fulfill essential United Nations functions, including ruling over U.S. laws even when our laws are different."

While we recognize that pollsters often structure their polling questions to achieve results that will influence rather than accurately reflect public opinion, and these surveys may be exaggerating the rise of pro-UN sentiments, there is little doubt that the world organization is experiencing a dramatic turnaround in citizen acceptance. In large measure, this has resulted from the enormously effective UN drum-beating campaigns of the Establishment news media.

The *New York Times*, *Los Angeles Times*, and *Washington Post* have led the way, with an avalanche of fawning editorials, news stories, and op-ed columns glorifying the alleged accomplishments and yet-to-be-realized potential of the UN. These pro-UN public relations pieces have been reprinted in thousands of newspapers and have also found their way into the mainstream of broadcast journalism.

Unfortunately, the religious media have followed along with their secular brethren in promoting this unquestioning faith in the salvific capability of the United Nations. One of the more egregious examples of this misplaced fervor appeared in a lengthy January 19, 1992 editorial in *Our Sunday Visitor*, the nation's largest Catholic publication. Headlined "UNsurpassed," the piece declared: "If the John Birch Society had its way and the United Nations had ceased to exist back in the 1950s, 1991 would have been a far more dismal year." The editorialist then proceeded to praise the UN's latest "accomplishments":

> It is unlikely that international support for the liberation of Kuwait and the dismantling of the Iraqi war machine would have been so easily marshaled by the United States. Cambodia's warring factions would most likely still be warring. Terry Anderson and his fellow hostages would still be languishing in Lebanon. Croats and Serbs would still be locked in their death grip with no international organization pressing for a cease-fire. And El Salvador would still be a vast cemetery slowly filling up with the victims of its fratricidal opponents....
>
> Now in its fifth decade of existence, the U.N. is finally coming into its own, thanks in part to the demise of the superpower standoff that hobbled the international organization for much of its existence. Nations are finding the mediation efforts of U.N. negotiators preferable to either unilateral actions or a bloody status quo of unwinnable conflicts.

Similar paeans of praise can be found in leading Protestant periodicals. New Age publications which have multiplied in number and influence in the past decade virtually worship the UN.

Readers of this book will be in a far better position to benefit from our presentation in the pages that follow, and to understand unfold-

ing world events, if they keep in mind the two major principles underlying virtually all of our federal government's foreign and domestic policies: "convergence" and "interdependence." The plan to bring
about a convergence or merger of the U.S. and the USSR is not a
recent policy response to the supposed reforms of Gorbachev and
Yeltsin. It first came to light officially in 1953 when public concern
over large tax-exempt foundation grants to communists and communist causes prompted Congress to investigate. Of particular concern were the funding activities of the Carnegie, Ford, and
Rockefeller Foundations. Perhaps the most startling revelation of
that investigation came when Ford Foundation president H. Rowan
Gaither admitted to Norman Dodd, staff director of the Congressional Special Committee to Investigate Tax-Exempt Foundations:

> Of course, you know that we at the executive level here were, at one
> time or another, active in either the OSS, the State Department, or
> the European Economic Administration. During those times, and with-
> out exception, we operated under directives issued by the White House.
> We are continuing to be guided by just such directives.... The substance
> [of these directives] was to the effect that we should make every effort
> to so alter life in the United States as to make possible a comfortable
> merger with the Soviet Union. [10]

At that time — even though the activities of the foundations coincided exactly with Gaither's startling admission — it was simply too
fantastic for many Americans to believe. It still is. Asked to assess
such information, most Americans ask: Why would some of our
nation's wealthiest and most powerful capitalists use their great fortunes to promote such a goal? This compelling question has stymied
many good Americans for decades.

If you, too, are perplexed about this seemingly suicidal practice,
you will find it explained — and condemned — in the pages that
follow. Of one thing there can be little doubt: Our nation is plunging
headlong toward "convergence" and the eventual "merger" referred
to by Rowan Gaither many years ago.

Simultaneously, our nation — along with the other nations of the
world — is being steadily drawn into the tightening noose of "inter-

dependence." Our political and economic systems are being intertwined and increasingly are being subjected to control by the United Nations and its adjunct international organizations. Unless this process can be stopped, it will culminate in the creation of omnipotent global governance and an "end to nationhood," as Walt Whitman Rostow once phrased the goal he shared with many others.[11] These were (and still are) the ultimate objectives of Gaither, his world order cronies, and their modern-day successors.

Thirty-five years after Mr. Gaither's admission, U.S. Senator Jesse Helms (R-NC) warned America of "establishment insiders" who are "bringing this one-world design — with a convergence of the Soviet and American systems as its centerpiece — into being." "The influence of establishment insiders over our foreign policy has become a fact of life in our time," the Senator charged. "... It is an influence which, if unchecked, could ultimately subvert our constitutional order." In this 1987 Senate speech, Senator Helms also identified the organizations through which these insiders operate:

A careful examination of what is happening behind the scenes reveals that all of these interests are working in concert with the masters of the Kremlin in order to create what some refer to as a new world order. Private organizations such as the Council on Foreign Relations, the Royal Institute of International Affairs, the Trilateral Commission, the Dartmouth Conference, the Aspen Institute for Humanistic Studies, the Atlantic Institute, and the Bilderberg Group serve to disseminate and to coordinate the plans for this so-called new world order in powerful business, financial, academic, and official circles.[12]

Unfortunately, because of the tremendous power that these Establishment Insiders* wield in our major media, Senator Helms's

---

* The terms "Establishment" and "Insiders" will be used throughout this text to refer generally to the elite coterie of one-world-minded individuals associated with the organizations named above by Senator Helms. For identification purposes, and to demonstrate the inordinate and dangerous influence these interests wield, individuals who are, or have been, members of the Council on Foreign Relations and the Trilateral Commission will be so noted parenthetically in the text as (CFR) or (TC) respectively.

warning never reached the American people. It was drowned under a flood of one-world propaganda on the Gorbachev "revolution" and the "new potentialities" for world peace through a revived and strengthened United Nations.

Yet, contrary to the many seductive pro-UN siren songs, the lessons of history about the relationship of man to government loudly and clearly proclaim that far from guaranteeing a new era of peace and security, the centralization of political and economic power on a planetary level can only bring about global tyranny and oppression on a scale never before imagined.

In late September of 1938, British Prime Minister Neville Chamberlain journeyed to Germany for his third meeting with Adolph Hitler. Blind to the menace of Hitler's "new world order" (Hitler's own words),[13] Chamberlain returned from that now-infamous meeting brandishing an agreement he had signed with *der Fuehrer* and proudly proclaiming that he had won "peace with honor" and "peace for our time." He was greeted with clamorous huzzahs by British politicians, the press, and throngs of citizens who also blindly called the betrayal "peace." Within months, Europe was convulsed in conflict, and soon even America was dragged into the bloodiest war in world history.

The peril America and the free world face today is every bit as real, though far greater in scope, than what a peace-hungry world faced in 1938. National sovereignty is threatened as never before. As UN power grows, the entire world stands on the brink of an era of totalitarian control. We must pull back before it is too late — too late to save our country, our freedoms, our families, and all we hold dear.

Here is what this book claims the new world order under the United Nations would mean:

- An end to your God-given rights guaranteed by the U.S. Constitution, i.e., freedom of religion, speech, press, and assembly, the right to trial by jury, etc. (Chapter 6)
- National and personal disarmament along with conscription of U.S. citizens into a United Nations Army or Police Force to serve at the pleasure of the UN hierarchy. (Chapters 1 and 2)
- The end of private property rights and the ability to control your

own home, farm, or business. (Chapters 6 and 7)
- Economic and environmental regulation at the hands of UN bureaucrats. (Chapter 10)
- Loss of your right as parents to raise and instruct your children in accordance with your personal beliefs. (Chapter 8)
- Coercive population control measures that will determine when — or if — you may have children. (Chapter 9)
- Unlimited global taxation. (Chapter 10)
- A centrally managed world monetary system that will lead all but the ruling elite into poverty. (Chapter 10)
- Environmental controls that will mean the end of single family homes and personal automobile ownership. (Chapter 6)
- The enthronement of an occult, New Age, new world religion. (Chapter 12)
- Communist-style totalitarian dictatorship and random, ruthless terror, torture, and extermination to cow all peoples into abject submission. (Chapters 2 & 14)

All of this need not happen. As late as the hour has become, it is still not too late to avert catastrophe and save our freedom. The world's future need not degenerate into what George Orwell wrote would resemble "a boot stamping on a human face — forever!" But the urgency of our situation cannot be overstated. Simply put, unless significant numbers of Americans can be awakened from their slumbers, shaken from their apathy and ignorance, pulled away from their diversions, and convinced to work, pray, vote, speak up, struggle, and fight against the powers arrayed against them, then such a horrible fate surely awaits all of us.

GLOBAL TYRANNY
...STEP BY STEP

*The people never give up their liberties
but under some delusion.*

— Edmund Burke (1784)

CHAPTER 1

The New World Army

*In the Gulf, we saw the United Nations playing the role
dreamed of by its founders, with the world's leading nations or-
chestrating and sanctioning collective action against aggression.*[1]
— President George Bush, August 1991
National Security Strategy of the United States

*The army of tomorrow is neither the Red Army nor the U.S.
Army.... If there is to be peace, it will be secured by a multinational force that monitors cease-fires ... and protects human
rights. Blue-helmeted United Nations peacekeepers are doing
just that....*
— "The Unsung New World Army"
New York Times editorial, May 11, 1992

*[I]t is time for the United States to lead in the creation of a
modest U.N. rapid-deployment force.*
— Republican Congressman James A. Leach
Foreign Affairs, Summer 1992

*The United States should strongly support efforts to expand
the U.N. peacekeeping role.*
— Democratic Congressman Lee H. Hamilton
Foreign Affairs, Summer 1992

Though few seemed to notice, January 31, 1992 was an historic
day on the march toward the new world order. To most New York-
ers, it simply meant worse than usual traffic jams, as motorcades
and security cordons for the many foreign dignitaries on their way
to United Nations headquarters tied up traffic for hours.

For the rest of America, the blur of headlines and evening news sound bites about the need for "collective security" coming from visiting potentates gave little hint of the significance of what was transpiring. Yet, this 3,046th meeting of the United Nations Security Council that attracted the dignitaries marked the first time that the body had convened at the level of heads of state or government.

The exalted group of world leaders representing the five permanent and ten rotating member states of the Security Council included a king, five presidents, six prime ministers, a chancellor, a premier, and two foreign ministers. They were gathering to launch a process that should have set off alarms worldwide: *the arming of the United Nations.*

The assemblage took on a religious aura as, one by one, the national leaders worshiped at the UN altar, referred to the UN Charter with a reverence usually reserved for Holy Writ, and recited the by-now-familiar doxology always heard at these increasingly frequent "summits": new world order; peace, equity, and justice; interdependence; global harmony; democracy; human rights; the rule of law; collective engagement; an enhanced and strengthened United Nations; etc.

President Bush enthusiastically extolled "the sacred principles enshrined in the United Nations Charter" and, recalling its messianic mission, proclaimed: "For perhaps the first time since that hopeful moment in San Francisco, we can look at our Charter as a living, breathing document."[2]

The UN's newly-installed Secretary-General, Egypt's Boutros Boutros-Ghali, was no less caught up with the spiritual purpose of the world organization. He called for additional summit-level meetings of the Security Council, since this "would also help to assure that transfiguration of this house which the world hopes to be completed before its fiftieth anniversary, in 1995."[3] How he divined what the world's "hopes" for the organization on its 50th birthday might be, he did not say. And he did not have to explain the motive behind his use of Biblical metaphor. That was transparent enough. *Webster* defines "transfigure" this way: "to give a new and typically exalted or spiritual appearance to." To the Christian mind, of course, "transfiguration" recalls the Gospel account of Christ's manifestation of his divine glory.

Boutros-Ghali undoubtedly knows the power of the symbolism he chose and, like his fellow true believers in the one-world gospel, he realized that much more of this evangelization is necessary if the masses are to be sold on the idea of the UN as the world's savior. When his turn at the UN podium came, even Boris Yeltsin was appropriately religious, referring to the organization as "the political Olympus of the contemporary world."[4] Venezuelan President Carlos Andres Perez proclaimed that "the United Nations is indispensable to us all."[5] Presumably, we cannot survive without it. "This means," said Perez, "placing our trust in its leadership and in its set-up, as well as in the decision-making machinery. The guiding principles must be those that inspired its establishment, now brought to complete fruition."[6] That's quite a contrast with the scriptural injunction to "trust in the Lord," and far indeed from the admonitions of our founding fathers to avoid putting trust in man (and government) but instead to "bind him down from mischief by the chains of the Constitution."[7]

A Bigger and Better UN?

Such quaint notions as national independence and limitation of government held no sway with these internationalists. The participants in this special convocation of the Security Council were virtually unanimous in their support of greatly expanded United Nations powers. This was necessary, they said, because of the rapid "acceleration of history," the "critical stage" of current world events, "global instability," "nuclear proliferation," and the many "threats to peace and security" presented by economic, social, humanitarian, and ecological "sources of instability."

The obsolete nation-state is incapable of meeting the world's needs, claimed one speaker after another. Boutros-Ghali explained that in his vision of the new world order, "State sovereignty takes a new meaning...." "[N]arrow nationalism," warned the Egyptian, "can disrupt a peaceful global existence. Nations are too interdependent, national frontiers are too porous and transnational realities ... too dangerous to permit egocentric isolationism."[8]

Repeated calls were made at this special UN session for increasing the powers of the Secretary-General, enhancing the jurisdiction of the World Court, expanding the membership of the Security Council, abolishing the veto power of the five permanent members, establishing a permanent funding mechanism for "peacekeeping," convening a summit meeting to address social development, increasing economic aid from North to South, and more. Hardly a speaker failed to hail the "end of the Cold War" and the demise of communism, but socialist thought was still the order of the day as one leader after another called for greater "global management" and redistribution of wealth.

French President Francois Mitterrand made the first concrete proposal to give military teeth to the world body with his call for establishing a rapid-deployment UN army. "I state that for its part France is ready to make available to the Secretary-General a 1,000-man contingent for peace-keeping operations, at any time, on 48-hours notice," said the internationalist Frenchman. And to buttress his enthusiasm for a UN military force, he added, "That figure could be doubled within a week."[9]

Belgian Prime Minister Wilfried Martens seconded Mitterrand's proposal and announced that "... Belgium will ensure rapid deployment of Belgian contingents in United Nations peace-keeping forces."[10] His idea was immediately endorsed by Russian President Boris Yeltsin and Hungarian Foreign Minister Geza Jeszenszky.

Going further, Yeltsin declared to the august assemblage: "I think the time has come to consider creating a global defence system for the world community. It could be based on a reorientation of the United States Strategic Defense Initiative, to make use of high technologies developed in Russia's defence complex." This magnanimous gesture on his part, said Yeltsin, could be made because "Russia regards the United States and the West not as mere partners but rather as allies."[11]

To reinforce his contentions that the "evil empire" is no more, and that his new-found devotion to human rights is genuine, Yeltsin announced: "A few days ago, the 10 remaining political prisoners were pardoned by a decree of the President of the Russian Federation. There are no longer any prisoners of conscience in free Russia."[12] There were no guffaws and no one had the inclination (or the guts) to ask what had happened to the consciences of millions more political, social, and religious prisoners still populating the gulags. Or why this former member of the Soviet Politburo wasn't being held accountable for his part in the USSR's long history of crimes against humanity. Likewise, when Red Chinese Premier Li Peng rose to speak of "human rights," "peaceful coexistence," and "social tranquility," he was met with respectful attentiveness. The Butcher of Tiananmen Square was politely given a world stage for the most outrageous totalitarian propaganda. China, he proclaimed, "will never become a threat to any country or any region of the world. China is of the view that no country should seek hegemony or practice power politics." His government, he said, looked forward to "the establishment of a new international order that will be stable, rational, just and conducive to world peace and development." [13] Not only was he not hooted down, he was granted the prestige of separate meetings with Presidents Bush and Yeltsin and Prime Ministers Major and Miyazawa.

Hundreds of Chinese demonstrators who came to protest this travesty were kept blocks away from the UN building by security forces. The *Los Angeles Times* reported the following lamentation uttered by one of the young demonstrators:

> "His [Li's] hand is full of the blood and tears of the Chinese people, and I don't understand why world leaders would shake hands with him," said a weeping Chai Ling, one of the leaders of the Tian An Men Square pro-democracy demonstrations. [14]

On the morning following this precedent-setting Security Council session, the Establishment media were ready to peddle the politically correct one-world view. For example, Joseph S. Nye Jr., whose Insider credentials include being the director of the Center for International Affairs, a member of the Council on Foreign Relations (CFR), a Harvard University professor, and a former Deputy Under Secretary of State, led off with an op-ed column in the *New York Times* entitled, "Create a U.N. Fire Brigade." Nye told readers: "If a new world order is ultimately to emerge from yesterday's summit meeting of the world's leaders at the U.N., they will have to stretch their imaginations."[15]

According to Nye, Messrs. Mitterrand, Martens, and company were thinking too small. "The U.S. should go beyond rhetoric to promote a new order.... To achieve this, the U.S. ought to propose the creation of a U.N. rapid-deployment force.... made up of 60,000 troops in brigades from 12 countries."[16]

That same morning, *Los Angeles Times* reporter Norman Kempster enthused: "Creating a standing army under the control of the United Nations Security Council would give the world organization a military punch it has never had before and could convert it into a full-time international police department." That should be a truly bone-chilling thought for anyone who values freedom. But Kempster didn't stop there, adding: "If adopted ... the plan would mark the transformation of the Security Council from a Cold War-hobbled debating society to an organization with the power to enforce its decisions...."[17] Even *more* chilling! But not, apparently, to the apostles of one-worldism who have been lustily cheering such proposals.

In the months following the summit, as the Bush Administration moved brazenly forward with never-announced plans to supplant the U.S. Constitution with the UN Charter, the Establishment news media, dominated by members of the Council on Foreign Relations and led by the *New York Times*, the *Washington Post*, the *Los Angeles Times*, and the CFR's own *Foreign Affairs*, provided both cover and support. So began the audacious propaganda campaign to resurrect a decades-old, one-world scheme to transfer U.S. military might to the United Nations.

In its March 6, 1992 lead editorial entitled "The New World Army," the *New York Times* came close to dropping all pretenses and subtlety:

> For years the United Nations has been notable mostly for its vocal cords. That's changed. Nowadays the U.N.'s muscle — its blue-helmeted soldiers — seems to be everywhere. And costs have soared. The bill for 11 peacekeeping missions could approach $3.7 billion this year. Never before have so many U.N. troops been committed to so many costly and diverse missions.

But don't get the idea that anyone at the *Times* is about to let fiscal worries stand in the way of its commitment to "world order" politics. The editorial ticked off the current count of blue-helmeted troops deployed worldwide: In Lebanon 5,900; Cyprus 2,200; Golan Heights 1,300; El Salvador 1,000; Iraq/Kuwait 540; Angola 440; Arab-Israel conflict 300; India/Pakistan 40; Cambodia 22,000; Yugoslavia 14,300; Western Sahara 2,700. This grand total of 50,720 UN troops is just the start of what these internationalists are planning. Any of these hot spots could, of course, develop into a major conflagration at any moment, requiring thousands — or tens of thousands — of UN reinforcements.

There are also numerous other trouble spots around the globe offering virtually unlimited opportunities for UN intervention: South Africa, Azerbaijan, Lithuania, Nicaragua, Northern Ireland, Korea, and Myanmar. Myanmar? Yes, although you probably remember it by its former name, Burma. The *Los Angeles Times* lead editorial for March 16, 1992 carried the title, "Next Target for World's Conscience: Myanmar — An apocalyptic 'killing field' for the former Burma?" It signaled that we may soon be seeing UN troops, possibly including American men and women, in that tragic land.

In the face of all of this support for a UN military arm, the only protests in Congress about the developing "New World Army" questioned merely the financial costs of the peacekeeping operations, including the disproportionate share (an automatic 30 percent) the U.S. is expected to shoulder. When Secretary of State James Baker appeared before a Senate subcommittee on March 5, 1992 to present the Bush Administration's request for an additional $810 million (above the $107 million already appropriated) for peacekeeping in 1992-93, he ran into resistance even from traditionally strong UN supporters. Senator Jim Sasser (D-TN) told Baker that although he believed the UN peacekeeping efforts were important, in this recessionary economy, constituent opposition to foreign aid had become "politically irresistible."[18] After the hearing, Sasser told an interviewer, "Our constituents are saying that they have borne the burden as long as they intend to."[19]

Yes, the bill for the UN's blue helmet operations is escalating rapidly. "Yet," said the *New York Times* in its "New World Army" editorial, "in hard cash terms, peacekeeping is a bargain.... Every war prevented saves blood and treasure, expands markets and trade." Though such an argument has a certain simplistic appeal, it breaks down rapidly under any close examination. And although the economic cost is a legitimate concern, a far more serious matter is the looming UN military threat to U.S. sovereignty. As the *Times* itself pointed out: "Now the peacekeepers are doing more than monitoring truce lines. They are becoming peacemakers, too. U.N. forces were asked to disarm guerrillas, conduct elections and enforce human rights, first in Namibia, then in Cambodia and El Salvador."[20]

The UN itself is finding new opportunities right and left to justify expansion of its armed forces. "The Security Council recently expanded the concept of threats to peace," the *Times* reported, "to include economic, social and ecological instability."[21] Talk about proliferation! This kind of assumed, open-ended authority virtually guarantees unlimited interference by the United Nations in the domestic affairs of sovereign states. And you can be sure that interference won't be directed primarily at stopping human rights violations in repressive communist/socialist regimes or petty third world dictatorships. It will be directed against what these internationalists consider the greatest threat to global peace and stability — the United States of America.

Yes, America is the target. According to an Associated Press report appearing on March 12, 1992, "a United Nations official said Wednesday ... that the United States is the greatest threat to the world's ecological health." That official, Canadian Maurice F. Strong, who served as secretary-general of the 1992 UN Earth Summit, declared: "In effect, the United States is committing environmental aggression against the rest of the world." He added: "At the environmental level, the United States is clearly the greatest risk."[22]

This would not be the first or last time Strong and other UN envirocrats would storm against what they consider the evils of U.S. consumption and production. It has become a standard theme at UN environmental conferences and was the major message at the world body's 1992 Earth Summit in Brazil. Judging from the vitriol these eco-globalists regularly throw at Americans, it's probably safe to assume they would eagerly deploy the blue helmets (or as some advocate, environmental police in green helmets) to close down much of the U.S. Will UN "peacekeepers" be deployed against the U.S. to rectify economic, social, or ecological "instabilities" determined by UN Marxists to be "threats to peace"? America would never stand for it, you say? But the stage is already being set to render nations incapable of blocking such moves by the UN.

Many of the UN's defenders claim that the organization can only send in its peacekeeping forces if they are officially invited. Yet, President Bush has already put the United States on record officially favoring UN action within the borders of sovereign nations. In his "Pax Universalis" speech delivered at UN headquarters on September 23, 1991, he said there was a need for UN action to settle "nationalist passions" within nations and also to remove an undesirable national leader from his post.[23] Even *New York Times* columnist Leslie Gelb (CFR) found the President's clearly stated policy "revolutionary" and "threatening."[24]

According to the CFR globalists, no single nation should have veto power over whether or not the UN should act. Writing in the Spring 1991 *Foreign Affairs* ("The U.N. in a New World Order"), Professors Bruce Russett and James S. Sutterlin concluded: "It is worth emphasizing that nothing in the [UN] charter prohibits the Security Council from deploying peacekeeping forces without the consent of all the parties, or from including troop contingents from the permanent members of the council in such forces where the need for deterrence arises." If this attitude prevails, UN eco-saviors can first declare your factory, your logging, ranching or farming practices, or even your use of an automobile a threat to the environment, and then decide under authority derived from the new definition of "peacekeeping" to send in the blue (or green) helmeted troops to address the breach of "peace" with force.

The Great Mutation

Although the UN has not yet used any of this steadily building "peacekeeping" muscle for enforcement of environmental or social dicta, the precedent for uninvited intervention has already been established under the assumed authority of "peacekeeping." As *Los*

Angeles Times columnist William Pfaff observed in his March 5, 1992 column appearing in the *International Herald Tribune*, the 1992 UN action in what was once Yugoslavia is a signal event, representing an overturning of national sovereignty. "Slowly, too slowly, the great mutation occurs," said Pfaff. "The principle of absolute national sovereignty is being overturned.... The civil war in Yugoslavia has rendered this service to us."

Pfaff, a committed internationalist, applauded the UN's "uninvited international intervention into the affairs of a state" which, until now, "has been held an unacceptable attack upon the principle of unlimited state sovereignty." He saw the intervention of the European Community and the UN in Yugoslavia as a new model of collective action that has many other potential applications. "What they have thus far done has been improvisation, but it is a start on something new," the Paris-based columnist noted approvingly. "We are now in a situation where improvisation and experiment are essential, in contrast to the big programmatic reforms of 1918 and 1945 — the League and the U.N." The "improvisation" Pfaff and his fellow globalists talk about is hardly spontaneous and is eminently predictable; it involves the expansion and concentration of the UN's political, economic, and military powers in response to global or regional or even local "crises."

The excuse for UN "peacekeeping" action in a crisis involving civil war and ethnic fighting is the supposed potential for the conflict to escalate to global dimensions if not checked by collective international force. "What may now be needed," said the *New York Times* in its March 6, 1992 editorial, "is a permanent force for rapid deployment in chaotic circumstances." The *Times* editorial continued: "One promising possibility is to make fuller use of the U.N. Charter. Article 43 already calls on members to make available 'armed forces, assistance and facilities' necessary to maintain international peace. To that end, the Charter established a Military Staff Committee...."

But, lamented the *Times*, this UN committee has never worked as intended, because "American armed forces have traditionally resisted [it] as a threat to command autonomy." Again, the far greater threat to national security and sovereignty was ignored.

"But in a transformed world," continued the *Times* editorial, "it makes sense to consider direct contributions of personnel and equipment to a rapid deployment force under real multinational control." Going still further, the article proposed that the UN military force be expanded with funds taken from the U.S. defense budget instead of from its foreign aid budget. "That won't be easy," the *Times* acknowledged. "But what a chance for President Bush to take the lead in giving real meaning to his still hazy vision of a New World Order."

A Long-Established Policy
The only haze surrounding either Mr. Bush's or that newspaper's vision of the new world order is that which they have deliberately created. They know that the real substance of the new world order was very clearly presented in 1961, more than 30 years ago, when President John F. Kennedy presented his plan for national disarmament to the United Nations. Crafted by his CFR-dominated State Department and entitled *Freedom From War: The United States Program for General and Complete Disarmament in a Peaceful World* (also known as Department of State Publication 7277), it presented a three-stage program for the gradual transfer of U.S. arms to the United Nations.[25]

During Stage II (the stage we are currently in), the document mandates: "The U.N. Peace Force shall be established and progressively strengthened." This will be accomplished "to the end that the United Nations can effectively in Stage III deter or suppress any threat or use of force in violation of the purposes and principles of the United Nations."[26]

This incredible policy — which has been actively but quietly brought along toward completion during successive administrations — concludes as follows:

In Stage III progressive controlled disarmament ... would proceed to a point where no state would have the military power to challenge the progressively strengthened U.N. Peace Force.[27]

Freedom From War was superseded in April 1962 by another disarmament document entitled *Blueprint for the Peace Race: Outline of Basic Provisions of a Treaty on General and Complete Disarmament in a Peaceful World.*[28] As before, its third stage calls for the strengthening of the UN Peace Force "until it had sufficient armed forces and armaments so that no state could challenge it."[29] That means, of course, that upon completion of this partially completed plan, every nation state, including the United States, would be subject to the unchallengeable military forces of the all-powerful United Nations.

But that was long ago; perhaps those policies and proposals have expired. Although that may be a comforting thought, unfortunately it is not true. On May 25, 1982, Congressman Ted Weiss (D-NY) called for the implementation of *Blueprint for the Peace Race* and entered its entire text into the *Congressional Record*.[30] He also pointed out that this disarmament proposal had never been formally withdrawn by the United States government. When questioned about the commitment of the United States to the *Blueprint*, A. Richard Richstein, General Counsel to the U.S. Arms Control and Disarmament Agency, confirmed in a letter on May 11th of that year that "the United States has never formally withdrawn this proposal."[31]

In January 1991, William Nary, the official historian of the Arms Control and Disarmament Agency, confirmed again that "the proposal has not been withdrawn." Mr. Nary also confirmed that "certain features of it have been incorporated into subsequent disarmament agreements."[32]

Indeed, significant portions of this long-range disarmament program have been already enacted into law. On September 23, 1961, Congress passed the "Arms Control and Disarmament Act," which was signed into law (Public Law 87-297) on September 26th by President Kennedy. According to the wording of the law itself, its purpose was to establish a U.S. Arms Control and Disarmament Agency that would advance efforts "toward ultimate world disarmament." But, is the objective really "world disarmament"? How can it be? Like *Freedom From War*, P.L. 87-297 calls not for the total elimination of arms — a completely utopian fantasy — but the *transfer* of arms from national to international control. Section 3 (a) of the Act states:

The terms "arms control" and "disarmament" mean the identification, verification, inspection, limitation, control, reduction, or elimination, of armed forces and *armaments of all kinds* under international agreement ... to establish an effective system of international control...." [Emphasis added]

By December 11, 1989, when President Bush signed the "Arms Control and Disarmament Amendments Act of 1989" (Public Law 101-216), the original Kennedy Administration legislation had already been amended nearly 20 times. This steadily growing body of law is moving us step by step toward surrender to a global UN military dictatorship. Like the original Act, the 1989 amendment contains the language "identification ... elimination" of "armaments of all kinds." Questions rush to the fore. Such as: Could the phrase "armaments of all kinds" be construed at some future date by a federal court or the UN's World Court to include the personal arms of private citizens? In view of the increasing onslaught of state and federal anti-gun legislation, the judicial activism of the federal courts, and the total absence in the UN Charter and UN "Rights" documents of any protection similar to our Second Amendment guarantee of the right to keep and bear arms, it could hardly be considered extreme to consider the possibility.

For apostles of the new world order, perhaps the closest thing to holy writ, and the scripture to which they all pay homage, is the 1958 volume *World Peace Through World Law* by Grenville Clark and Louis B. Sohn.[33] In this venerated text, Clark and Sohn proposed a socialist world government through a revised UN Charter. The key to this global superstate would be a United Nations "world police force" invested with "a coercive force of overwhelming power." "This world police force would be the only *military* force permitted anywhere in the world after the process of national disarmament has been completed." And what about the civilian police and private firearms owners? The authors warned "that even with the complete elimination of all [national] *military* forces," local "police forces, supplemented by civilians armed with sporting rifles and fowling pieces, might conceivably constitute a serious threat to a neighboring country...." (Emphasis in original) Accordingly, they recommend extremely rigid controls on *all* firearms and ammunition possessed by civil police and private citizens. [34]

Top Military Post

If these proposals are implemented, who will control these supreme United Nations forces? Isn't that a question everyone should be concerned with? In the past, the person in charge of all UN military activities has been the UN Under-Secretary-General for Political and Security Council Affairs. Since the UN was created, 14 individuals have held that post. *All have been communists and all but one have come from the Soviet Union.* This is no coincidence. Secretary-General Trygve Lie revealed that U.S. Secretary of State Edward Stettinius (CFR) had agreed to naming a Soviet national to this strategic post, which Lie described as "the premier Assistant Secretaryship." [35] Lie said he first learned of the agreement from Soviet representative Andrei Vishinsky, and that "Mr. Stettinius confirmed to me that he had agreed with the Soviet Delegation in the matter." [36] The surprised Secretary-General Lie wrote:

> The preservation of international peace and security was the Organization's highest responsibility, and it was to entrusting the direction of the Secretariat department most concerned with this to a Soviet national that the Americans had agreed. What did the Americans want for themselves? To my surprise, they did not ask for a department concerned with comparable substantive affairs, like the economic or the social. Rather, Mr. Stettinius proposed that an American citizen be appointed Assistant Secretary-General for the Administrative and Financial Services. [37]

The communists have remained in control ever since, even though, Lie maintained, this was not intended as a permanent arrangement. In January 1992, newly elected Secretary-General Boutros-Ghali reorganized the UN's bureaucracy. There are now two posts of Under-Secretary-General for Political Affairs (the "Security Council" part of the title was dropped) with joint responsibilities for military affairs. Named to the positions were Vladimir E. Petrovsky, a former deputy foreign minister in the Gorbachev regime, and

James O.C. Jonah of Sierra Leone, who has been a career UN bureaucrat since 1963. The historical roster of the men who have held this "premier Assistant Secretaryship" reads as follows:

1946–1949 .... Arkady Sobolev (USSR)
1949–1953 .... Konstatin Zinchenko (USSR)
1953–1954 .... Ilya Tchernychev (USSR)
1954–1957 .... Dragoslav Protitch (Yugoslavia)
1958–1960 .... Anatoly Dobrynin (USSR)
1960–1962 .... Georgy Arkadev (USSR)
1962–1963 .... E.D. Kiselev (USSR)
1963–1965 .... V.P. Suslov (USSR)
1965–1968 .... Alexei E. Nesterenko (USSR)
1968–1973 .... Leonid N. Kutakov (USSR)
1973–1978 .... Arkady N. Shevchenko (USSR)
1978–1981 .... Mikhail D. Sytenko (USSR)
1981–1986 .... Viacheslav A. Ustinov (USSR)
1987–1992 .... Vasiliy S. Safronchuk (USSR)
1992–   .... Vladimir Petrovsky (Russia, "former USSR")
                     James O.C. Jonah (Sierra Leone)

Surrendering our military capabilities to the United Nations (or any other international body) should be unthinkable to every American, even if there were guarantees that a *U.S. citizen* would always hold the position of Under-Secretary-General for Political Affairs. To consider doing so in the face of the current and historical facts just mentioned above is treasonous.

A more colossal betrayal of one's country would be difficult to conceive. But the *Los Angeles Times*, for one, is more than willing to assist in preparing the public's mind for the sellout. On January 5, 1992, the newspaper gave generous space for an op-ed article entitled "Dream of Total Disarmament Could Become Reality," written by radical leftists Gar Alperovitz and Kai Bird. In it, Alperovitz, a senior fellow at the Washington DC-based Institute for Policy Studies, and Bird, a research associate at this same rabidly anti-American organization, urged a formal reaffirmation of the 30-year-old Kennedy disarmament proposals and praised the vision of the CFR "wise men" who had designed them. The IPS duo quoted the *Freedom From War* Stage III passage ("No state shall have the military power ...") and declared: "We could refine and implement the ... disarmament plan by requiring all countries to cut defense budgets by, say, 15%-20% per year." Those nations that refused to go along "could be penalized with economic sanctions or — in the extreme — military intervention."

UN Leader Paves the Way

At the close of the special Security Council meeting convened on January 31, 1992, Secretary-General Boutros-Ghali was instructed by the Council to prepare by July 1st his "recommendations on ways of strengthening" the UN's peacekeeping capabilities. In June, the energetic Egyptian completed his assignment and issued *An Agenda for Peace*.[38] A more apt title would have been, *An Agenda for Global Socialistic Rule*. Signaling a new direction, the report notes that, in the past, "United Nations operations in areas of crisis have generally been established after conflict has occurred." But now, the "time has come to plan for circumstances warranting preventive deployment." The Secretary-General explains:

> Under Article 42 of the Charter, the Security Council has the authority to take military action to maintain or restore international peace and security. While such action should only be taken when all peaceful means have failed, the option of taking it is essential to the credibility of the United Nations as a guarantor of international security. This will require ... special agreements ... whereby Member States undertake to make armed forces, assistance and facilities available to the Security Council ... not only on an ad hoc basis but *on a permanent basis*.[39] [Emphasis added]

As a sop to anyone concerned about national independence, he promised: "The foundation-stone of this work is and must remain the State. Respect for its fundamental sovereignty and integrity are crucial to any common international progress." But in the next breath, he showed his real intentions by noting, "The time of absolute and exclusive sovereignty ... has passed."[40] Yes, national sovereignty will remain, but only *as defined by the United Nations*. As the Secretary-General himself said, the concept of sovereignty "takes a new meaning."

The new agenda championed by the UN's top official calls for "a United Nations capable of maintaining international peace and security, of securing justice and human rights and of promoting ... 'social progress and better standards of life in larger freedom.'"[41] If that sounds to you like the globalists intend to blur the distinction between foreign and domestic matters, then you have begun to grasp the evolving meaning of "peacekeeping," "peacemaking," and "peacebuilding."

For further evidence that the UN leader intends the world body to become a global Big Brother meddling in every aspect of our lives, consider the following from the Boutros-Ghali report: "The sources of conflict and war are pervasive and deep.... To reach them will require our utmost effort ... to promote sustainable economic and social development...."[42]

In what social or economic spheres, if any, will the world orderites *not* find a pretext for intervention? According to the new UN agenda, there are none. Among the "new risks for stability" listed by the Secretary-General are "ecological damage" and "disruption of family and community life." Other "sources of conflict" include "unchecked population growth," "drugs and the growing disparity between rich and poor," "[p]overty, disease, famine," "drought," "a porous ozone shield," and about anything else you might imagine.[43]

According to the UN leader, "the efforts of the Organization to build peace, stability and security must encompass matters beyond military threats in order to break the fetters of strife and warfare that have characterized the past."[44] In other words, under the new UN definitions of "peacekeeping," virtually any circumstance or condition in any part of the world might conceivably constitute a "risk for stability" or a "threat" to peace, and therefore justify UN intervention, including military intervention.

What is so incredible about all of this is not the arrogance and effrontery of Boutros-Ghali and his many like-minded associates in proposing such a colossal power grab. What else can be expected from a gang of megalomaniacs? The far more incredible feature of this developing nightmare is the almost complete ignorance of, and near total absence of opposition to it. What should be strikingly obvious to anyone — particularly to Americans, who should have a special appreciation for the limitation of governmental force — is that an organization powerful enough to enforce world "peace" would also be powerful enough to enforce world tyranny. No organization should ever have that kind of power!

Americans should have been shocked and outraged then, when President Bush, in his address to the United Nations General Assembly on September 21, 1992, announced: "I welcome the Secretary General's call for a new agenda to strengthen the United Nations' ability to prevent, contain, and resolve conflict across the globe.... Robust peace-keeping requires men and equipment that only member states can provide.... These forces must be available on short notice at the request of the Security Council...." Mr. Bush said the challenges "as we enter the 21st century" will "require us to transform our collective institutions." He pledged to work with the UN "to best employ our considerable lift, logistics, communications, and intelligence capabilities," and stated: "The United States is prepared to make available our bases and facilities for multinational training and field exercises. One such base, nearby, with facilities is Fort Dix."[45]

Other than the John Birch Society, which has warned about these impending developments for decades, very few have raised a voice to spread the alarm. One who has is syndicated columnist Sam Francis. Commenting on *An Agenda for Peace*, he wrote: "If Americans would like to preserve the national independence and sovereignty they and their forebears have fought for, they need to pull down the one-world monstrosity Boutros-Ghali is planning before he and his planners have a chance to build it."[46]

And to that every freedom-loving American should say, Amen!

UN PHOTO

The UN Security Council on January 31, 1992 met for the first time at the level of heads of state or government. The exalted group included (from the left): Foreign Minister Nathan Shamuyarira of Zimbabwe, Prime Minister Carlos Veiga of Cape Verde, Prime Minster P. V. Narasimha Rao of India, Prime Minister Kiichi Miyazawa of Japan, President Rodrigo Borja-Cevallos of Ecuador, King Hassan II of Morocco, President George Bush of the United States, Prime Minister John Major of the United Kingdom, Secretary-General Boutros Boutros-Ghali, President Boris Yeltsin of the Russian Federation, President Francois Mitterrand of France, President Carlos Perez of Venezuela, Prime Minister Li Peng of China, Chancellor Franz Vranitzky of Austria, Prime Minister Wilfried Martens of Belgium, and Foreign Minister Geza Jeszenszky of Hungary.

21

Before the UN General Assembly on September 21, 1992, President George Bush endorsed Secretary-General Boutros-Ghali's call for a permanent UN army.

France's Socialist President Francois Mitterrand pledged 2,000 men for UN rapid deployment force.

Red Chinese Premier Li Peng, the Butcher of Tiananmen Square, speaks at UN of "human rights" and "social tranquility."

UN troops disarmed anti-communist Nicaraguan forces in 1990. The UN did not disarm the much more heavily armed communist Sandinista forces supplied by Cuba and the Soviet Union.

Communist-instigated "ethnic conflict" in Yugoslavia provides pretext for UN military intervention and appeals for greatly enlarged UN peacekeeping forces.

23

President John F. Kennedy signed *Freedom From War* and *Blueprint for the Peace Race* in September 1961 and April 1962, respectively. Both documents called for tansferring U.S. armaments and forces to an all-powerful UN military.

Secretary of State Edward Stettinius signs the UN Charter as President Harry Truman looks on. Stettinius agreed to the naming of a Soviet as UN Under-Secretary-General for Political and Security Council Affairs, the post in charge of UN military actions. Communists have held the post ever since.

Russian Vladimir E. Petrovsky (right) was named in January 1992 as Under-Secretary-General for Political Affairs (the "Security Council" part of the title was dropped).

CHAPTER 2

In the Name of Peace

The U.N. jets next turned their attention to the center of the city. Screaming in at treetop level ... they blasted the post office and the radio station, severing Katanga's communications with the outside world.... One came to the conclusion that the U.N.'s action was intended to make it more difficult for correspondents to let the world know what was going on in Katanga.... [1]

— Smith Hempstone
Rebels, Mercenaries, and Dividends, 1962

Early in 1987, millions of American television viewers tuned in to watch the dramatic ABC mini-series, *Amerika.* What they saw was a grim, menacing portrayal of life in our nation after it had been taken over by a Soviet-controlled United Nations force. Their TV sets showed a foreboding picture of America as an occupied police-state, complete with concentration camps, brainwashing, neighborhood spies, and Soviet-UN troops, tanks and helicopter gunships enforcing "the rule of law."

Liberals angrily denounced the mini-series, claiming it demonized both the Soviets and the UN and insisting that it would rekindle anti-communist hysteria at a time when Soviet-American relations were at their best point since the end of World War II. The fact that Soviet troops were at that very time committing real atrocities against the peoples of Afghanistan didn't matter. UN officials, furious about the way their organization was being portrayed, even tried to have the program cancelled. [2]

Why all the furor? Is the UN's image so sacrosanct or the goal of U.S.-Soviet rapprochement so sacred that even fictional tarnishing is akin to blasphemy? After all, it was just a television program. Haven't there been scores of highly acclaimed Hollywood productions depicting the U.S. military and American patriots in similarly bad or even far worse light? Besides, the totalitarianism depicted in *Amerika* could never happen here. Could it?

Dress Rehearsal?

You may be surprised to learn that *it has already happened here*. No, not in the same manner and on the same scale as viewers saw in the television series, but in an alarming real-life parallel of that dramatic production. What follows is the true, but little-known story of the "invasion" of about a dozen American cities by "UN forces," as told by economist/author Dr. V. Orval Watts in his 1955 book, *The United Nations: Planned Tyranny*.

At Fort MacArthur, California, and in other centers, considerable numbers of American military forces went into training in 1951 as "Military Government Reserve Units." What they were for may appear from their practice maneuvers during the two years, 1951-1952.

Their first sally took place on July 31, 1951, when they simulated an invasion and seizure of nine California cities: Compton, Culver City, Inglewood, Hawthorne, Huntington Park, Long Beach, Redondo Beach, South Gate and Torrance. The invading forces, however, did not fly the American flag. They came in under the flag of the United Nations, and their officers stated that they represented the United Nations.

These forces arrested the mayors and police chiefs, and pictures later appeared in the newspapers showing these men in jail. The officers issued manifestoes reading "by virtue of the authority vested in me by the United Nations Security Council." At Huntington Park they held a flag-raising ceremony, taking down the American flag and running up in its place the United Nations banner.

On April 3, 1952, other units did the same thing at Lampasas, Texas. They took over the town, closed churches, strutted their authority over the teachers and posted guards in classrooms, set up concentration camps, and interned businessmen after holding brief one-sided trials without *habeas corpus*.

Said a newspaper report of that Texas invasion: "But the staged action almost became actual drama when one student and two troopers forgot it was only make-believe. 'Ain't nobody going to make me get up,' cried John Snell, 17, his face beet-red. One of the paratroopers shoved the butt of his rifle within inches of Snell's face and snarled, 'You want this butt placed in your teeth? Get up.' "

The invaders put up posters listing many offenses for which citizens would be punished. One of them read: "25. Publishing or circulating or having in his possession with intent to publish or circulate, any printed or written matter ... hostile, detrimental, or disrespectful ... to the Government of any other of the United Nations."

Think back to the freedom-of-speech clause of the United States Constitution which every American officer and official is sworn to support and defend. What was in the minds of those who prepared, approved and posted these UN proclamations?

The third practice seizure under the United Nations flag occurred at Watertown, New York, August 20, 1952, more than a year later than the first ones. It followed the same pattern set in the earlier seizures in California and Texas.

Is this a foretaste of World Government, which so many Americans seem to want?[3]

Who ordered these "mock" UN invasions? And to what purpose were they carried out? Do answers to these questions really matter? Or are these merely idle concerns about curious but irrelevant events that happened decades ago and have no bearing on our lives today?

Events, developments, and official policies in the succeeding years, under both Republican and Democratic administrations, indicate that the mock invasions of the early 1950s do matter and that they do have a bearing on our lives today. The dress-rehearsal takeovers of American cities described above occurred just six years after the founding of the United Nations, while the organization was still enjoying widespread public support. American military personnel were at that very time fighting and dying under the UN flag in Korea. But as recounted in our previous chapter, a decade later in September of 1961, the President of the United States would propose a phased transfer of America's military forces to the UN. Under such a plan, our Army, Navy, Air Force, Marine Corps, even our nuclear arsenal, would be given over to UN command, making it possible for our nation's military forces to be used in a *real* UN invasion at some future date anywhere in the world.

Interestingly, the Kennedy *Freedom From War* plan differed little from one proposed earlier that same month by the Soviet-dominated "nonaligned" nations at a conference held in Belgrade, Yugoslavia.[4] And it was merely an expansion of the policy enunciated by Secretary of State Christian Herter (CFR) during the latter days of the Eisenhower Administration. But few Americans even saw, and fewer still ever read and understood the incredible disarmament document. For those who did see, read and understand it, however, there could be no doubt that it created a path leading to global dictatorship.

If the American public had been aware of *Freedom From War* and a number of then-classified government studies being prepared at that time — each of which spelled out even more explicitly the intent of government and Establishment elitists to surrender America to an all-powerful United Nations — there may well have been a popular uprising that would have swept all of the internationalist schemers from public office and public trust.

In February 1961, seven months before the President released the *Freedom From War* plan to the public, his State Department, led by Secretary of State Dean Rusk (CFR), hired the private Institute for Defense Analyses (contract No. SCC 28270) to prepare a study showing how disarmament could be employed to lead to world government. On March 10, 1962, the Institute delivered Study Memorandum No. 7, *A World Effectively Controlled By the United Nations*, written by Lincoln P. Bloomfield (CFR).[5] Dr. Bloomfield had himself recently served with the State Department's disarmament staff, and while writing his important work was serving as an associate professor of political science and director of the Arms Control Project at the Center for International Studies, Massachusetts Institute of Technology.

This Bloomfield/IDA report is especially significant because the author is uncharacteristically candid, eschewing the usual euphemisms, code words, and double-talk found in typical "world order" pronouncements meant for public consumption. The author believed he was addressing fellow internationalists in a classified memorandum that would never be made available for public scrutiny. So he felt he could speak plainly.

Here is the document's opening passage, labelled *SUMMARY*:

A world effectively controlled by the United Nations is one in which "world government" would come about through the establishment of supranational institutions, characterized by mandatory universal membership and some ability to employ physical force. Effective control would thus entail a preponderance of political power in the hands of a supranational organization.... [T]he present UN Charter could theoretically be revised in order to erect such an organization equal to the task envisaged, thereby codifying a radical rearrangement of power in the world.

Dr. Bloomfield was still fudging a little as he began. The phrase "some ability to employ physical force" was more than a slight understatement, as the bulk of the report makes abundantly clear. He continued:

The principal features of a model system would include the following: (1) powers sufficient to monitor and enforce disarmament, settle disputes, and keep the peace — including taxing powers — with all other powers reserved to the nations; (2) an international force, balanced appropriately among ground, sea, air, and space elements, consisting of 500,000 men, recruited individually, wearing a UN uniform, and controlling a nuclear force composed of 50-100 mixed land-based mobile and undersea-based missiles, averaging one megaton per weapon; (3) governmental powers distributed among three branches...; (4) compulsory jurisdiction of the International Court....[6]

"The notion of a 'UN-controlled world' is today a fantastic one," the professor wrote. "... Political scientists have generally come to despair of quantum jumps to world order as utopian and unmindful of political realities. But fresh minds from military, scientific, and industrial life ... have sometimes found the logic of world government — and it is world government we are discussing here — inescapable."[7]

Dr. Bloomfield then cited Christian Herter's speech of February 18, 1960, in which the Secretary of State called for disarmament "to the point where no single nation or group of nations could effectively oppose this enforcement of international law by international machinery."[8] To this CFR-affiliated academic, who had recently worked for the disarmament agency where Herter's speech had most likely been written, there was no question about the meaning of the Secretary of State's words.

"Here, then," said Bloomfield, "is the basis in recent American policy for the notion of a world 'effectively controlled by the United Nations.' It was not made explicit, but the United States position carried the unmistakable meaning, by whatever name, of world government, sufficiently powerful in any event to keep the peace and enforce its judgments."[9]

Then, to be absolutely certain that there would be no confusion or misunderstanding about his meaning, he carefully defined his terms:

> "World" means that the system is global, with no exceptions to its fiat: universal membership. "Effectively controlled" connotes ... a relative monopoly of physical force at the center of the system, and thus a preponderance of political power in the hands of a supranational organization.... "The United Nations" is not necessarily precisely the organization as it now exists.... *Finally, to avoid endless euphemism and evasive verbiage, the contemplated regime will occasionally be referred to unblushingly as a "world government."*[10] [Emphasis added]

If government is "force" — as George Washington so simply and accurately defined it — then world government is "world force." Which means that Bloomfield and those who commissioned his report and agreed with its overall recommendations wanted to create a global entity with a monopoly of force — a political, even military power undisputedly superior to any single nation-state or any possible alliance of national or regional forces. It is as simple as that.

"The appropriate degree of relative force," the Bloomfield/IDA study concluded, "would ... involve total disarmament down to police and internal security levels for the constituent units, as against a significant conventional capability at the center backed by a marginally significant nuclear capability."[11] Again and again as the following excerpts demonstrate, the study drives its essential points home:

- "National disarmament is a condition *sine qua non* for effective UN control.... [W]ithout it, effective UN control is not possible."[12]
- "The essential point is the transfer of the most vital element of sovereign power from the states to a supranational government."[13]
- "The overwhelming central fact would still be the loss of control of their military power by individual nations."[14]

Putting Theory Into Practice

While Dr. Bloomfield was still writing his treatise for global rule, the hapless residents of a small corner of Africa were experiencing the terrible reality of "a world effectively controlled by the United Nations." The site chosen for the debut of the UN's version of "peace-keeping" was Katanga, a province in what was then known as the Belgian Congo. The center of world attention 30 years ago, the name Katanga draws a complete blank from most people today.

Katanga and its tragic experience have been expunged from history, consigned to the memory hole. The region appears on today's maps as the Province of Shaba in Zaire. But for one brief, shining moment, the courageous people in this infant nation stood as the singular testament to the capability of the newly independent Africans to govern themselves as free people with a sense of peace, order, and justice.

While all around them swirled a maelstrom of violent, communist-inspired revolution and bloody tribal warfare, the Katangese distinguished themselves as a paradigm of racial, tribal, and class harmony.[15] What they stood for could not be tolerated by the forces of "anti-colonialism" in the Kremlin, the U.S. State Department, the Western news media, and especially the United Nations.[16]

The stage was already set for the horrible drama that would soon unfold when Belgium's King Baudouin announced independence for the Belgian Congo on June 30, 1960. The Soviets, who had been agitating and organizing in the Congo for years, were ready. Patrice Lumumba was their man, bought and paid for with cash, arms, luxuries, and all the women, gin, and hashish he wanted. With his

Soviet and Czech "diplomats" and "technicians" who swarmed all over the Congo, Lumumba was able to control the Congo elections. [17] With Lumumba as premier and Joseph Kasavubu as president, peaceful independence lasted one week. Then Lumumba unleashed a communist reign of terror against the populace, murdering and torturing men, women, and children. Amidst this sea of carnage and terror, the province of Katanga remained, by comparison, an island of peace, order, and stability. Under the able leadership of the courageous Moise Kapenda Tshombe, Katanga declared its independence from the central Congolese regime. "I am seceding from chaos," declared President Tshombe, a devout Christian and an ardent anti-communist. [18]

These were the days when the whole world witnessed the cry and the reality of "self determination" as it swept through the African continent. Anyone should have expected that Katanga's declaration of independence would have been greeted with the same huzzahs at the UN and elsewhere that similar declarations from dozens of communist revolutionary movements and pip-squeak dictatorships had evoked.

But it was Tshombe's misfortune to be pro-Western, pro-free enterprise, and pro-constitutionally limited government at a time when the governments of both the U.S. and the USSR were supporting Marxist "liberators" throughout the world. Nikita Khrushchev declared Tshombe to be "a turncoat, a traitor to the interests of the Congolese people." [19] American liberals and the rabble at the UN dutifully echoed the hue and cry.

To our nation's everlasting shame, on July 14, 1960, the U.S. joined with the USSR in support of a UN resolution authorizing the world body to send troops to the Congo. [20] These troops were used, *not* to stop the bloody reign of terror being visited on the rest of the Congo, but to assist Lumumba, the chief terrorist, in his efforts to subjugate Katanga. Within four days of the passage of that resolution, thousands of UN troops were flown on U.S. transports into the Congo, where they joined in the campaign against the only island of sanity in all of black Africa.

Smith Hempstone, African correspondent for the *Chicago Daily News*, gave this firsthand account of the December 1961 UN attack on Elisabethville, the capital of Katanga:

> The U.N. jets next turned their attention to the center of the city.
> Screaming in at treetop level ... they blasted the post office and the
> radio station, severing Katanga's communications with the outside
> world.... One came to the conclusion that the U.N.'s action was in-
> tended to make it more difficult for correspondents to let the world
> know what was going on in Katanga....
>   A car pulled up in front of the Grand Hotel Leopold II where all of
> us were staying. "Look at the work of the American criminals," sobbed
> the Belgian driver. "Take a picture and send it to Kennedy!" In the
> backseat, his eyes glazed with shock, sat a wounded African man cra-
> dling in his arms the body of his ten-year-old son. The child's face and
> belly had been smashed to jelly by mortar fragments. [21]

The 46 doctors of Elisabethville — Belgian, Swiss, Hungarian,
Brazilian, and Spanish — unanimously issued a joint report indict-
ing the United Nations atrocities against innocent civilians. This is
part of their account of a UN attack on a hospital:

> The Shinkolobwe hospital is visibly marked with an enormous red
> cross on the roof.... In the maternity, roof, ceilings, walls, beds, tables
> and chairs are riddled with bullets.... 4 Katangan women who had just
> been delivered and one new-born child are wounded, a visiting child of
> 4 years old is killed; two men and one child are killed.... [22]

The UN atrocities escalated. Unfortunately, we do not have space
here to devote to relating more of the details of this incredibly vi-
cious chapter of UN history — even though the progress toward establishing a permanent UN army makes full knowledge of every
part of it more vital than ever. Among the considerable body of additional testimony about the atrocities, we highly recommend *The
Fearful Master* by G. Edward Griffin; *Who Killed the Congo?* by
Philippa Schuyler; *Rebels, Mercenaries, and Dividends* by Smith
Hempstone; and *46 Angry Men* by the 46 doctors of Elisabethville.
    In 1962, a private group of Americans, outraged at our govern-
ment's actions against the freedom-seeking Katangese, attempted

to capture on film the truth about what was happening in the Congo. They produced *Katanga: The Untold Story*, an hour-long documentary narrated by Congressman Donald L. Jackson. With newsreel footage and testimony from eyewitnesses, including a compelling interview with Tshombe himself, the program exposed the criminal activities and brutal betrayal perpetrated on a peaceful people by the Kennedy Administration, other Western leaders, and top UN officials. It documents the fact that UN (including U.S.) planes deliberately bombed Katanga's schools, hospitals, and churches, while UN troops machine-gunned and bayoneted civilians, school children, and Red Cross workers who tried to help the wounded. This film is now available on videotape,[23] and is "must-viewing" for Americans who are determined that this land or any other land shall never experience similar UN atrocities.

After waging three major offensive campaigns against the fledgling state, the UN "peace" forces overwhelmed Katanga and forced it back under communist rule. Even though numerous international observers witnessed and publicly protested the many atrocities committed by the UN's forces, the world body has never apologized for or admitted to its wrongdoing. In fact, the UN and its internationalist cheering section continue to refer to this shameful episode as a resounding success.[24] Which indeed it was, if one keeps in mind the true goal of the organization.

Following the Policy Line

Why did the government of the United States side with the Soviet Union and the United Nations in their support of communists Lumumba and Kasavubu and their denunciation of Tshombe? Why did our nation supply military assistance to and an official endorsement of the UN's military action against Katanga? The answer to both questions is that our government was guided by the same "world order" policy line laid out by the *New York Times* in its hard-to-believe editorial of August 16, 1961:

[W]e must seek to discourage anti-Communist revolts in order to avert bloodshed and war. We must, under our own principles, live with evil even if by doing so we help to stabilize tottering Communist regimes, as in East Germany, and perhaps even expose citadels of freedom, like West Berlin, to slow death by strangulation.[25]

Further elaboration on this theme is revealed in a 1963 study conducted for the United States Arms Control and Disarmament Agency by the Peace Research Institute. Published in April of that year, here's what our tax dollars produced:

> Whether we admit it to ourselves or not, we benefit enormously from the capability of the Soviet police system to keep law and order over the 200 million odd Russians and the many additional millions in the satellite states. The break-up of the Russian Communist empire today would doubtless be conducive to freedom, but would be a good deal more catastrophic for world order....[26]

"We benefit enormously?" Who is this "we"? Certainly not the American taxpayer, who carried the tax burden for the enormous military expenditures needed to "contain" Soviet expansionism.

And who determined that freedom must be sacrificed in the name of "world order"?

Dr. Bloomfield, in the same classified IDA study cited earlier, again let the world-government cat out of the bag. If the communists remained too militant and threatening, he observed, "the subordination of states to a true world government appears impossible; *but if the communist dynamic were greatly abated, the West might well lose whatever incentive it has for world government.*"[27] (Emphasis added)

In other words, the world order Insiders were faced with the following conundrum: How do we make the Soviets menacing enough to convince Americans that world government is the only answer because confrontation is untenable; but, at the same time, not make the Soviets so menacing that Americans would decide to fight rather than become subject to communist tyrants?

Are we unfairly stretching these admissions? Not at all. Keep in mind that from the end of World War II, up to the very time these statements were being written, the communists had brutally added Albania, Bulgaria, Yugoslavia, Poland, Romania, Czechoslovakia,

North Korea, Hungary, East Germany, China, Tibet, North Vietnam, and Cuba to their satellite empire and were aggressively instigating revolutions throughout Africa, Asia, Latin America, and the Middle East.

And, as was later demonstrated by the historical research of Dr. Antony Sutton and other scholars, all of these Soviet conquests had been immeasurably helped by massive and continuous transfusions from the West to the Kremlin of money, credit, technology, and scientific knowledge.[28] It was arranged for and provided by the same CFR-affiliated policy elitists who recognized in the "communist dynamic" they created an "incentive" for the people in the West to accept "world government."

Project Phoenix
The U.S. Departments of State and Defense funded numerous other studies about U.S.-USSR convergence and world order under UN control. In 1964, the surfacing of the Project Phoenix reports generated sufficient constituent concern to prompt several members of Congress to protest the funding of such studies.[29] But there was not enough pressure to force Congress to launch full investigations that could have led to putting an end to taxpayer funding of these serious attacks on American security and our constitutional system of government.

Produced by the Institute for Defense Analyses for the U.S. Arms Control and Disarmament Agency, the Phoenix studies openly advocated "unification" of the U.S. and USSR.[30] The following passages taken from *Study Phoenix Paper* dated June 4, 1963 leaves no doubt about this goal:

Unification — ... At present the approach ... may appear so radical that it will be dismissed out of hand; nevertheless, its logical simplicity ... is so compelling that it seems to warrant more systematic investigation....

Today, the United States and the Soviet Union combined have for all practical purposes a near monopoly of force in the world. If the use and direction of this power could somehow be synchronized, stability and, indeed even unity might be within reach.[31]

The Phoenix studies, like many other government reports before and after, urged increased U.S. economic, scientific, and agricultural assistance to the Soviet Union. These recommendations are totally consistent with the long-range "merger" plans admitted to a decade before by Ford Foundation President Rowan Gaither. And both Republican and Democratic administrations have followed the same overall policy ever since. But world order think-tank specialists like Bloomfield realized that the incremental progress made through these programs was too slow. He even lamented that reaching the final goal "could take up to two hundred years."[32]

Bloomfield then noted that there was "an alternate road" to merger and eventual world government, one that "relies on a grave crisis or war to bring about a sudden transformation in national attitudes sufficient for the purpose."[33] The taxpayer-funded academic explained that "the order we examine may be brought into existence as a result of a series of sudden, nasty, and traumatic shocks."[34]

Incredible? Impossible? Couldn't happen here? Many Americans thought so 30 years ago — before "perestroika," the Persian Gulf War, propaganda about global warming, and other highly publicized developments. But by the fall of 1990, *Newsweek* magazine would be reporting on the emerging reality of "Superpowers as Superpartners" and "a new order.... the United States and the Soviet Union, united for *crisis management* around the globe."[35] (Emphasis added)

In a seeming tipping of his hat to Bloomfield, President Bush would state in his official August 1991 report, *National Security Strategy of The United States*: "I hope history will record that the Gulf crisis was the crucible of the new world order."[36]

The CFR's house academics were already beating the convergence drums. Writing in the Winter 1990 issue of *Foreign Policy* (published by the Carnegie Endowment for International Peace), Thomas G. Weiss (CFR) and Meryl A. Kessler exhorted: "If Washington is to seize the full potential of this opportunity, it will have to ... begin to treat the Soviet Union as a real partner."

The long-planned partnership began to take form officially with the signing of "A Charter for American-Russian Partnership and Friendship" by Presidents Bush and Yeltsin on June 17, 1992.

Among the many commitments for joint action in this agreement, we find the following:

- "... Summit meetings will be held on a regular basis";
- "The United States of America and the Russian Federation recognize the importance of the United Nations Security Council" and support "the strengthening of UN peace-keeping";
- The parties are determined "to cooperate in the development of ballistic missile defense capabilities and technologies," and work toward creation of a joint "Ballistic Missile Early Warning Center";
- "In view of the potential for building a strategic partnership between the United States of America and the Russian Federation, the parties intend to accelerate defense cooperation between their military establishments ..."; and
- "The parties will also pursue cooperation in peacekeeping, counter-terrorism, and counter-narcotics missions."[37]

Before this charter had even been signed, however, our new "partners" were already landing their bombers on American soil. *Airman*, a magazine for the U.S. Air Force, reported in large headlines for the cover story of its July 1992 issue: "The Russians Have Landed." The cover also featured a photo of the two Russian Tu-95 Bear bombers and an An-124 transport which had landed on May 9th at Barksdale Air Force Base in Louisiana. An accompanying article noted that the Russians were given "a rousing salute from a brass band and a thrilled gathering of Air Force people and civilians who waved U.S. and Commonwealth of Independent States flags."

The long-standing plan of the Insiders calls for a merger of the U.S. and the USSR (or Commonwealth of Independent States as it has become) and then world government under the United Nations (see Chapter 5). Details leading to completion of the plan are unfolding week after week, month after month, before an almost totally unaware America.

UN "invasion" of Lampasas, Texas, 1952 (top); U.S. forces under UN flag "arrest" mayor of Culver City, California, 1951 (center); sign on Lampasas bank reads: "Closed by order of Military Government."

UN soldier stands guard over airfield in Elisabethville, Katanga, where U.S. Air Force planes transported UN troops, weapons, supplies.

Presidents Bush and Yeltsin meet in June 1992 to sign "A Charter for American-Russian Partnership and Friendship."

With UN help, Soviet stooge "Premier" Patrice Lumumba (left) unleashed reign of terror on Congo.

"President" Joseph Kasavubu, with Lumumba's help, imposed dictatorship on Congo.

Moise Tshombe, the Christian, anti-communist, pro-American president of peaceful Katanga, was attacked by UN-U.S.-Soviet coalition.

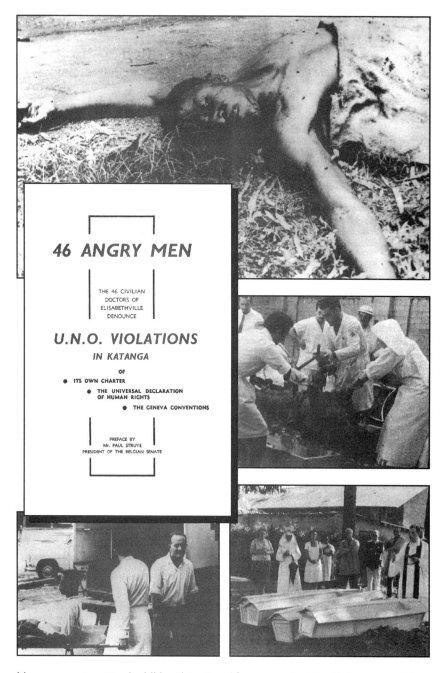

46 ANGRY MEN

THE 46 CIVILIAN
DOCTORS OF
ELISABETHVILLE
DENOUNCE

U.N.O. VIOLATIONS
IN KATANGA

OF
● ITS OWN CHARTER
   ● THE UNIVERSAL DECLARATION
      OF HUMAN RIGHTS
      ● THE GENEVA CONVENTIONS

PREFACE BY
Mr. PAUL STRUYE
PRESIDENT OF THE BELGIAN SENATE

Numerous atrocities by UN multinational forces against the Katangese civilian population were detailed by foreign correspondents and the 46 doctors of Elisabethville, Katanga. Women, children, the elderly, hospitals, ambulances, and medical personnel were not spared in the savage attacks.

Airman

Magazine of America's Air Force

July 1992

Soviet Bombers Land On U.S. Soil

Joint Ops Is a Mixed Profession

Two Soviet Tu-95 Bear bombers and a Soviet An-124 transport landed on American soil at Barksdale Air Force Base in Louisiana in May 1992. The Soviet "visit," arranged by Air Force Chief of Staff Gen. Merrill A. McPeak (CFR), is one of the many programs and efforts underway to condition Americans for the planned U.S.-Soviet "merger" outlined by Ford Foundation President H. Rowan Gaither in 1953.

CHAPTER 3

The UN Founders

We're now in sight of a United Nations that performs as envisioned by its founders. [1]
— George Bush, September 11, 1990
Televised address before a Joint Session of Congress

At last the United Nations is beginning to fulfill the security mission its founders intended.
— Democratic Congressman Lee H. Hamilton
Foreign Affairs, Summer 1992

With the United Nations finally beginning to function as its framers intended, it is time for the United States to lead....
— Republican Congressman James A. Leach
Foreign Affairs, Summer 1992

The United Nations has begun to fulfill the vision of its founders. [2]
— *Changing Our Ways*, 1992 report of the
Carnegie Endowment for International Peace

After suffering years of declining prestige, the United Nations is once again basking in the same glory it enjoyed in the immediate post-World War II years. Solemn references to the "ideals," "vision," and "wisdom" of the UN founders abound in current speeches and articles as we experience another round of historical revisionism. In 1945, we are told, a peace-hungry world groped for solutions that would put an end to war. Atomic weapons made their quest an absolute necessity, because an atomic exchange could put an end to mankind. Statesmen of great vision seized the opportunity and fashioned an instrument — the United Nations — to attain that lofty and elusive goal: world peace.

Creation of the CFR

That, of course, is the standard textbook rendering and the interpretation of history most frequently encountered today. Unfortunately, it is not accurate. The organization known as the United Nations did indeed officially come into being with the signing of the UN Charter by representatives from 50 nations meeting in San Francisco on June 26, 1945. But that signal event was the culmination of years of planning by a private, high-level policy group that had gained de facto control of our foreign policy during the Roosevelt Administration. Immediately after our entry into the war, that organization, the Council on Foreign Relations (CFR), planted the idea of a world-governing "peace" organization. At the instigation of our State Department, the 26 nations at war against the Axis powers proclaimed themselves the United Nations in January 1942. Historian Clarence Carson observed:

> Roosevelt worked to avoid the pitfalls that had helped to keep the United States out of the League of Nations. His hand is clearly apparent in trying to get the name accepted even before the organization had been formed. (Americans continued to refer to their side as the "Allies" during World War II, not the "United Nations," but officially the term was being used anyhow.)[3]

President Roosevelt, however, was merely implementing the policies that were being handed to him. In his 1988 exposé, *The Shadows of Power: The Council on Foreign Relations and the American Decline,* James Perloff outlined the genesis of the UN plan:

> In January 1943, Secretary of State Cordell Hull formed a steering committee composed of himself, Leo Pasvolsky, Isaiah Bowman, Sumner Welles, Norman Davis, and Morton Taylor. All of these men — with the exception of Hull — were in the CFR. Later known as the Informal Agenda Group, they drafted the original proposal for the United Nations. It was Bowman — a founder of the CFR and member of Colonel House's old "Inquiry" — who first put forward the concept.

They called in three attorneys, all CFR men, who ruled that it was constitutional. Then they discussed it with FDR on June 15, 1944. The President approved the plan, and announced it to the public that same day.[4]

The list of those in the U.S. delegation to the UN's founding San Francisco Conference reads like a CFR roll call. Delegates who were, had been, or would later become members of the Council included:[5]

Theodore C. Achilles	Foy D. Kohler
James W. Angell	John E. Lockwood
Hamilton Fish Armstrong	Archibald MacLeish
Charles E. Bohlen	John J. McCloy
Isaiah Bowman	Cord Meyer, Jr.
Ralph Bunche	Edward G. Miller, Jr.
John M. Cabot	Hugh Moore
Mitchell B. Carroll	Leo Pasvolsky
Andrew W. Cordier	Dewitt C. Poole
John S. Dickey	William L. Ransom
John Foster Dulles	Nelson A. Rockefeller
James Clement Dunn	James T. Shotwell
Clyde Eagleton	Harold E. Stassen
Clark M. Eichelberger	Edward R. Stettinius, Jr.
Muir S. Fairchild	Adlai E. Stevenson
Thomas K. Finletter	Arthur Sweetser
Artemus Gates	James Swihart
Arthur J. Hepburn	Llewellyn E. Thompson
Julius C. Holmes	Herman B. Wells
Philip C. Jessup	Francis Wilcox
Joseph E. Johnson	Charles W. Yost
R. Keith Kane	

The secretary-general of the conference was U.S. State Department official Alger Hiss, a member of the CFR and a secret Soviet agent. Other high-level American communists who served as delegates included: Noel Field, Harold Glasser, Irving Kaplan, Nathan Gregory Silvermaster, Victor Perlo, Henry Julian Wadley, and

Harry Dexter White. Some — like Hiss, Lauchlin Currie, and Lawrence Duggan — shared the odious distinction of membership in both the Council and the Communist Party. In the next chapter, we will explore the important relationship between these two seemingly disparate organizations as well as the communist leadership role at the conference. But for now, let us concentrate on the Council.

What the historical record shows, and what is essential for all people of good will to understand, is that the United Nations is completely a creature of the Council on Foreign Relations and was designed by that organization eventually to become an instrument for an all-powerful world government. In order to establish the factual basis for this claim, and to permit an appreciation for the significance of it, we must revisit some murky pages of the history of this century.

Some Necessary Background

Hitler's invasion of Poland, the *casus belli* of World War II, was launched on September 1, 1939. Although the United States would not enter the war for two more years (December 1941), within days of the German invasion top members of the CFR were taking over *post-war* planning for the Roosevelt Administration. In 1947, the Council published its own version of how it came to run FDR's State Department:

> Within a week [of the war's start], Hamilton Fish Armstrong, Editor of *Foreign Affairs*, and Walter H. Mallory, Executive Director of the Council, paid a visit to the Department of State to offer such aid on the part of the Council as might be useful and appropriate in view of the war.
>
> The Department was already greatly overworked as a result of the crisis.... The Council representatives suggested that, pending the time when the Department itself would be able to assemble a staff and begin research and analysis on the proper scale, the Council might undertake work in certain fields, without, of course, any formal assignment of responsibility on the one side or restriction of independent action on the other....
>
> The Department officers welcomed the Council's suggestion and en-

couraged the Council to formulate a more detailed plan. This was done in consultation with Department officials. The Rockefeller Foundation was then approached for a grant of funds to put the plan into operation. When assurances had been received that the necessary funds would be available, the personnel of the groups were selected and on December 8, 1939, an organization meeting was held in Washington....[6]

Following that meeting, as Robert W. Lee explained in his 1981 book, *The United Nations Conspiracy*, the State Department established a Committee on Post-War Problems. It was assisted by a research staff that was organized in February 1941 into a Division of Special Research. "After the Japanese attack on Pearl Harbor," wrote Lee, "the research facilities were expanded and the overall project was reorganized into an Advisory Committee on Post-War Foreign Policies. Serving on the Committee were a number of influential CFR members, including Hamilton Fish Armstrong, Sumner Welles, Isaiah Bowman, Norman H. Davis, James T. Shotwell, Myron C. Taylor, and Leo Pasvolsky. The Russian-born Pasvolsky became the Committee's Director of Research."[7]

The Council and its defenders insist that it has no sinister agenda; that, in fact, it has no agenda at all. "The Council shall not take any position on questions of foreign policy," the organization officially declares.[8] It is simply a study group, its spokesmen regularly maintain, and its civic-minded members offered their expertise in service of their country during an hour of great peril. And they have continued to provide their services ever since.

One who heartily disagreed with those protestations of innocence and benevolence was Admiral Chester Ward, a former Judge Advocate General of the Navy, who was himself a member of the Council for 16 years. His experience led him to conclude that the group was formed for the "purpose of promoting disarmament and submergence of U.S. sovereignty and national independence into an all-powerful one-world government." Together with coauthor Phyllis Schlafly, he wrote that the most influential clique within the CFR "is composed of the one-world-global-government ideologists — more respectfully referred to as the organized internationalists. They are the ones who carry on the tradition of the founders." Moreover, he charged, "this lust to surrender the sovereignty and independence of the United States is pervasive throughout most of the membership.... The majority visualize the utopian submergence of the United States as a subsidiary administrative unit of a global government...."[9] These are serious charges from a man of considerable distinction who enjoyed the benefit of an inside look at the Insiders of the American Establishment.

Admiral Ward is far from alone in rendering this harsh judgement of the CFR. After surveying the colossal damage done to America and the Free World from the foreign and domestic policies imposed by members of the Council, many patriotic Americans have arrived at the same conclusion. These include historians, journalists, academicians, members of Congress, and other civic leaders. We will be introducing some of their statements further along in this book. More immediately, however, let us examine the origins of the Council on Foreign Relations.

Origins of the CFR
According to the CFR's own history:

> The origins of the Council on Foreign Relations lay in the concern of the founders at what they regarded as the disappointing conduct of the Versailles negotiations ... and at the short-sighted, as they saw it, rejection by the United States of membership in the League of Nations. In 1921 they founded the Council as a privately funded, nonprofit and nonpartisan organization of individual members.[10]

Accompanying President Woodrow Wilson to the Versailles Peace Conference at the end of World War I were a number of men who would become founders of the CFR. Preeminent among these was Wilson's closest adviser, the mysterious Colonel Edward Mandell House. So dependent was Wilson upon House that he referred to him as "my second personality," "my independent self," "my alter ego." Further, he asserted, "His thoughts and mine are one."[11] According to Wilson biographer George Sylvester Viereck, "Woodrow Wilson stalks through history on the feet of Edward Mandell House."[12] An appreciation of this abnormal dependency, what

Viereck would call "The Strangest Friendship in History,"[13] is essential to understanding the course of American statecraft in the ensuing decades.

It was Colonel House who penned the first draft of the covenant of the League of Nations.[14] He also prevailed on Wilson to convene the group known as the "Inquiry," a cabal of American one-worlders who formulated much of Wilson's "Fourteen Points" peace program. Hand-picked by House, the group included Walter Lippman, Allen W. Dulles, John Foster Dulles, Christian A. Herter, and Norman Thomas. Director of the Inquiry was Dr. Sidney Mezes, House's brother-in-law.[15]

Perhaps one of the best sources of insight into the mind and character of Wilson's "alter ego" is a novel authored by House entitled *Philip Dru: Administrator.*[16] Although it was published anonymously during the presidential campaign of 1912, the colonel later acknowledged the book as his own. He admitted it was "not much of a novel," but that fiction was the best format for disseminating his political ideas to a large audience.[17] One need barely open the book's cover to discover the author's radical ideals. The title page prominently features a quotation by the 19th century revolutionist and arch-conspirator Giuseppe Mazzini. Identified on the same page is the book's publisher, B. W. Huebsch, a longtime publisher of left-wing literature who was affiliated with numerous Communist Party fronts. The dedication page declares, in typical Marxist fashion, that "in the starting, the world-wide social structure was wrongly begun." The novel's hero, Philip Dru, opines that American society is "a miserable travesty" and believes in "Socialism as dreamed of by Karl Marx," modified with a "spiritual leavening." Dru leads a military coup, establishes himself as dictator of the United States, abolishes the constitution and institutes Marxist reforms.

Many of Administrator Dru's "reforms" would later be adopted by President Wilson. Viereck observed that "The Wilson Administration transferred the Colonel's ideas from the pages of fiction to the pages of history."[18] House's novel, commented Dr. J. B. Matthews, "is an indispensable source book on the origins of Woodrow Wilson's New Freedom and Franklin D. Roosevelt's New Deal."[19] Through *Philip Dru,* House also proposed a "league of nations" — anticipating by seven years Wilson's appeal at Versailles for an identically-named world body.

In its 1928 *Survey of American Foreign Relations*, the CFR reported, "In the first months of the World War a new movement sprang up spontaneously — the League to Enforce Peace."[20] Actually, it didn't spring up "spontaneously" at all. The League was the creation of one Theodore Marburg, a wealthy internationalist from Maryland, and was funded primarily by Andrew Carnegie, at the time reputed to be the richest man in the world.[21] The CFR history recounts that "the four years' activity of the League to Enforce Peace served the League [of Nations] cause by preparing the public mind for its reception and by popularizing the ideal of international organization in behalf of peace."[22] Concerning Wilson's involvement with the Marburg/Carnegie League to Enforce Peace, the 1928 volume reported:

> As early as the autumn of 1914 Wilson said, when looking ahead to the end of the war; "all nations must be absorbed into some great association of nations...." When Wilson was persuaded to speak at the League to Enforce Peace banquet in Washington on May 27, 1916, he endorsed the program of that organization only indirectly, making no mention of force; but he advocated the general idea of a league with such ardor that he was henceforth regarded as its champion.[23]

The U.S. Senate, however, led by "irreconcilables" Henry Cabot Lodge of Massachusetts and William Borah of Idaho, refused to ratify the Covenant. Americans were suspicious of entanglements with the constantly warring European powers and wanted no part of submersion in a world super-state. Without American participation, the one-worlders' plans for a global government would come to naught.

"Wilson had done his best in his individualistic way from 1914 to stimulate a public desire for a liberal peace and a new world order," said the CFR's director of research Charles P. Howland. But, he wrote, "Men's minds were not ready for great decisions in a new political field; the mass opinion of 120,000,000 people orientates itself slowly in novel situations."[24]

Obviously, men's minds needed to be made "ready." It was for this purpose that the Council on Foreign Relations was launched at a May 1919 meeting held at the Majestic Hotel in Paris. Joining American members of the Inquiry were like-minded internationalists from Britain belonging to the elite, semi-secret Round Table group begun by that diamond and gold mogul of fabled wealth, Cecil Rhodes.[25] According to Rhodes biographer Sarah Millin, "The government of the world was Rhodes' simple desire."[26]

The Paris meeting was hosted by Colonel House.[27] Out of that gathering was born an Institute of International Affairs, which would have branches in London and New York. The locations were appropriate, since as one historian of the Council observed, "nearly all of them [the CFR's founding members] were bankers and lawyers."[28] Not just your ordinary, run-of-the-mill bankers and lawyers, mind you, these were the top international barristers and financiers of Wall Street who were associated with the magic name of J. P. Morgan.

"The founding president of the CFR," wrote author James Perloff, "was John W. Davis, who was J. P. Morgan's personal attorney and a millionaire in his own right. Founding vice-president was Paul Cravath, whose law firm also represented the Morgan interests. Morgan partner Russell Leffingwell would later become the Council's first chairman. A variety of other Morgan partners, attorneys and agents crowded the CFR's early membership rolls."[29]

In 1921, the American branch of the organization launched in Paris was incorporated in New York as the Council on Foreign Relations. The British branch became the Royal Institute of International Affairs, otherwise known as Chatham House.

CFR Globalist Influence Grows

To propagate its "internationalist" world view among a select intelligentsia, the Council launched a quarterly journal, *Foreign Affairs*. *Time* magazine called *Foreign Affairs* "the most influential periodical in print,"[30] while the CFR itself boasts that its journal provides an "insider's look at world politics."[31] Admiral Ward said of its influence: "By following the evolution of this propaganda in the most prestigious scholarly journal in the world, *Foreign Affairs*, anyone can determine years in advance what the future defense and foreign policies of the United States will be. If a certain proposition is repeated often enough in that journal, then the U.S. Administration in power — be it Republican or Democratic — begins to act as *if* that proposition or assumption were an established fact."[32] (Emphasis in original)

The CFR's globalist bent was evident from the first issue of *Foreign Affairs*, where readers were told, "Our government should enter heartily into the existing League of Nations...."[33] With CFR members in charge of dispersing tens of millions of dollars from the major tax-exempt foundations (Carnegie, Rockefeller, Twentieth Century Fund) each year, it was not long before an entire nationwide network of one-world support groups was established. By 1928 the CFR's research division could report to the Council:

> University courses dealing with international affairs have trebled in number since the war; there has been an outpouring of books on foreign relations, diplomatic history, and international law; periodicals such as *Foreign Affairs*, *Current History*, and the *American Journal of International Law*, and the information service of the Foreign Policy Association are supplying materials for a sound background; and associations and organizations devoted to an impartial discussion of international relations and the supplying of authentic information have sprung up in almost every great city. As yet, however, these agencies for furnishing adequate standards of judgment and accurate current information have not penetrated very far down in society.[34]

Whether or not the Council's approved sources provided "impartial discussion," "authentic information," and "adequate standards of judgment" is something for each reader to decide for himself. It is worth noting, however, that a congressional investigation by the Special House Committee to Investigate Tax-Exempt Foundations (the Reece Committee) concluded in 1954 that the CFR "productions are not objective but are directed overwhelmingly at promoting the globalist concept," and that it had become "in essence an agency of the United States Government ... carrying its internationalist bias with it."[35]

The director of research for that investigative committee was the same Norman Dodd whom we quoted in our Introduction (about the astonishing admission to him by Ford Foundation President H. Rowan Gaither). If Dodd was jarred (and he was) by Gaither's confessed involvement in a master scheme to merge the U.S. and the Soviet Union, he was no less shocked by what his investigative team found in the minutes of the Carnegie Endowment for International Peace.

In his 1980 exposé, *The Tax-Exempt Foundations*, William H. McIlhany, II interviewed Norman Dodd, who repeated what his investigator Kathryn Casey had found in the "peace" organization's minutes compiled several years before the start of World War I:

> [In the minutes] the trustees raised a question. And they discussed the question and the question was specific, "Is there any means known to man more effective than war, assuming you wish to alter the life of an entire people?" And they discussed this and at the end of a year they came to the conclusion that there was no more effective means to that end known to man. So, then they raised question number two, and the question was, "How do we involve the United States in a war?"
>
> And then they raised the question, "How do we control the diplomatic machinery of the United States?" And the answer came out, "We" must control the State Department. At this point we catch up with what we had already found out and that was that through an agency set up by the Carnegie Endowment every high appointment in the State Department was cleared. Finally, we were in a war. These trustees in a meeting about 1917 had the brashness to congratulate themselves on the wisdom of their original decision because already the impact of war had indicated it would alter life and can alter life in this country. This was the date of our entry in the war; we were involved. *They even had the brashness to word and to dispatch a telegram to Mr. Wilson, cautioning him to see that the war did not end too quickly.* [Emphasis added]
>
> The war was over. Then the concern became, as expressed by the trustees, seeing to it that there was no reversion to life in this country as it existed prior to 1914. And they came to the conclusion that, to prevent a reversion, they must control education. And then they ap-

proached the Rockefeller Foundation and they said, "Will you take on the acquisition of control of education as it involves subjects that are domestic in their significance? We'll take it on the basis of subjects that have an international significance." And it was agreed.

Then, together, they decided the key to it is the teaching of American history and they must change that. So, they then approached the most prominent of what we might call American historians at that time with the idea of getting them to alter the manner in which they presented the subject.[36]

The first president of the Endowment was Theodore Roosevelt's Secretary of State, Elihu Root,[37] who became an honorary member of the CFR in 1922 and from 1931-37 served as honorary president of the group. Later a U.S. senator and Nobel Peace Prize recipient, Root stated in his address to the CFR, at the opening of its new headquarters in 1930, that to achieve its goals the Council would have to engage in "steady, continuous, and unspectacular labor."[38]

That it has surely done. A host of adjunct organizations were created to promote the CFR viewpoint: the United World Federalists, Atlantic Council, Trilateral Commission, Aspen Institute, Business Council, Foreign Policy Association, etc. Through its members, the CFR steadily gained influence in and dominance of the executive branch of the federal government, both major political parties, important organs of the news media, major universities, influential think tanks, large tax-exempt foundations, huge multi-national corporations, international banks, and other power centers.

Historian Arthur M. Schlesinger (CFR), who served as a special assistant to President Kennedy, wrote in 1965 of "the New York financial and legal community — that arsenal of talent which had so long furnished a steady supply ... to Democratic as well as Republican administrations. This community was the heart of the American Establishment ... its front organizations [are] the Rockefeller, Ford and Carnegie foundations and the Council on Foreign Relations; its organs, the *New York Times* and *Foreign Affairs*."[39]

John J. McCloy was known in CFR Insider circles as "the chairman of the Establishment." Besides serving as chairman of the CFR from 1953 to 1970, and as chairman of both the Ford Foundation and the Rockefellers' Chase Manhattan Bank for long periods, he was friend and advisor to nine U.S. presidents, from Franklin Roosevelt to Ronald Reagan.[40] McCloy recalled: "Whenever we needed a man we thumbed through the roll of the Council members and put through a call to New York."[41]

The Council's imprimatur has become so essential for many top posts that veteran CFR member Richard Barnet has stated, "failure to be asked to be a member of the Council has been regarded for a generation as a presumption of unsuitability for high office in the national security bureaucracy."[42]

Commenting decades ago on this Insider lockgrip on our government, newspaper columnist Edith Kermit Roosevelt (a granddaughter of Theodore Roosevelt) wrote:

> What is the Establishment's view-point? Through the Roosevelt, Truman, Eisenhower and Kennedy administrations its ideology is constant: That the best way to fight Communism is by a One World Socialist state governed by "experts" like themselves. The result has been policies which favor the growth of the superstate, gradual surrender of United States sovereignty to the United Nations and a steady retreat in the face of Communist aggression.[43]

That CFR lockhold on the White House and other top positions in the federal government has continued through to the present. Writing in the September 21, 1992 issue of *The New American*, Robert W. Lee briefly cited some key indicators of continuing CFR dominance:

> At least 13 of the 18 men to serve as Secretary of State since the CFR's founding have belonged to the organization, not counting current Acting Secretary of State Lawrence Eagleburger, who is also a member. Our last eight CIA directors have also belonged, including current chief Robert M. Gates.
>
> During the past four decades alone, the major-party candidates for President and Vice President who were, or eventually became, members of the CFR include: Dwight D. Eisenhower, Adlai Stevenson, John F. Kennedy, Richard Nixon, Hubert Humphrey, George McGovern,

Gerald Ford, Jimmy Carter, Walter Mondale, Michael Dukakis, George Bush, Bill Clinton, Henry Cabot Lodge, Nelson A. Rockefeller, Edmund Muskie, and Geraldine Ferraro.

President Bush was a CFR director in the 1970s. Members of his Administration who belong include Secretary of Defense Dick Cheney, National Security Advisor Brent Scowcroft, CIA Director William Webster, and Chairman of the Joint Chiefs of Staff General Colin Powell.

The UN founders so highly lauded today were carrying out a decades-old plan of — in the words of Admiral Ward — "promoting disarmament and submergence of U.S. sovereignty and independence into an all-powerful one-world government."[44] They were "one-world-global-government-ideologists," who conspired with totalitarian communists to subvert and destroy the constitutional system of government they had sworn under oath to protect and uphold. Their treasonous actions, "ideals" and "vision" deserve not honor but utter contempt.

UN founding conference in San Francisco, 1945.

Soviet agent and Council on Foreign Relations member Alger Hiss was UN's first Secretary-General at San Francisco conference.

U.S. delegation to San Francisco conference included (from left, seated at table, facing camera): Rep. Sol Bloom; Senator Tom Connally; Secretary of State Edward Stettinius; Senator Arthur Vandenberg; Rep. Charles A. Eaton; Harold E. Stassen.

Council on Foreign Relations headquarters at the Harold Pratt House, 58 East 68th Street, in New York City. *Time* magazine calls the CFR journal *Foreign Affairs* "the most influential periodical in print."

60

Admiral Chester Ward, a CFR member for 16 years, charged the Council with trying to "submerge U.S. sovereignty and independence into an all-powerful one-world government."

President Wilson was so dependent upon the mysterious Col. House he referred to him as "my second personality," "my alter ego."

Norman Dodd, director of research for the special House Committee to Investigate Tax-Exempt Foundations, learned from Ford Foundation president H. Rowan Gaither that the large foundations were working under directives aimed at so altering "life in the United States as to make possible a comfortable merger with the Soviet Union."

Dwight D. Eisenhower

Adlai Stevenson

John F. Kennedy

Henry Cabot Lodge

Richard Nixon

Hubert Humphrey

Edmund Muskie

George McGovern

Gerald Ford

Nelson Rockefeller

Jimmy Carter

Walter Mondale

Geraldine Ferraro

Michael Dukakis

George Bush

Bill Clinton

The CFR Wins Again! During the past four decades, through both Republican and Democratic administrations, the CFR has had a lockhold on the White House, as evidenced by the Council members pictured above. In some elections the presidential and/or vice presidential candidates of both major parties have been CFR members. In 1992, CFR candidate Bill Clinton beat out CFR candidate George Bush.

62

CHAPTER 4

Reds

I am appalled at the extensive evidence indicating that there is today in the UN among the American employees there, the greatest concentration of Communists that this Committee has ever encountered.... These people occupy high positions. They have very high salaries and almost all of these people have, in the past, been employees in the U.S. government in high and sensitive positions. [1]

— U.S. Senator James O. Eastland
Activities of U.S. Citizens Employed by the UN
Hearings, Senate Committee on the Judiciary, 1952

The creation of the United Nations, as we saw in the previous chapter, was the culmination of an intensive campaign begun in the early days of this century by those who could only be described as the pillars of the American Establishment. Names like Carnegie, Morgan, Warburg, Schiff, Marburg, and Rockefeller headed the list of those promoting "world order."

It is interesting then, though a source of confusion to many, to learn that not only were the ideas of world government in general and the League of Nations and United Nations in particular especially fond goals of these "arch-capitalists," but they were also the ultimate objects of desire for world socialist and communist movements. This is not idle speculation but a matter of historical record so overwhelmingly evident as to hardly need proving. Unfortunately, that record is not widely known.

As long ago as 1915, before the Bolshevik Revolution, Lenin himself proposed a "United States of the World." [2] In 1936, the official program of the Communist International proclaimed: "Dictatorship can be established only by a victory of socialism in different countries or groups of countries, after which the proletariat republics would unite on federal lines with those already in existence, and this system of federal unions would expand ... at length forming the World Union of Socialist Soviet Republics."[3] Shortly after the founding of the UN, in March of 1946, Soviet dictator and mass-murderer Joseph Stalin declared: "I attribute great importance to U.N.O. [United Nations Organization, as it was then commonly called] since it is a serious instrument for preservation of peace and international security."[4]

The American communists, too, left no doubt about their commitment to Soviet-style, one-world government. In his 1932 book *Toward Soviet America*, William Z. Foster, national chairman of the Communist Party USA (CPUSA), wrote:

> The American Soviet government will join with the other Soviet governments in a world Soviet Union.... Not christianity [sic] but Communism will bring peace on earth. A Communist world will be a unified, organized world. The economic system will be one great organization, based upon the principle of planning now dawning in the U.S.S.R. The American Soviet government will be an important section in this world organization.[5]

Earl Browder, general secretary of the CPUSA, stated in his book, *Victory and After*, that "the American Communists worked energetically and tirelessly to lay the foundations for the United Nations which we were sure would come into existence."[6] Moreover, this leader of the American Reds declared:

> It can be said, without exaggeration, that ever closer relations between our nation and the Soviet Union are an unconditional requirement for the United Nations as a world coalition....[7]

> The United Nations is the instrument for victory. Victory is required for the survival of our nation. The Soviet Union is an essential part of the United Nations. Mutual confidence between our country and the Soviet Union and joint work in the leadership of the United Nations are absolutely necessary.[8]

Some indication of the importance the Kremlin attached to the creation of the UN can be gained from the April 1945 issue of *Political Affairs*, its official mouthpiece in the United States directed principally at Party members. The American comrades were told:

> After the Charter is passed at San Francisco, it will have to be approved by two thirds of the Senate, and this action will establish a weighty precedent for other treaties and agreements still to come. But the victory cannot be won in the Senate alone; it must emanate from the organized and broadening national support built up for the President's policy, on the eve of the San Francisco gathering and after.... Great popular support and enthusiasm for the United Nations policies should be built up, well organized and fully articulate. But it is also necessary to do more than that. The opposition must be rendered so impotent that it will be unable to gather any significant support in the Senate against the United Nations Charter and the treaties which will follow.[9]

Support for the UN was even written into the Communist Party's basic document. The preamble to the constitution of the Communist Party, USA states:

> The Communist party of the United States ... fights uncompromisingly against ... all forms of chauvinism.... It holds further that the true national interest of our country and the cause of peace and progress require ... the strengthening of the United Nations as a universal instrument of peace.[10]

We have also the testimony of many former communists which reveals the value the Party placed on the world organization. In her autobiography, *School of Darkness*, former top CPUSA official Dr. Bella Dodd told of her role in the Party's campaign for the UN:

> When the Yalta conference had ended, the Communists prepared to support the United Nations Charter which was to be adopted at the San Francisco conference to be held in May and June, 1945. For this I organized a corps of speakers and we took to the street corners and held open-air meetings in the millinery and clothing sections of New

York where thousands of people congregate at the lunch hour. We spoke of the need for world unity and in support of the Yalta decisions.[11]

Another former top Communist Party member, Joseph Z. Kornfeder, revealed in 1955:

> Now, as to the United Nations. If you were, let's say, a building engineer, and someone were to show you a set of blueprints about a certain building, you would know from those blueprints how that building was going to look. Organization "blueprints" can be read the same way. I need not be a member of the United Nations Secretariat to know that the UN "blueprint" is a Communist one. I was at the Moscow headquarters of the world Communist party for nearly three years and was acquainted with most of the top leaders, and, of course, I was also a leading party worker. I went to their colleges; I learned their pattern of operations, and if I see that pattern in effect anywhere, I can recognize it....
>
> From the point of view of its master designers meeting at Dumbarton Oaks and Bretton Woods, and which included such masterful agents as Alger Hiss, Harry Dexter White, Lauchlin Currie, and others, the UN was, and is, *not* a failure. They and the Kremlin masterminds behind them never intended the UN as a peace-keeping organization. What they had in mind was a fancy and colossal Trojan horse under the wings of which their smaller agencies could more effectively operate. And in that they succeeded, even beyond their expectations....
>
> Its [the UN's] internal setup, Communist designed, is a pattern for sociological conquest; a pattern aimed to serve the purpose of Communist penetration of the West. It is ingenious and deceptive.[12]

Two years earlier (1953), a congressional committee heard testimony from Colonel Jan Bukar, a Czechoslovakian intelligence officer who had defected to the West. Among the revelations he supplied was a lecture given by Soviet General Bondarenko at the Frunze Military Academy in Moscow. In that lecture, Bondarenko told the elite trainees: "From the rostrum of the United Nations, we shall convince the colonial and semicolonial people to liberate themselves and to spread the Communist theory all over the world."[13]

Kornfeder was not suffering delusions when he claimed to see a communist design and a "pattern for sociological conquest" in the UN's setup. The historical record amply demonstrates that American citizens who were conscious Soviet agents operating at high levels of the U.S. government were very instrumental in the planning and formation of both the United Nations Charter and the organization itself. State Department and Treasury Department officials who were key figures in planning the UN, and who were later exposed during official investigations as Soviet agents, include:[14]

Soloman Adler	Abraham G. Silverman
Virginius Frank Coe	Nathan G. Silvermaster
Lawrence Duggan	William H. Taylor
Noel Field	William L. Ullman
Harold Glasser	John Carter Vincent
Alger Hiss	Henry Julian Wadleigh
Irving Kaplan	David Weintraub
Victor Perlo	Harry Dexter White

The UN's Top Men

As we have noted, the first secretary-general of the United Nations at the organization's founding conference was Alger Hiss. Since that time, six other men have held the position of secretary-general, the highest office in the world organization. Each of these individuals has advanced the causes of world communism and world government, while endangering American sovereignty and liberty. Because the leaders of any group tell much about the organization they represent, the records of each of these men deserve close examination. Unfortunately, we have space here for only a very brief look at the men who have led the UN.

Alger Hiss. As far back as 1939, the FBI had presented solid evidence concerning Hiss's Communist activities to the executive branch. It continued to issue repeated warnings concerning him. But, as had happened in so many previous cases and would continue to occur with a frequency that became an established pattern, the reports were disregarded. In 1944, Hiss was made acting director of the State Department's Office of Special Political Affairs in charge of all postwar planning. He was the executive secretary of the critically important 1944 Dumbarton Oaks Conference, where Stalin's expert Vyacheslav Molotov and "our" expert Hiss worked together on the UN Charter. It was Hiss who accompanied President Roosevelt to the infamous Yalta Conference, where he served as the dying President's "top international organization specialist." It was at that conference in the Soviet Crimea during February 1945 that FDR agreed to give the Soviets three votes in the UN General Assembly to our one. As critics pointed out when that secret agreement became known, giving the Soviets separate votes for the Ukraine and Byelorussia made as much sense as giving extra votes to the United States for Texas and California.

It was Hiss's starring role at San Francisco, however, that was most important. As the acting secretary-general, he was the chief planner and executive of that conference. *Time* magazine, reporting about Hiss and the upcoming conference, stated in its April 16, 1945 issue: "As secretary-general, managing the agenda, he will have a lot to say behind the scenes about who gets the breaks." At San Francisco, Hiss also served on the steering and executive committees, which put the finishing touches on the UN Charter. And it was Alger Hiss, who at the conclusion of the conference, personally carried the new charter back to Washington for Senate ratification.

Hiss was later exposed as a Soviet spy, and in 1950 was convicted for perjuring himself before a federal Grand Jury while being questioned about his communist activities.[15] The statute of limitations on his espionage charges had run out, but he served 44 months in the federal penitentiary for the perjury charges. His trial was one of the most celebrated in American history. Not only did communists, socialists, liberals, and radical leftists turn out to support Hiss, so too did the CFR-dominated Establishment media.

As we have noted, Hiss was himself a member of the CFR. Following his stint at the UN founding in San Francisco, he was named president of the Carnegie Endowment for International Peace. The man responsible for hiring him was the chairman of the Endowment, John Foster Dulles, a founder of the CFR. Dulles, who would later serve as Secretary of State (1953-59), was informed of Hiss's communist background in 1946, but ignored this information until February 1948, just one month before Hiss went before the Grand Jury.[16] **Trygve Lie.** The first elected secretary-general of the United Nations, Trygve Lie, was a Norwegian socialist. Lie was a high-ranking member of the Social Democratic Labor Party in Norway, an offshoot of the early Communist International, and a strong supporter of the Soviet Union on virtually every issue. It was hardly surprising then that the Soviet Union led the campaign to elect Lie as secretary-general. One of Lie's principal causes was the admission of Red China to the UN, which was also a primary objective of the Soviet Union.

Dag Hammarskjöld. Lie was succeeded by another Scandinavian socialist who was openly sympathetic to the world communist revolution. Hammarskjöld once stated in a letter to a friend that "... Chou En-lai to me appears as the most superior brain I have so far met in the field of foreign politics." This he spoke of the man who, together with Mao Tse-tung, was responsible for the murder of between 34 million and 64 million Chinese.[17]

It was Hammarskjöld who was primarily responsible for the early planning and direction of the UN's brutal war against Katanga (see Chapter 2). When Soviet troops invaded Hungary to crush the 1956 uprising, Hammarskjöld turned a deaf ear to the Hungarian freedom fighters. As secretary-general, he persecuted the courageous Danish UN diplomat Povl Bang-Jensen, who refused to turn over the names of Hungarian refugees who had testified in confidence to a special UN committee.

U Thant. Burmese Marxist U Thant continued and intensified an anti-American, pro-Soviet tradition begun by his predecessors. While ignoring the massive human rights abuses — torture, slaughter, imprisonment — of the communist regimes, Thant slavishly followed the Soviet line by condemning Rhodesia and South Africa as terrible human rights violators. During the Vietnam War, Thant continually used the rostrum of the Secretariat to place the blame for the war on the United States. Secretary-General Thant revealed a great deal about both himself and the organization which he headed with his statement in 1970 that the "ideals" of Bolshevik dictator and mass-murderer Lenin were in accord with the UN Charter. "Lenin was a man with a mind of great clarity and incisiveness," Thant said, "and his ideas have had a profound influence on the course of contemporary history." The Burmese Marxist continued: "[Lenin's] ideals of peace and peaceful coexistence among states have won widespread international acceptance and they are in line with the aims of the U.N. Charter."[18]

For his personal staff assistant, Thant chose Soviet KGB officer Viktor Lessiovsky with whom he had established a friendship in the early 1950s.[19]

Kurt Waldheim. When U Thant retired on December 31, 1971, the Soviet Union was ready with a replacement. Austrian Kurt Waldheim was its choice, and for good reason. He had deep, dark secrets that would assure his usefulness to them. During World War II, Waldheim not only wore the uniform of the Third Reich, but also worked with Yugoslavian communist leader Tito. "As soon as he was safely in office [as UN secretary-general], Waldheim planted over 250 Russians in key posts," revealed foreign affairs expert Hilaire du Berrier. "His immediate circle was composed almost completely of Titoists.... When Tito met his old friend at the UN, he hugged him to his breast and gave him a decoration — a great honor for a man who had massacred Serbs, Slovenes, Montenegrans and other Yugoslavs."[20] During his reign as secretary-general, the Establishment media kept Waldheim's Nazi-Communist past under wraps.

During the 1970s, while Waldheim was praising communist dictators and dictatorships, The John Birch Society, through its publications, was virtually the only source for this important information about the Secretary-General's background.[21] Finally, in 1986, the *New York Times* and other CFR media "discovered" the Waldheim Nazi connection, when the by-that-time "former" secretary-general was running for president of Austria.

Javier Perez de Cuellar. This Peruvian diplomat took the UN helm in 1981 and is credited with greatly burnishing the UN image. "Under his tutelage," said *Wall Street Journal* reporter Frederick Kempe, "the U.N. has been midwife to more peace agreements than ever before."[22] Perez de Cuellar helped convene and also addressed the Global Forum of Spiritual and Parliamentary Leaders on Human Survival, the New Age-ecology-world religion confab convened by Mikhail Gorbachev in 1990. He penned the Foreword to the radical socialist New Age publication, *Gaia Peace Atlas*.[23] Perez de Cuellar has distinguished himself as a man of "peace." Like the other men who have held his post, however, he finds it impossible to condemn communist oppression. Speaking of the 1989 Tiananmen Square massacre, an event that occurred during his watch at the UN, Perez de Cuellar has said: "Tiananmen was exaggerated. I think it was a really cruel oppression, but from there to say it was a tremendous, dramatic, tragic violation of human rights is an exaggeration."[24] If an estimated 5,000 dead, 10,000 wounded, the subsequent torture and imprisonment of tens of thousands, and the execution of a still unknown number do not qualify as a "tremendous, dramatic, tragic violation of human rights," what does?

Boutros Boutros-Ghali. A former professor of international relations, Boutros-Ghali began his political career in the regime of the pro-Soviet Egyptian dictator Gamal Abdel Nasser. As editor of the official *Economic Ahram*, it was his job to give credibility to the communistic ideas of the Nasser revolution. As with all of the men who have held the UN's top post, Boutros-Ghali had the support of the communists. As we have previously noted (Chapter 2), Boutros-Ghali has initiated revolutionary advances in the UN's march toward world government. He has called for the forming of a permanent UN Army and is pressing for taxing authority for the UN globocrats.

Espionage and Propaganda

Through the decades, communist leaders and their clients certainly have used the United Nations for world propaganda, as advocated by Soviet General Bondarenko. Red dictators and terrorists from Khrushchev, Tito, and Ceaucescu to Nkrumah, Castro, Lumumba, Arafat, and Mandela have been honored with rousing ovations at the UN. Their anti-American tirades have been broadcast to the world from that forum of "world peace and brotherhood."

The Communists' use of the UN as a principal center of espionage against the United States has been exposed time and again. FBI Director J. Edgar Hoover stated in 1963 that communist diplomats assigned to the UN "represent the backbone of Russian intelligence operations in this country."[25] British espionage authority Chapman Pincher has observed:

> Because of the protection and cover they afford, all the major United Nations institutions have been heavily penetrated.... Whole books have been published listing the abuse and manipulation of the United Nations by the Soviets. The area most blatantly used for active measures and espionage is the main headquarters in New York.[26]

Among the many defectors from the communist bloc countries who have testified about the importance of the UN in the Soviet scheme of things is former KGB operative Ladislav Bittman. In his book *The KGB and Soviet Disinformation: An Insider's View*, Bittman wrote:

> The United Nations is an international organization that deserves special attention for the role it plays in overt and clandestine propaganda campaigns conducted by the Soviets. As an organization that helps to shape world public opinion and plays a vital peacekeeping role, the United Nations is a major battlefield for the Soviet Union and the United States.... But the Soviet Union maintains the most impressive intelligence organization, consisting of the largest single concentration of Soviet spies anywhere in the West.... Spying in New York is so pervasive that some diplomats refer to the United Nations as "the stock exchange of global intelligence operations."[27]

Arkady Shevchenko, who was an under-secretary-general at the UN when he defected in 1978, has described the United Nations as a "gold mine for Russian spying."[28] The most senior Soviet official to defect to the West, Shevchenko was a personal assistant to Soviet Foreign Secretary Andrei Gromyko from 1970 to 1973. He then became Under-Secretary-General for Political and Security Council Affairs at the United Nations. Shevchenko confirmed what anti-communists had been saying all along: The Soviet Politburo regarded détente as simply "a tactical manoeuvre which would in no way supersede the Marxist-Leninist idea of the final victory of the worldwide revolutionary process."[29] And the United Nations was continuing to play an essential role in that process.

"In spite of this and other exposures," said Pincher in 1985, "the International Department and the KGB have not reduced the scale of their operations out of the United Nations and its offshoots, being unable to resist the facility, denied to ordinary diplomats, that renders UN staff free to travel, without restriction, in the countries where they are based."[30]

KGB defector Oleg Gordievsky gave a similar assessment:

> The size of the KGB presence in both the United States and the UN delegation in New York increased more rapidly at the height of détente than at any other period: from about 120 officers in 1970 to 220 in 1975. At the very moment when the London residency was being sharply cut back, those in the United States were almost doubling in size.[31]

It should be of no small concern to American taxpayers to learn that they have been subsidizing these KGB campaigns of espionage, subversion, and disinformation against their own country. In his massive 1974 study, *KGB: The Secret Work of Soviet Secret Agents*, John Barron revealed:

> The KGB derives still another advantage from placing its officers on the United Nations payroll. Since the United States pays 25 percent of the entire U.N. operating budget, it pays 25 percent of the bountiful salaries granted KGB officers insinuated into U.N. jobs. American taxpayers thus are compelled to finance KGB operations against themselves and the noncommunist world. Moreover, the Soviet Union requires its citizens paid by international organizations to rebate the greater part of their salaries to the government. Thus, it actually makes money each time it plants a KGB officer in the U.N.[32]

The UN has also proved useful for the opportunity it offers the Soviets to make contact with and transfer funds to their agents in the CPUSA. John Barron's *KGB Today: The Hidden Hand* (1983) reported concerning the Soviet *modus operandi*:

> From the United Nations, KGB officers additionally maintain clan-

destine contact with the U.S. Communist Party, delivering money and instructions in behalf of the International Department. The U.S. Party exists almost entirely on secret Soviet subsidies....[33]

Considering the fact that locating the UN headquarters in the United States, and in New York City in particular, has afforded the enemies of America unparalleled opportunities for espionage, sabotage, terrorism, propaganda, subversion, and disinformation, it is important to note how the site for the world-body's headquarters was chosen. Americans have been encouraged to believe that the decision to build the United Nations in the United States was a great diplomatic coup for our country. Nothing could be more patently false. In reality, it was exactly what the communists and one-worlders wanted.

In his book *In the Cause of Peace*, the UN's first elected secretary-general described the "long and heated discussions" concerning the future location of the permanent headquarters. Lie and many of his fellow socialists saw the merit of establishing the UN in the U.S. to overcome America's "isolationism." Lie asked: "Why not locate the headquarters of the future international organization within the United States' own borders, so that the concept of international cooperation could match forces on the spot with those of its arch-enemy, isolationism — utilizing at all times the American people's own democratic media?"[34] The Kremlin certainly could see the merit of the plan. Lie wrote:

> The Americans declared their neutrality as soon as the Preparatory Commission opened its deliberations. The Russians disappointed most Western Europeans by coming out at once for a site in America....
> ... Andrei Gromyko of the U.S.S.R. had come out flatly for the United States. As to where in the United States, let the American Government decide, he had blandly told his colleagues. Later the Soviet Union modified its stand to support the east coast.[35]

Even so, these best-laid plans almost fell apart for lack of funds to purchase a site. At that point, Lie said, he advised New York Mayor William O'Dwyer to "Get in touch with Nelson Rockefeller tonight by phone." With the help of Nelson Rockefeller (CFR), Lie and his UN team were soon in "secret consultations with the Rockefeller brothers and with their father, John D. Rockefeller, Jr." In very short order the Rockefellers produced "a gift of $8,500,000 with which to purchase the East River property as a Headquarters site."[36]

The More Things Change ...

The world's most famous capitalists provided the Kremlin with an incredible bonanza. But that is all ancient history, according to current prevailing wisdom. As most news stories have it, the Soviet KGB has been disbanded and its archives completely thrown open. The Cold War is now over. Or is it?

On October 24, 1991, the *Wall Street Journal's* deputy features editor Amity Shlaes commented on evidence indicating that the UN Secretariat headquartered in New York City was still under the domination of old-line communists and Third World Marxist ideo- logues. Shlaes wrote that rather than becoming "the cornerstone in President Bush's oft-mentioned 'new world order.' ... [M]any of those working within the Secretariat, or at its missions in its vicinity, ar- gue that communism left a legacy.... 'It works like a scorpion's stinger,' says one U.N. professional. 'The scorpion — East bloc so- cialism — dies. But the stinger remains poisonous, and strikes new victims.'" Shlaes reported that "Westerners who worked at the U.N. ... found themselves surrounded by what many have called a com- munist mafia."

The KGB has undergone a number of recent permutations, but to paraphrase Mark Twain, reports of its death are highly exaggerated. Zdzislaw Rurarz, the former Polish ambassador to Japan who de- fected to the United States in 1981, was one of the few Soviet ex- perts to take notice of Boris Yeltsin's sinister new security superagency, the MSIA. Rurarz reported in January 1992 that Boris's MSIA "is an amalgam of four previously existing institutions: the USSR MVD, or the Ministry of Internal Affairs, the Russian MVD, the ISS, or Interrepublican Security Service, which was mainly the former KGB, and the FSA, the Federal Security Agency, or the Russian equivalent of the former KGB."

"The MSIA has inherited the network of informers and collaborators of the former KGB and ISS which was in place throughout the USSR. Why," asks Rurarz, "should Russia need such a network in the remaining former Soviet republics, now 'independent states'?"[37] An obvious question — that yields an obvious answer — except to "liberals" who are too busy planning new welfare schemes on which to spend the "peace dividend," and to "conservatives" who are too busy celebrating and congratulating themselves on their victory over communism.

Commenting on the Kremlin security reshuffling, Albert L. Weeks wrote in April 1992 that the "new" Russian agency under Viktor Barannikov "means that 500,000 officials and informers function today as a separate entity, going about their business largely as before. Thousands of other ex-KGBists work for Yevgeny Primakov, director of the Russian Foreign Intelligence Agency." Dr. Weeks, professor emeritus of New York University and author of numerous articles and books about the Soviet Union, also noted that "90-95% of middle-ranking KGB officers remain in the same positions as before the August, 1991, coup attempt, according to a recent defector...."[38]

The "thawing" of U.S.-Russian relations has *not* ended Communist espionage and disinformation activities in the West. To the contrary, it appears to have added new impetus to these operations in many areas. According to R. Patrick Watson, deputy assistant director of the FBI's intelligence division, "It is clear that the foreign intelligence threat from the Soviet Union has not abated, and in fact it has become more difficult to counter." Watson, addressing the National Security Institute on March 13, 1991, said: "In recent months the KGB has emphasized the recruitment of scientists and businessmen to obtain information of economic value." Watson said the KGB and its military counterpart, the GRU, have intensified their efforts and regularly plant their agents in groups of Soviets visiting the United States. A primary task of these agents is to identify Americans with access to technology or information sought by their organizations.[39]

In October 1992, FBI spokesman Steve Markardt confirmed that the espionage agencies of the East European bloc and the "former" Soviet Union "are still highly active in this country engaged in espionage ... particularly against economic and technological targets."[40]

As KGB defector Anatoliy Golitsyn revealed, however, espionage — the stealing of technology and state secrets — has always been of minor importance compared to the KGB's primary purpose of *strategic deception.* Golitsyn, arguably the most important Soviet agent ever to defect to the West, exposed the inner workings and methodology of this critically important disinformation process. He demonstrated how, time after time, the Soviets had thoroughly deceived the West concerning developments in the USSR and Moscow's geopolitical objectives. Through the use of elaborate, long-range programs of strategic deception, the Kremlin has been incredibly successful, he showed, at manipulating the policy decisions of Western governments.

Golitsyn's signal warning to the West, *New Lies For Old,* [41] published in the prophetic year 1984, has proven to be the most reliable and prescient commentary on the acclaimed changes in the communist world. Years before they occurred, Golitsyn predicted the "liberalization" policies in the Soviet Union and Eastern Europe, the glasnost and perestroika campaigns, the rise of independence movements, the political restructuring, the ascendance of "liberal" leaders like Gorbachev and Yeltsin, the dismantling of the Berlin Wall, the breakup of the USSR, the dissolution of the Communist Party, the dismantling of the KGB, and many other developments. He was able to do this with such uncanny accuracy because he had been involved, as a member of the KGB inner circle on strategic disinformation, in planning these types of deceptions. What Golitsyn apparently did not know was that the suicidal course we are taking is not so much the result of our *leaders* being duped by "masters of deceit" in the Kremlin as it is a case of one-world Insiders in the West, conjointly with his former KGB masters, deceiving the American public in order to build the ultimate monopoly: world government.

Space permitting, a great deal more evidence could be cited demonstrating the dangerous folly of current wishful thinking regarding the "demise" of the KGB. Suffice to say, the world's most ruthless and bloody-handed police-state apparatus has not transformed itself into a benign bunch of Boy Scouts or a superfluous bureaucracy. Nor has it abandoned its "stock exchange of global intelligence operations" at the UN.

Top: Alger Hiss, FDR's top adviser at Yalta and the chief planner and executive of the UN founding conference, denied — and continues to deny — that he was an agent for Soviets. Bottom: Detailed testimony by ex-Communist Party members Whittaker Chambers (at microphone) and Elizabeth Bentley (not shown) proved the Hiss denial to be a lie. Hiss, also identified as a Soviet agent by ex-Communists Hede Massing and Nathaniel Weyl, was convicted of perjury in 1950.

Earl Browder, general secretary of the Communist Party USA, stated in his book, *Victory and After:* "American Communists worked energetically and tirelessly to lay the foundations for the United Nations, which we were sure would come into existence."

Former top communist Dr. Bella Dodd told of organizing support for the UN.

Norwegian socialist Trygve Lie, the first elected UN secretary-general, supported Soviets on virtually every issue.

Dag Hammarskjöld praised Red Chinese mass murderer Chou En-lai and launched a brutal UN war against Katanga.

Burmese Marxist U Thant praised Lenin's "ideals of peace," which he said are in line with aims of UN Charter.

Former World War II Nazi Kurt Waldheim was pal of Yugoslavian communist boss Tito.

Javier Perez de Cuellar used UN post to push New Age religion and promote Gorbachev's perestroika.

U Thant chose Soviet KGB agent Viktor Lessiovsky (right) for his personal staff assistant at UN Secretariat. FBI Director J. Edgar Hoover said communist diplomats assigned to UN "represent the backbone of Russian intelligence operations in this country."

Nelson Mandela, leader of the terrorist African National Congress, receives tumultous welcome at UN.

Boutros Boutros-Ghali leads campaign for a UN army and global taxing and regulatory agencies.

March 1947: John D. Rockefeller III (right), on behalf of his father, presents UN Secretary-General Trygvie Lie with a check for $8.5 million to purchase land for UN headquarters in Manhattan, pictured below.

CHAPTER 5

The Drive for World Government

[T]here is going to be no steady progress in civilization or self-government among the more backward peoples until some kind of international system is created which will put an end to the diplomatic struggles incident to the attempt of every nation to make itself secure... The real problem today is that of world government.[1]

— Philip Kerr
Foreign Affairs, December 1922

There is no indication that American public opinion, for example, would approve the establishment of a super state, or permit American membership in it. In other words, time — a long time — will be needed before world government is politically feasible.... [T]his time element might seemingly be shortened so far as American opinion is concerned by an active propaganda campaign in this country....[2]

— Allen W. Dulles (CFR) and Beatrice Pitney Lamb
Foreign Policy Association, 1946

[T]here is no longer a question of whether or not there will be world government by the year 2000. As I see it, the questions we should be addressing to ourselves are: how it will come into being — by cataclysm, drift, more or less rational design — and whether it will be totalitarian, benignly elitist, or participatory (the probabilities being in that order.)[3]

— Saul H. Mendlovitz, director
World Order Models Project, 1975

A major obstacle to alerting Americans about plans to cancel our national sovereignty and personal freedoms and to submerge the United States in a world government is the dissembling double-talk and outright lying routinely employed by the world government advocates. While groups like Planetary Citizens, the World Federalist Association, the Association of World Citizens, the Committee to Frame a World Constitution, the World Constitution and Parliament Association, the World Association for World Federation, etc. have usually flown their world government flags openly, the Council on Foreign Relations and other Establishment groups seeking world government prefer to obfuscate their aims with terms like "collective security," "the rule of law," "world law," "global institutions," "interdependence," and "world order."

As we have already shown and will further demonstrate, the CFR and its influential members are also on record favoring and promoting world government. However, most of these public CFR utterances have appeared in publications and speeches intended for a select, sympathetic audience where the new world order adepts can "unblushingly" (in the words of Lincoln Bloomfield) contemplate and discuss "world government."[4]

World government is not a subject to which most Americans, or other peoples of the world for that matter, give much serious thought. However, if John Q. Citizen does become cognizant of and disturbed about the threat of an emerging global leviathan, and if he expresses this concern to his congressman, senator, or local newspaper editor, he either meets with derisive charges that he is chasing chimera, or he is provided with solemn denials that plans for world government are even being considered.

This writer experienced a typical example of this derision/denial paradigm in November 1990 at a branch of Purdue University in Fort Wayne, Indiana. The occasion was a Citizens Forum to discuss "America's Role in the New World Order." It featured as its three leading participants: Charles William Maynes (CFR), editor of *Foreign Policy*; Pulitzer Prize-winning columnist David Broder; and Senator Richard Lugar (R-IN), former chairman of the Senate Foreign Relations Committee.

All three of these Establishment internationalists enthusiastically touted the newly enhanced role of the United Nations as a result of the Persian Gulf War and embraced President Bush's oft-mentioned new world order. Attending as a member of the press, I questioned each of them concerning the meaning of the term "new world order" and its relationship to "a strengthened UN." All denied that there were any plans to transform the UN into a world government. "Nobody even talks about world government anymore, or seriously considers it," said Charles Maynes. "People gave up on that idea 30 years ago." Maynes, whose journal is published by the Carnegie Endowment for International Peace, one of the premier fountains of world government propaganda, obviously knows better because he regularly publishes the Establishment world order line.

Most Americans, however, find it difficult to believe that individuals in prestigious positions, like Maynes, their senator, or the President, would lie to them or deceive them. But it is time to face facts: The historical record and the unfolding of current events patently contradict the denials and expose them for lies.

It daily becomes more obvious that the world government advocates are pushing toward their goal with increased zeal and audacity. At the time of the Purdue conference, President Bush was pressing for the most far-reaching transfers of authority, prestige, and power to the United Nations that have taken place since its founding. Under the pretext of saving the people of Kuwait from the "naked aggression" of Saddam Hussein, he trumpeted his "new world order" gospel almost daily, even including as its centerpiece a call for new military muscle for the world body. In the succeeding months, as we have mentioned in previous chapters, he went even further, supporting UN Secretary-General Boutros-Ghali's call for a permanent UN Army and pledging America's economic and military support for the revolutionary venture.

Extensive Evidence of Intent

Anyone who is willing to spend a little time in a library researching this issue will have little difficulty verifying that the movement for world government has been underway in earnest for many decades. It has been led and supported by CFR members and their kindred spirits for most of this century. They have left a revealing trail of books, articles, studies, proclamations, and other documents — some blatantly obvious, others more discreetly veiled — that unmistakably confirm their intention.

During the 1930s, '40s, and '50s, many influential works by noted political leaders and intellectuals openly called for the supplanting of national governments by a one-world government. In his 1940 book, *The New World Order*, for instance, popular British novelist/historian H. G. Wells denounced "nationalist individualism" as "the world's disease" and proposed as an alternative a "collectivist one-world state."[5] Wells, a leading member of the Fabian Socialist Society, stated further:

> [T]hese two things, the manifest necessity for some collective world control to eliminate warfare and the less generally admitted necessity for a collective control of the economic and biological life of mankind, are *aspects of one and the same process.*[6] [Emphasis in original]

That same year saw publication of *The City of Man: A Declaration on World Democracy*, which called for a "new order" where "All states, deflated and disciplined, must align themselves under the law of the world-state...."[7] Penned by radical theologian Reinhold Niebuhr, socialist philosopher Lewis Mumford, and other famous literati, it was greeted with critical acclaim by the CFR Establishment media. "Universal peace," these one-worlders declared, "can be founded only on the unity of man under one law and one government."[8] No, they were not envisioning the Second Coming of Jesus Christ and a world subject to God's rule; they had in mind a worldly kingdom of their own making.

In the fall of 1945, immediately following the UN founding conference in San Francisco, some of America's most famous educators met at the Rockefeller-endowed University of Chicago to propose the creation of an Institute of World Government. Their proposal resulted in the Committee to Frame a World Constitution, under the chairmanship of University of Chicago Chancellor Robert Maynard Hutchins.[9] Chancellor Hutchins was the Establishment's "golden boy" of academe and the logical choice to lead the One-World crusade among the nation's intelligentsia. The Committee was heavy with "Hutchins' boys" from the University of Chicago faculty: Mortimer Adler, Richard McKeon, Robert Redfield, Wilbur Katz, and Rexford Guy Tugwell. They were joined by such luminaries as

Stringfellow Barr (St. John's College), Albert Guérard (Stanford), Harold Innis (Toronto), Charles McIlwain (Harvard), and Erich Kahler (Princeton).[10]

In 1948, the Committee unveiled its *Preliminary Draft of a World Constitution*, published by the University of Chicago Press.[11] The principal author of this document was the Committee's secretary-general, G.A. Borgese, a renowned author of books dealing with literary criticism, history, and political science and a professor of romance languages at the University of Chicago.

The following year, Senator Glen Taylor of Idaho introduced a resolution in the U.S. Senate stating that "the present Charter of the United Nations should be changed to provide a true world government constitution."[12] Authored by Borgese, Hutchins, Tugwell, et al., it was reintroduced in 1950.[13]

John Foster Dulles (CFR), who would become President Eisenhower's first Secretary of State, added his considerable influence to the world government campaign in 1950 with the publication of his book, *War or Peace.* "The United Nations," he wrote, "represents not a *final* stage in the development of world order, but only a primitive stage. Therefore its primary task is to create the conditions which will make possible a more highly developed organization."[14]

A founding member of the CFR and one of Colonel House's young protégés, Dulles was a delegate to the UN founding conference. He had married into the Rockefeller family and eventually served as chairman of both the Rockefeller Foundation and the Carnegie Endowment. It was Chairman Dulles who chose Communist Alger Hiss to be president of the Carnegie Endowment for International Peace.[15]

Earlier, Dulles had turned his attention toward religion and, in 1941, had become the first chairman of the Commission on a Just and Durable Peace of the subversive Federal Council of Churches. The efforts to draft a set of internationalist principles on which peace might be built sounded to him, he said, like an echo of the Gospels.[16] His commission's first order of business was to pass a resolution proclaiming that

... a world of irresponsible, competing and unrestrained national sovereignties, whether acting alone or in alliance or in coalition, is a world of international anarchy. It must make place for a higher and more inclusive authority.[17]

Dulles's credentials as a certified, top-level Establishment Insider intimately involved in the design and creation of the UN make this following quote from *War or Peace* especially significant. He wrote:

> I have never seen any proposal made for collective security with "teeth" in it, or for "world government" or for "world federation," which could not be carried out either by the United Nations or under the United Nations Charter.[18]

That same year, 1950, fellow one-world Insider James P. Warburg (CFR) would testify before the Senate Foreign Relations Subcommittee, claiming:

> We shall have world government, whether or not we like it. The question is only whether world government will be achieved by consent or by conquest.[19]

Additional intellectual ammunition for the campaign came with publication of *Foundations of the World Republic* by Professor Borgese in 1953. There was no mistaking the book's intent; the publisher (again, the University of Chicago Press) had this to say in the opening sentences of the promotional fly-leaf of the book's dust jacket:

> WORLD GOVERNMENT, asserts Mr. Borgese, is inevitable. It will be born in one of two ways. It may come as a World Empire, with mass enslavement imposed by the victor of World War III; or it may take the form of a World Federal Republic, established by gradual integration of the United Nations.[20] [Emphasis in original]

Immediately below that promotional blurb appeared this endorsement from University of Chicago Professor Robert Redfield: "This book is about the necessary interdependence of peace, justice, and power. It is an argument for world government. It is a revelation that justice is, in the end, love."

At about the same time *Saturday Review* was candidly editorializing:

> If UNESCO is attacked on the grounds that it is helping to prepare the world's peoples for world government, then it is an error to burst forth with apologetic statements and denials. Let us face it: the job of UNESCO is to help create and promote the elements of world citizenship. When faced with such a "charge," let us by all means affirm it from the housetops. [21]

Lewis Mumford added more endorsements for the idea of a world state with statements like the following from *The Transformations of Man*:

> [T]he destiny of mankind, after its long preparatory period of separation and differentiation, is at last to become one.... This unity is on the point of being politically expressed in a world government that will unite nations and regions in transactions beyond their individual capacity.... [22]

In his 1959 book *The West in Crisis*, CFR member James P. Warburg (who was also an Insider banker, economist and former member of FDR's socialist "brain trust") proclaimed:

> ... a world order without world law is an anachronism ... since war now means the extinction of civilization, a world which fails to establish the rule of law over the nation-states cannot long continue to exist.
>
> We are living in a perilous period of transition from the era of the fully sovereign nation-state to the era of world government. [23]

Moreover, said Warburg, we must initiate "a deliberate search for methods and means by which American children may best be educated into ... responsible citizens not merely of the United States but of the world." [24]

In 1960, Atlantic Union Committee treasurer Elmo Roper (CFR) delivered an address and authored a pamphlet, both of which were entitled, "The Goal is Government of All the World." In his appeal for global rule, Roper said: "For it becomes clear that the first step toward world government cannot be completed until we have advanced on the four fronts: the economic, the military, the political, and the social."[25]

Just the Tip of the Iceberg

We have, thus far, barely scratched the surface of the massive accumulation of world-government propaganda issued during the past several decades. Several additional chapters could easily be devoted to further presentation of examples from Establishment sources. We could turn to the late Norman Cousins (CFR, Planetary Citizens, United World Federalists, editor of *Saturday Review*), a one-worlder who tended to wear his colors openly. On Earth Day, April 22, 1970, he asserted, "Humanity needs a world order. The fully sovereign nation is incapable of dealing with the poisoning of the environment.... The management of the planet, therefore — whether we are talking about the need to prevent war or the need to prevent ultimate damage to the conditions of life — requires a world-government."[26]

We could also cite the *Humanist Manifesto II* (1973), a blatantly anti-Christian, anti-American document openly endorsed by some of America's most prominent authors, educators, academicians, scientists, and philosophers. It declares:

> We deplore the division of humankind on nationalistic grounds. We have reached a turning point in human history where the best option is to *transcend the limits of national sovereignty* and to move toward the building of a world community.... a system of world law and a world order based upon transnational federal government.[27] [Emphasis in original]

It would also be worthwhile to discuss the campaign during the 1960s and '70s for *A Constitution for the World*, another effort of Messrs. Tugwell, Hutchins, et al., funded and promoted by the Ford Foundation through the Fund for the Republic and the Center for the Study of Democratic Institutions.[28] Or, we could examine the growing momentum behind more recent efforts, such as those of the

World Constitution and Parliament Association, which have attracted the support of political figures, jurists, celebrities, and intellectuals from 85 countries.

In 1991, the World Constitution and Parliament Association launched a "3-year intensive global ratification campaign" for a proposed "Constitution for the Federation of Earth." The organization enjoys the support of such "Honorary Sponsors" as Nobel laureates George Wald, Glenn T. Seaborg (CFR), and Desmond Tutu, and other notables such as actor Ed Asner, *Scientific American* editor and publisher Gerard Piel (CFR), SWAPO terrorist leader and President of Namibia Sam Nujoma, psychologist Kenneth Clark, and former Attorney General Ramsey Clark.[29]

We have space here, however, for presentation of only a small selection of material out of a vast deposit of globalist agit-prop. Those who require more evidence to become convinced that Americans have been subjected to — and are being subjected to — a conscious, well-orchestrated, long-range propaganda campaign by the CFR Establishment and its vast network of transmission belts and allies need only spend some time in a major library perusing the literature under the subject headings "world government," "world order," "interdependence," "internationalism," and "globalism."

Attacks on National Sovereignty

However, while many of the passages we have cited are straightforward appeals for world government, the CFR Insiders and their one-world propagandists more frequently resort to the oblique approach of advancing "world order" through attacks on national sovereignty. Since a one-world government is impossible as long as nations retain their sovereign powers to conduct their own affairs as they see fit, it makes sense for the globalists to undermine the whole concept of national sovereignty. Over a period of time, the peoples of the world might be convinced gradually to surrender aspects of national sovereignty to international institutions until, ultimately, world government is an established fact.

This internationalist theme was delivered to the *Foreign Affairs* reading audience 70 years ago in the CFR journal's second issue. "Obviously there is going to be no peace or prosperity for mankind," the December 1922 *Foreign Affairs* claimed, "so long as it remains divided into fifty or sixty independent states."[30]

The problem for the CFR was overcoming the American people's "sovereignty fetish." The Council pondered this difficulty in its 1944 publication entitled *American Public Opinion and Postwar Security Commitments.* Therein we find:

> The sovereignty fetish is still so strong in the public mind, that there would appear to be little chance of winning popular assent to American membership in anything approaching a super-state organization. Much will depend on the kind of approach which is used in further popular education.[31]

The gradualist approach, as outlined for instance in *The International Problem of Governing Mankind,* by Columbia University professor and later World Court justice Philip C. Jessup (CFR), was the strategy most often adopted by the Insider internationalists. "I agree that national sovereignty is the root of the evil," Jessup wrote in his 1947 book. But, he noted: "The question of procedure remains. Can the root be pulled up by one mighty revolutionary heave, or should it first be loosened by digging around it and cutting the rootlets one by one?"[32] Like most of his elitist confreres, he opted for the piecemeal approach.

Archetypal CFR Insider and former FDR Secretary of the Treasury Henry Morgenthau recognized the need for the step-by-step approach: "We can hardly expect the nation-state to make itself superfluous, at least not overnight. Rather what we must aim for is recognition in the minds of all responsible statesmen that they are really nothing more than caretakers of a bankrupt international machine which will have to be transformed slowly into a new one. The transition will not be dramatic, but a gradual one. People will still cling to national symbols."[33]

Years later, in 1975, former Secretary of the Treasury C. Douglas Dillon, an ardent CFR globalist and honorary chairman of the Institute for World Order, admitted that it would still "take a while before people in this country as a whole will be ready for any substantial giving-up of sovereignty to handle global problems."[34]

Not that members of the CFR crowd were taking a lackadaisical attitude. Far from it — they had been engaged in full-scale sovereignty-bashing for decades.

In his 1960 book *The United States in the World Arena,* Walt Whitman Rostow (CFR), who would rise to become chairman of the State Department's Policy Planning Board and the President's national security advisor, declared:

> [I]t is a legitimate American national objective to see removed from all nations — including the United States — the right to use substantial military force to pursue their own interests. Since this residual right is the root of national sovereignty and the basis for the existence of an international arena of power, it is, therefore, an American interest to see *an end to nationhood* as it has been historically defined.[35] [Emphasis added]

That kind of statement — literally advocating an end to our nation and our constitutional system of government — should have immediately disqualified Rostow for any government position. It would be impossible for him, in good faith, to take the oath of office to defend and protect the U.S. Constitution while adhering to such a position. However, quite to the contrary, it was this very same subversive, internationalist commitment that guaranteed his promotion by fellow one-world Insiders.

Meanwhile, on Capitol Hill, the war against national sovereignty was being led by the likes of Senator J. William Fulbright, longtime chairman of the Senate Foreign Relations Committee and one of the most influential members of Congress. In his 1964 book *Old Myths and New Realities*, Fulbright declared:

> Indeed, the concept of national sovereignty has become in our time a principle of international anarchy....[36]
>
> * * *
>
> ... the sovereign nation can no longer serve as the ultimate unit of personal loyalty and responsibility.[37]

New York Governor and perennial presidential aspirant Nelson

Rockefeller also certified his globalist credentials with frequent attacks on nationalism. Echoing the familiar Establishment theme at the 1962 Godkin lectures at Harvard University, he averred that "the nation-state, standing alone, threatens, in many ways, to seem as anachronistic as the Greek city-state eventually became in ancient times."[38]

In his Harvard lectures, published in 1964 under the title *The Future of Federalism*, Rockefeller warned against the "fever of nationalism" and declared that "the nation-state is becoming less and less competent to perform its international political tasks."[39] His solutions? "All these, then, are some of the reasons — economic, military, political — pressing us to lead vigorously toward the true building of a *new world order*."[40] (Emphasis added) "More specifically, I hope and urge," stated Mr. Rockefeller, "... there will evolve the bases for a federal structure of the free world."[41]

In his 1972 book *World Without Borders*, Worldwatch Institute President Lester Brown (CFR) noted the continuing "problem" faced by himself and his fellow globalists: "Needless to say, sovereign nation-states steadfastly resist the transfer of power necessary to create strong supranational institutions."[42] He continued:

> There is discussion from time to time on the need for a full-fledged world government. Realistically, this is not likely to come about in the short run. If we can build some of the supranational institutions that are needed in various areas ... adding them to the International Monetary Fund, INTELSAT and the many others already in existence, these will eventually come to constitute an effective, though initially limited world government.[43]

The "existing international system," Brown has declared, "... must be replaced by *a new world order*."[44] (Emphasis added)

"Declaration of INTERdependence"

One of the Insiders' most audacious propaganda gambits in support of the new world order was the world-government-promoting "Declaration of INTERdependence," unveiled in 1975 during the planning for our nation's 1976 bicentennial.[45] Sponsored by the

World Affairs Council of Philadelphia and written by Establishment historian Henry Steele Commager (CFR), the "Declaration of INTERdependence" turned the Founding Fathers upside-down, declaring:

> When in the course of history the threat of extinction confronts mankind, it is necessary for the people of The United States to declare their *interdependence* with the people of all nations....
>
> To establish a *new world order* of compassion, peace, justice and security, it is essential that mankind free itself from the limitations of national prejudice, and acknowledge ... that all people are part of one global community.... [Emphasis added]

The document's penultimate paragraph, and its real *raison d'être*, declares: "We affirm that *a world without law is a world without order,* and we call upon all nations *to strengthen and to sustain the United Nations* and its specialized agencies, and other institutions of *world order*...." (Emphasis added)

Amazingly, 124 members of Congress endorsed this attack on our constitutional system of limited government. One of those who did not support this declaration was the late Congressman John Ashbrook (R-OH), who charged:

> Unlike the Declaration of Independence, whose great hallmarks are guarantees of individual personal freedom and dignity for all Americans and an American Nation under God, the declaration abandons those principles in favor of cultural relativism, international citizenship, and supremacy over all nations by a world government.
>
> The declaration of interdependence is an attack on loyalty to American freedom and institutions, which the document calls "chauvinistic nationalism," "national prejudice," and "narrow notions of national sovereignty."[46]

To accompany, promote, and expand upon the "Declaration of INTERdependence," the World Affairs Council of Philadelphia and the Aspen Institute published *The Third Try at World Order: U.S. Policy for an Interdependent World* written by Harlan Cleveland

(CFR).* In that book, Cleveland, a former Assistant Secretary of State and U.S. Ambassador to NATO, lamented that the first try at "world order" collapsed with the failure to secure U.S. entry into the League of Nations and that the second failure resulted from a United Nations that was not invested with sufficient authority and power to enact and enforce world law.[47]

According to Cleveland, the "third try," now underway, is an attempt to arrive at "world governance" piecemeal, by strengthening the UN to deal with various global "crises" involving, for instance,

---

* Like many of his fellow Establishment Insiders — Walt and Eugene Rostow, Dean Acheson, John McCloy, and Robert McNamara — Cleveland had a long career on the far left that is worthy of note. Dr. Francis X. Gannon, in his authoritative *Biographical Dictionary of the Left,* recorded: "At Princeton, Cleveland was president of the Anti-War Society for three years and in the Princeton yearbook he listed himself as a 'Socialist.'" Intelligence expert Frank A. Capell reported in his column for *The Review Of The News* for August 21, 1974: "Cleveland wrote articles for *Far Eastern Survey* and *Pacific Affairs,* publications of the Institute of Pacific Relations, a subversive organization described by the Senate Judiciary Committee as 'an instrument of Communist policy, propaganda and military intelligence.' He worked with John Abt and other key Reds on the staff of the LaFollette Civil Liberties Committee. He worked as deputy to Soviet agent Harold Glasser inside U.N.R.R.A. [United Nations Relief and Rehabilitation Administration] and took part in 'Operation Keelhaul,' sending nearly five million Europeans into Russian concentration camps." William J. Gill's shocking 1969 exposé of the extensive subversion in the U.S. government, *The Ordeal of Otto Otepka* (New Rochelle, NY: Arlington House), devotes more than two chapters to the pro-communist exploits of Harlan Cleveland. After having been brought into the State Department during the Kennedy Administration on a security waiver signed by Dean Rusk, Cleveland began to load up his staff with other security risks. One of those he tried to hire was his longtime friend Irving Swerdlow, who had been discharged eight years earlier as a security risk. He then stunned Otto Otepka, the chief of the State Department's personnel security, by asking: "What are the chances of getting Alger Hiss back into the Government?" In 1962, the State Department's Advisory Committee on International Organizations, chaired by Cleveland, attempted to devise an end run around the security checks on Americans employed by the United Nations. The new security procedures had been instituted in the wake of the Hiss espionage scandal and the revelations that he and his brother, Donald Hiss, had personally recruited more than 200 people for UN jobs. (For further information, see also *State Department Security 1963-65: The Otepka Case,* Senate Internal Security Subcommittee Hearings, 1963-65.)

"the global environment," "food reserve[s]," "energy supplies," "fertility rates," "military stalemate," and "conflict in a world of proliferating weapons."[48] It was a recapitulation of what he had written in 1964 in the foreword to Richard N. Gardner's book, *In Pursuit of World Order*, wherein Cleveland stated: "A decent world order will only be built brick by brick."[49]

Piece by Piece, Brick by Brick

CFR luminary Richard N. Gardner took this same message of patient, persistent plodding to the Council's members and followers in 1974, with his now-famous article in *Foreign Affairs* entitled "The Hard Road to World Order." Since hopes for "instant world government" had proven illusory, he wrote, "the house of world order" would have to be built through "an end run around national sovereignty, eroding it piece by piece." This could be done, he noted, on an ad hoc basis with treaties and international "arrangements" that could later be brought within "the central institutions of the U.N. system."[50]

As we shall see, this gradualist road to world order, as outlined by Jessup, Cleveland, Gardner, et al. — "root by root," "brick by brick," "piece by piece" — has been followed assiduously by the one-worlders and is now rapidly approaching completion. However, even at this late hour, it still is not too late to throw a wrench into their well-oiled machine and topple their planned "house of world order" like a house of cards.

Globalist Saul Mendlovitz (CFR), head of World Order Models Project, sees world government as reality by the year 2000.

A founding member of the CFR and a leading U.S. delegate to the UN founding conference, John Foster Dulles became Ike's Secretary of State.

Philosopher Lewis Mumford (CFR) added his call for "transformation" to "world government."

Radical theologian Reinhold Niebuhr (CFR) urged a "new order" "under the law of the world-state."

World Court justice Philip C. Jessup (CFR) says "national sovereignty is the root of the evil."

Senator J. William Fulbright claims national sovereignty is akin to "international anarchy."

Kennedy national security adviser Walt W. Rostow (CFR) asserts it is "an American interest to see an end to nationhood as it has been historically defined."

Henry Steele Commager (CFR) penned subversive 1976 "Declaration of INTERdependence."

Congressman John Ashbrook (R-OH) charged "Declaration of INTERdependence" was a dangerous attack on basic American principles and institutions.

Apostle of "World Order," Harlan Cleveland (CFR) brought many security risks into JFK State Department, tried to sabotage security checks on Americans employed by UN, and even tried to bring Alger Hiss back into the federal government.

CHAPTER 6

Treaties and Treason

*I say the same as to the opinion of those who consider the grant
of the treaty-making power as boundless. If it is, then we have
no Constitution.* [1]

— Thomas Jefferson
September 1803

*Treaties make international law and also they make domestic
law. Under our Constitution, treaties become the supreme law of
the land.... [T]reaty law can override the Constitution. Treaties,
for example, ... can cut across the rights given the people by their
constitutional Bill of Rights.* [2]

— Secretary of State John Foster Dulles
April 11, 1952

[A]fter all, the UN Charter is the law of the land.... [3]

— George L. Sherry (CFR)
The United Nations Reborn, 1990

The main political obstacle to the new world order envisioned by the
one-world schemers has been, and remains, the Constitution of the
United States of America. Unique in both its foundational principles
and structure, the constitutional system established by America's
Founding Fathers — abused though it may be by decades of sustained assault on the one hand and neglect on the other — continues to stymie the architects of totalitarian global government.

From their own experience, and from an acquaintance with history, the Americans of 1776 and 1787 well understood that the dangers to liberty from an unrestrained government were, more often
than not, far greater than the threat of tyranny from a conquering
foreign power. The limitations placed on government by the design-

101

ers of our founding document, therefore, served as formidable bulwarks against the dangerous centralization of power in the national government; those limitations also rendered any transfers of constitutional powers of governance to an international government virtually impossible.

One of 20th century America's most passionate defenders of liberty against the encroachments of omnipotent government was Frank Chodorov, editor of *The Freeman*. Writing in 1955, in a special issue devoted to exposing and opposing "One Worldism and the United Nations," he noted:

> Government is the monopoly of coercion. Its function is to prevent individuals from using violence or other coercive methods on one another, so that the business of Society — the exchange of goods, services and ideas — may be carried on in safety and tranquility. Its contribution to social progress, though necessary, is purely negative. In this country, tradition and the Constitution hold that the function of government is to protect the individual in the enjoyment of those rights which inhere in him by virtue of existence, and which are the gifts of the Creator. And in the beginning, before tradition and the spirit of the Constitution were perverted, Americans took for granted that government had no other competence.[4]

"But the hard fact," said Chodorov, "is that this monopoly of coercion is vested in humans — of which government is necessarily composed — and that these humans are no different in make-up from those they are called upon to coerce."[5] That is indeed a hard fact that no amount of wishful thinking or high-flown rhetoric about global brotherhood can change. It was the recognition of just such hard realities as these that prompted Thomas Jefferson to issue his famous dictum: "In questions of power let no more be heard of confidence in man, but bind him down from mischief by the chains of the constitution."[6] The failure of peoples to keep government rigidly contained have time after time tragically proven the wisdom of Jefferson's admonition. Chodorov agreed and noted:

> Thus in time the agency established for the purpose of protecting

Society becomes its master.

This tendency of government to expand upon its power and its prerogatives is inherent in it simply because it is composed of men.... Therefore, the concern of Society, particularly in the last few centuries, has been to find some way to keep government within bounds. Thus came constitutionalism. Thus came the idea that to safeguard freedom — from government, of course — it is necessary to keep government small, so that it can be subject to constant surveillance, and poor, so that it cannot get out of hand.[7]

Chodorov was confirming what the founders believed, that government itself must be made subject to "the rule of law." The American republic, as a result, in its earlier years, could proudly claim to be "a government of laws, not of men." Another champion of freedom, John F. McManus, more recently offered the following observation about the unique foundation of American constitutionalism:

The underlying premise of the American system is the thunderous assertion in the Declaration of Independence that "all men ... are endowed by their Creator with certain unalienable Rights." Because they are endowed with rights, the Declaration reasons, men have the power to protect their rights collectively. In other words, they have the power to form a government. The government they create is to have as its sole purpose the protection of the God-given rights of the individual. Government is not to be the distributor of wealth, the regulator of the law-abiding citizenry, or the ruler of the people.[8]

Unfortunately, there are in our midst today many powerful individuals and organizations who find such personal freedom, and the principles of governance that make it possible, totally repugnant. For both personal freedom and limitations on government power obstruct their plans to create a "new world order" for the planet.

CFR Versus the Constitution

To the Council on Foreign Relations, for example, our exquisite system with its checks and balances and separation of powers, which has earned the plaudits of renowned political observers worldwide, erects impenetrable obstacles that "militate against the development of responsible government." In one of its very early and revealing reports, *Survey of American Relations* (1928), we find the Council lamenting:

> The Roman republic and the Hanoverian monarchy described by Montesquieu and Blackstone were both governments of separation of powers maintained by checks and balances. Both were forced to achieve unity by the increase of international complications. One went the way of executive sovereignty; the other that of parliamentary sovereignty. The difficulties in the way of either such development in the United States are obvious. While presidents have sometimes acted like dictators in brief emergencies, an intensive reaction of congressional control has always followed. The jealous control of the purse by Congress is a check which would inevitably curb an ambitious president if the electorate's opposition to a third term should wane. Furthermore, the physical separation of the cabinet from Congress, the comparative equality of power of the two houses, rendering each a check upon the other, the "states' rights" sentiment which prevents a gradual subordination of the Senate, and the position of the Supreme Court as final interpreter of the constitutional separation of powers — *all these militate against the development of responsible government.*[9] [Emphasis added]

The Council was, at this point, still struggling mightily against the triumphant "isolationism" that had ruined the internationalists' "first try at world order," the League of Nations. It was the one-worlders' failure to secure the constitutionally required two-thirds majority in the Senate necessary for ratification of all treaties that doomed the League. Thus, the 1928 Council report stressed at length the need to remove this constitutional obstacle to "responsible government." The CFR report stated:

> The seriousness of the situation is increased by the apparent rigidity of the Senate's attitude. Charles Cheney Hyde, former solicitor of the Department of State, believes that "Any constructive proposal designed to make a successful appeal to those possessed of the treaty-

making power of the United States must reckon with the following conditions: first, that this nation has a passion for independence; secondly, that it will not agree to be drawn into a war between other states; and, thirdly, that it will not delegate to any outside body the right to determine what is the nature of a controversy or how it ought to be adjusted. These are facts." From this Professor Hyde assumes that the United States must limit her participation in international organization accordingly. Others have argued from the same premises that the Constitution must be amended to eliminate the two-thirds rule in the Senate.[10]

The Council report made clear its support for the elimination of this vital restraint on executive power. The 1928 report argued:

Substitution of a majority of both houses for two-thirds of the Senate in treaty ratification would accord with the practice of most continental European governments. It would obviate the complaints of the House and eliminate the ever-present possibility of inability to execute a treaty, valid at international law, because of the refusal of the House to agree to appropriations or necessary legislation. This would seem reasonable, in view of the constitutional provision that treaties are the supreme law of the land, and on this score was suggested in the Federal convention of 1787. It would also render deadlocks less frequent, because one political party is much more likely to control a majority of both houses than two-thirds of the Senate.... In any case, the desirability of preventing deadlocks when treaties are as necessary as legislation should overrule these objections.[11]

The two-thirds requirement "exceeds the need for a check on administrative usurpation," said the Council's *Survey*. "... Such a division of powers," it held, far from providing needed protection, "... has too often resulted in weakness, muddle, and delay, sometimes even in the paralysis of one of the most vital functions of modern government."[12] It is certain that the CFR hand-wringers would have found little if any sympathy among this nation's founders for their interpretation of "the most vital functions of modern government."

More than half a century later, the Establishment's brain trust-

venting their spleen over the aggravation the Constitu-
ues to cause them. In his *The Power to Lead* (1984), Professor James MacGregor Burns stated: "Let us face reality. The
framers [of the U.S. Constitution] have simply been too shrewd for
us. They have outwitted us. They designed separated institutions
that cannot be unified by mechanical linkages, frail bridges, tinker-
ing. If we are to 'turn the founders upside down' — to put together
what they put asunder — we must directly confront the constitutional structure they erected."[13]

Professor Burns has served as co-director of Project '87 and as a
board member of the Committee on the Constitutional System
(CCS), two of the Establishment's most important agencies working
to radically change the Constitution. Both organizations, heavily
larded with CFR members, are ready with proposals that would
drastically alter our system of government should a constitutional
convention be called. Most Americans are completely unaware that
our nation is dangerously close to completing the process to convene
a constitutional convention.[14]

Professor Charles Hardin, a CCS founder, has written in the
Committee's important 1985 book of essays, *Reforming American
Government*, that the Senate "should be deprived of its power to approve treaties and presidential nominations."[15] Moreover, Hardin
believes: "The ideal is to create conditions so that the conduct of *government itself will be ruled largely by conventions rather than by
fixed laws.*"[16] (Emphasis added)

The one-worlders have failed thus far to effect the "major surgery"
on the Constitution advocated by Hardin, Burns, et al.,[17] but they
continue undeterred on their subversive course. Since the Constitution's amendment process was purposefully made difficult by the
framers so as to protect against the very tampering and aggrandize-
ment the internationalists propose, their primary strategy to create
"world order," as we have seen, has involved revising the Constitution "piece by piece" by means of "treaty law." This gigantic fraud
has been perpetrated against the American people by CFR Insiders
working in concert with the media, academe, and the federal executive, legislative, and judicial branches during much of this century.

It is highly doubtful that the UN Charter would have been ratified by the U.S., or by many other countries for that matter, without inclusion of Article 2, Paragraph 7, which provides:

> Nothing contained in the present Charter shall authorize the United Nations to intervene in matters which are essentially within the domestic jurisdiction of any state or shall require the Members to submit such matters to settlement under the present Charter....[18]

The wording and meaning seem clear enough: Membership in the UN, as indicated by acceptance of the Charter, in no way constitutes surrender of control over domestic affairs to the world organization. As successful as the CFR's internationalist propaganda campaign was in selling the UN idea in 1945, it would have failed if there had been any admission that the real intent was to allow other nations and international bureaucrats to meddle in and dictate policies concerning our internal affairs.

However, what the UN provides with one hand it takes with the other. Article 2, Paragraph 7 of the UN Charter also states: "... but this principle shall not prejudice the application of enforcement measures under Chapter VII." This wording could well be used by UN officials to authorize intervention by the organization in the domestic affairs of a member nation. So, even though the first portion of Paragraph 7 would seem to prohibit any such meddling, the final portion could be construed as a loophole that would allow such intervention.

Many other UN documents contain ambiguous wording of this type. Should the UN ever decide to act contrary to its own clear prohibitions, internationalist legal scholars will focus on whichever portion of the ambiguous wording suits their fancy.

Indeed, almost before the ink on the Charter had dried, a well-orchestrated campaign was underway to undercut and reverse the meaning of Article 2, Paragraph 7. In 1946, William G. Carr, a consultant for the United States delegation at the San Francisco Conference, wrote in his book *One World In the Making*:

> Under modern conditions, few acts of a nation affect only its own people.... It seems clear that *no nation which signs this [UN] Charter*

can justly maintain that any of its acts are its own business, or within its own domestic jurisdiction, if the Security Council says that these acts are a threat to the peace.[19] [Emphasis added]

Soon thereafter, this same theme was being transmitted via many respected sources. The April 1949 *American Bar Association Journal*, for instance, carried an article by UN staff member Moses Moskowitz contending that

... once a matter has become, in one way or another, the subject of regulation by the United Nations, be it by resolution of the General Assembly or by convention between member states at the insistence of the United Nations, that subject ceases to be a matter being "essentially within the domestic jurisdiction of the Member States." As a matter of fact, such a position represents the official view of the United Nations, as well as of the member states that have voted in favor of the Universal Declaration of Human Rights.[20]

Such incredibly arrogant advocacy of the usurpation of sovereign national powers should have met with immediate rebuke from American officials. Instead, it was embraced as our nation's official position with President Harry S Truman's claim in 1950 that "There is now no longer any real difference between domestic and foreign affairs."[21]

In like manner, President Dwight Eisenhower subsequently declared: "For us indeed there are no longer 'foreign affairs' and 'foreign policy.' Since such affairs belong to and affect the entire world, they are essentially local affairs for every nation, including our own."[22]

Dulles and Treaty Law

It was Eisenhower's Secretary of State John Foster Dulles, however, who touched off heated national debate about the issue with his highly controversial speech before the regional meeting of the American Bar Association at Louisville, Kentucky in 1952. In his formal address, Dulles asserted:

Treaties make international law and also they make domestic law.

Under our Constitution, treaties become the supreme law of the land. They are, indeed, more supreme than ordinary laws for congressional laws are invalid if they do not conform to the Constitution, whereas treaty law can override the Constitution. Treaties, for example, can take powers away from the Congress and give them to the President; they can take powers from the States and give them to the Federal Government or to some international body, and they can cut across the rights given the people by their constitutional Bill of Rights.[23]

Dulles was grossly misinterpreting the Constitution on several very important points. In fact, his dissertation was an outright assault on the basic premises of our constitutional system. It would behoove us at this point to see what the Constitution, "the supreme law of the land," has to say about treaties and the treaty power. In the Constitution we find:

> Article II, Sec. 2: "[The President] shall have Power, by and with the Advice and Consent of the Senate, to make Treaties, provided two-thirds of the Senators present concur...."
>
> Article III, Sec. 2: "The judicial Power shall extend to all Cases, in Law and Equity, arising under this Constitution, the Laws of the United States, and Treaties made, or which shall be made, under their Authority...."
>
> Article VI: "This Constitution, and the Laws of the United States which shall be made in Pursuance thereof; and all Treaties made, or which shall be made, under the Authority of the United States, shall be the supreme Law of the Land; and the Judges in every State shall be bound thereby, any Thing in the Constitution or Laws of any State to the Contrary notwithstanding."

John F. McManus, writing in *The New American*, commented on an important distinction regarding the wording of Article VI that is rarely mentioned. "It must be carefully noted," he observed, "that, within the body of the Constitution itself, the founders frequently referred to the document they had crafted as 'this' Constitution. At the close of the above passage, they referred to 'the' Constitution, and what they meant was that no state constitution or state law

109

shall stand above the U.S. Constitution. There is no justification for holding that the document empowers the makers of treaties to undo the Constitution itself."[24]

According to Dulles, Moskowitz, and modern Supreme Court interpretations, however, Article VI amounts to an unlimited grant of power through which the President and two-thirds of a quorum of the Senate may do virtually anything. President Eisenhower, Secretary Dulles, and their internationalist cohorts even went so far as to claim that the real danger to the Constitution came not from an expansive interpretation of the treaty power, but from attempts to explicitly and unequivocally guarantee that "treaty law" would not be able to override the Constitution.[25]

A close examination of the Constitution's wording and the "original intent" of the framers, however, make abundantly clear that the position espoused by McManus is far more in tune with what was intended in our founding document than the opinion taken by Dulles, Moskowitz, et al. James Madison, who was the secretary of the Philadelphia Convention, the principal author of the Constitution, and has justly been called "the Father of the Constitution," said of the scope of the treaty power:

> I do not conceive that power is given to the President and the Senate to dismember the empire, or alienate any great, essential right. I do not think the whole legislative authority have this power. The exercise of the power must be consistent with the object of the delegation.[26]

In 1801, the year he began his presidency, Thomas Jefferson published his authoritative reference work, *A Manual of Parliamentary Practice*, which went through many printings and became a standard handbook used in both the House and Senate. In that book, Jefferson declared of treaty power:

> 1. It is admitted that it must concern the foreign nation, party to the contract, or it would be a mere nullity *res inter alias [sic] acta.* 2. By the general power to make treaties, the Constitution must have intended to comprehend only those objects which are usually regulated by treaty, and cannot be otherwise regulated. 3. It must have meant to

except out of those the rights reserved to the states; for surely the President and Senate cannot do by treaty what the whole government is interdicted from doing in any way.[27]

This is not only sound legal opinion; it is plain, common sense. If the Bill of Rights and the whole Constitution were to have any lasting force and meaning, it could not have been intended that they could be completely undone by means of treaty.* Or as Jefferson rightly observed: "I say the same as to the opinion of those who consider the grant of the treaty-making power as boundless. If it is, then we have no Constitution."[28]

Alexander Hamilton, one of the most forceful of the Federalists and one who often clashed with Jefferson, nevertheless agreed with his distinguished adversary on this important point. Hamilton wrote:

> The only constitutional exception to the power of making treaties is, that it shall not change the Constitution.... On natural principles, a

---

* It is worth noting that the legal status of the United Nations Charter itself is, or should be, very much in question. Speaking before the House of Representatives in 1954, Congressman Usher L. Burdick of North Dakota noted that although ratified as a treaty, the UN Charter could not legally be considered as such. Rep. Burdick charged: "The first move was made at San Francisco, where many nations met, drew up a charter, and submitted that charter to the Senate for approval as a treaty. This document had none of the earmarks of a treaty, because the Supreme Court of the United States has held in many cases that a treaty is an agreement made between nations, to do or not to do particular things. In the case of the Charter of the United Nations, it was not an agreement between nations. It was an agreement made by the agents of several governments, and there is no contention from any quarter that the United Nations at that time was a nation with which we could make a treaty, but intended to make it an integral power at the first opportunity. How these forces for evil planned to make the United Nations a nation is clear now, since they propose at this time to build a world government by simply amending the Charter of the United Nations." (*Congressional Record*, April 28, 1954)

Congressman Burdick was standing on firm ground. For as Hamilton pointed out in essay No. 75 of *The Federalist Papers* regarding the power of making treaties: "Its objects are *CONTRACTS with foreign nations* which have the force of law, but derive it from the obligations of good faith. They are not rules prescribed by the sovereign to the subject, but *agreements between sovereign and sovereign*." (Emphasis added) treaty, which should manifestly betray or sacrifice primary interests of the state, would be null.[29]

"A treaty cannot be made," Hamilton maintained, "which alters the Constitution of the country or which infringes any express exceptions to the power of the Constitution of the United States."[30]

Until recent times, this was also the opinion of the vast majority of legal scholars and the federal judiciary. Supreme Court Justice Joseph Story, for instance, expressed the view commonly held by 19th century jurists when he opined:

> [T]hough the power is thus general and unrestricted, it is not to be so construed as to destroy the fundamental laws of the state. A power given by the Constitution cannot be construed to authorize a destruction of other powers given in the same instrument.... A treaty to change the organization of the Government, or to annihilate its sovereignty, to overturn its republican form, or to deprive it of its constitutional powers, would be void; because it would destroy, what it was designed merely to fulfill, the will of the people.[31]

Justice Stephen J. Field's dictum in the 1890 case of *Geofroy v. Riggs* buttressed Story's opinion. It stated:

> That the treaty power of the United States extends to all proper subjects of negotiation between our government and the governments of other nations, is clear.... It would not be contended that it extends so far as to authorize what the Constitution forbids, or a change in the character of the government or in that of one of the States, or a cession of any portion of the territory of the latter, without its consent.[32]

In *New Orleans vs. United States* (1836), the Supreme Court held:

> The government of the United States, as was well observed in the argument, is one of limited powers. It can exercise authority over no subjects except those which have been delegated to it. *Congress cannot, by legislation, enlarge the federal jurisdiction, nor can it be enlarged under the treaty-making power.*[33] [Emphasis added]

One of the most dedicated and articulate defenders of this view of the subordination of treaties to the Constitution was Frank Holman, past president of the American Bar Association. Beginning in 1948 with his first speech on the danger of "treaty law" given at the State Bar of California, he launched a nationwide educational effort to marshal opposition to this dangerous encroachment. "The doctrine that the treaty power is unlimited and omnipotent and may be used to override the Constitution and the Bill of Rights," said Holman, "... *is a doctrine of recent origin* and largely derived from *Missouri vs. Holland.*"[34] (Emphasis in original)

Concurring with Holman, constitutional scholar Roger MacBride maintained that the Supreme Court's 1920 *Missouri* decision "ushered in a new era of treaty jurisprudence"[35] by holding that a treaty does supersede the Constitution.

Treaty Traps Proliferating

Through the misuse of the treaty-making provision, the one-worlders have taken huge strides in their effort to "turn the founders upside down." It is of paramount importance, therefore, that Americans exercise special vigilance concerning all treaties. Unfortunately, we find just the opposite to be the case; the American public appears to be totally oblivious to the flood of treaties intended to sweep away our constitutional protections.

There was no fanfare, no opposition, and scant media coverage, for example, when the United Nations International Covenant on Civil and Political Rights sailed through the Senate on April 2, 1992 on an unrecorded vote. There was none of the intense, emotional public debate that attended the Panama Canal Treaty ratification a few years earlier, but the Civil and Political Rights Covenant (hereafter CP Covenant) represents a far greater danger to our constitutional system and to the rights of every American citizen.

During hearings on the treaty conducted by the Senate Committee on Foreign Relations, Senator Jesse Helms was the only member to register opposition. "Now this Senator and every other Member of Congress has taken an oath of office to protect and defend the Constitution of the United States," the North Carolina solon reminded his colleagues. "And that means we should be fully committed to the rights of the individual, which are enshrined in our Constitution. And we should be committed to the protection of these individual rights. We cannot keep the commitment if we agree to the terms of this covenant."[36]

Why the conflict? Because, said Helms, the "covenant calls into question the right of freedom of speech, and freedom of the press, and just punishments — they are clearly constitutional, and even the Federal/State structure of our legal system. Now any agreement that undercuts these rights is an attack on human rights, not a safeguarding of human rights. This covenant, in sum, is a step backward into authoritarianism...."[37]

Serious charges. But they were summarily dismissed by the more "sophisticated," internationally-minded members of the committee as the paranoid ravings of a hopeless super-nationalist. The serious flaws in the Covenant, however, are obvious and by no means inconsequential. In wording typical of that found in the constitutions of communist states, the Covenant acknowledges various rights of individuals, then negates those rights with all manner of conditions.

Article 14, for example, states "everyone shall be entitled to a fair and public hearing...." Sound similar to the U.S. Constitution's guarantee "to a speedy and public trial"? Ah, but the article then declares: "The Press and the public may be excluded from all or part of a trial for reasons of morals, public order...."[38] It, in essence, provides legitimacy for secret trials, a hallmark of despotism throughout history.

The enormous contrast between our Bill of Rights and the UN's so-called "human rights" conventions should be evident to anyone willing to compare the documents. Article I of the U.S. Bill of Rights, for example, declares without qualification, "Congress shall make no law respecting an establishment of religion, or prohibiting the free exercise thereof; or abridging the freedom of speech or of the press...."

By way of contrast, Article 18 of the CP Covenant states, in part, "Everyone shall have the right to freedom of thought, conscience and religion." But then it goes on to assert: "... Freedom to manifest one's religion or beliefs may be subject only to such limitations as are prescribed by law and are necessary...."[39]

Likewise, Article 21 purports to guarantee the right of peaceful assembly, but then permits the state to limit this right for "national security or public safety, public order, ... the protection of public health or morals...."[40] What dictator couldn't drive a tank through that opening? So it goes with the UN's treatment of all rights we take for granted under our Constitution.

The Bush Administration, seeking to blunt criticism of these glaring defects, came up with five reservations, five understandings, four declarations, and numerous explanations (filling 18 pages) that it attached to the treaty. Declaration Number 2 shows the weakness of Mr. Bush's commitment to rights: "[I]t is the view of the United States that States Party to the Covenant should wherever possible refrain from imposing any restrictions or limitations on the exercise of the rights recognized and protected by the Covenant, even when such restrictions and limitations are permissible under the terms of the Covenant."[41] Read it again: "should wherever possible refrain." Translation: "Please use your dictatorial powers sparingly — if you can help it."

As Senator Helms noted: "Many countries controlled by totalitarian governments have signed on to this covenant, laughing all the way back to the garage." He also said, "I have no doubt that these countries will not acknowledge our reservations, but they will use U.S. ratification to make false charges of violations of the covenant. Mark my words, that is precisely what will happen. Meanwhile, they will use the serious weaknesses of this covenant to justify their own cruel regimes."[42]

It is not only foreign dictators who put little store in the power of reservations and declarations. The State Department's claim, for instance, that its Declaration Number 1 makes the treaty "non-self-executing" (that is, it "will not create a cause of private action in U.S. courts") is rejected by many treaty proponents here in the United States. The International Human Rights Law Group stated: "It is not clear that such a declaration would be binding on the judiciary. Scholars and court decisions support the view that the issue whether a treaty is self-executing or not is one of construction by the courts."[43]

Abraham Katz, president of the United States Council for International Business, concurred, stating to the Senate committee:

> There are, however, no precise rules for determining whether a treaty is self executing and, consequently, there is no certain method for making this determination. Indeed the courts frequently disagree.... [S]ome federal courts may not feel bound by such a Senate declaration attached to the resolution of ratification and might nevertheless treat the ratification as being self executing....[44]

The World Court

When the U.S. Constitution and the rights of American citizens conflict with treaties and UN covenants, as is likely to happen with increasing frequency, there are certain to be many politicians, "legal experts," and judges who will hold that American national interests, individual rights, and domestic law must yield to the higher purposes of "world order" and "the rule of law." In the interests of expediting this process, Establishment Insiders have been trying for decades to expand the jurisdiction and authority of the International Court of Justice (more commonly known as the World Court).[45] This makes all the more alarming the recently renewed campaign simultaneously to strengthen the Court and entangle the U.S. in a welter of new treaties.

Writing in the Summer 1992 issue of the CFR's *Foreign Affairs*, Representative Jim Leach (R-IA) declared: "Since one of the most effective antidotes to the irrationality of ancient enmity is the swift justice of the law, a turn (or in the case of the United States, return) to the compulsory jurisdiction of the World Court would appear to be one of the most appropriate and achievable objectives of the decades ahead."

Although the U.S. automatically became a member of the World Court in 1945 when the Senate ratified the UN Charter, we were not bound to accept its compulsory jurisdiction. The Senate resolution recognizing the Court's compulsory jurisdiction excepted those "disputes with regard to matters which are essentially within the domestic jurisdiction of the United States." That was not enough to satisfy many Americans who rightly asked: "But who will define 'domestic jurisdiction?'" It was apparent that if the definition were left up to the UN or its World Court to decide, there would be very little if any "domestic jurisdiction."

To assuage these fears, Senate Foreign Relations Committee Chairman Tom Connally (D-TX), who favored the resolution, proposed the addition of these eight words: "as determined by the United States of America." These eight words comprise what is known as the Connally Reservation.[46] And, as author G. Edward Griffin has pointed out, these words "are all that stand between us and complete legal subjection to the whims of fifteen or nine or five or even two men [of the World Court] whose legal backgrounds and personal ideologies may be strongly antipathetic to the free world in general and to the United States in particular."[47]

Even that scant protection, however, may soon disappear — by outright repeal or by "overriding" agreements, treaties or court rulings — unless a significant portion of the American public can be roused to a robust, determined opposition to this treachery.

The deluge of treaties now in various stages of readiness and preparation — regarding the "environment" (see Chapter 7), "children's rights" (see Chapter 8), "peace and disarmament" (see Chapters 1 and 2), and a host of other issues — has the capability of utterly destroying our Republic if they are approved.

But it is not treaties alone that constitute this threat; the U.S. Department of State includes the following in its "sources of international law making": "treaties, executive agreements, legislation, ... testimony and statements before Congressional and international bodies...."[48] The period of 1990-99 has been declared by the United Nations General Assembly to be "the United Nations Decade of International Law."[49] As such, it being used to propel additional assaults on national sovereignty.

Americans must face up to the reality that our heritage of freedom under the "rule of law" of the Constitution is being replaced piecemeal by the tyrannical "rule of men" under the Charter of the United Nations. We must decide now, while there is yet time, which future we will choose for ourselves and our posterity.

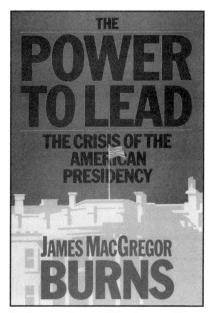

Professor James MacGregor Burns, a leader of Project '87 and Committee on the Constitutional System, two Establishment groups trying to alter the U.S. Constitution, writes in his book *The Power to Lead* of wanting to "turn the founders upside down."

John Birch Society President John F. McManus: Purpose of government is to defend God-given rights.

Frank Chodorov — author, editor, champion of freedom — exposed UN threat.

Eisenhower wanted treaty power to override Constitution.

President Truman: "no ... difference between domestic and foreign affairs."

Madison opposed currently prevailing thought that treaty power is unrestrained.

Hamilton: Treaties contrary to the Constitution are null and void.

The International Court of Justice (or World Court) could dictate to Americans if U.S. accepts compulsory jurisdiction.

Senator Tom Connally, delegate to the UN founding conference and staunch UN supporter, authored Connally Reservation to calm fears of UN opponents. It restricts World Court from interfering in domestic matters "as determined by the United States of America."

CHAPTER 7

The Global Green Regime

In searching for a new enemy to unite us, we came up with the idea that pollution, the threat of global warming, water shortages, famine and the like would fit the bill.... All these dangers are caused by human intervention.... The real enemy, then, is humanity itself. [1]

— *The First Global Revolution*
The Council of the Club of Rome, 1991

There are genuine ecological problems today challenging mankind's intelligence, wisdom, and resourcefulness. Very few will deny that fact. One need not investigate very deeply into the organized "environmental movement," however, or examine the "science" on which it hangs its hat, to realize that its repeated prophesies of apocalyptic doom have far more to do with increasing and centralizing government control over mankind than with protecting man and nature from environmentally harmful practices.

Over the past two decades, a flood of books, articles, television documentaries, and news broadcasts has given the public such a frightening forecast of ecological catastrophe that far too many individuals now appear willing to give up their freedom for "solutions" that seem always to involve massive increases in government.

It is not our purpose here to present the hard, factual evidence assembled by prominent scientific authorities to refute the many false claims of the environmental disaster lobby. There are already many excellent volumes that capably expose the fraudulent theories about ozone depletion, global warming, pollution, pesticides, cancer risks, nuclear power, PCBs, asbestos, acid rain, deforestation, carbon dioxide, biodiversity, soil depletion, etc. [2] Rather, we hope to demonstrate convincingly that concerns about the environment (some overblown, others completely fabricated) are being cynically exploited by influential individuals and organizations whose goal includes building a global tyranny.

Central Planning Nightmare

The horrifying political, economic, and social consequences wrought by totalitarian government in the former communist world have been so thoroughly exposed over the past several years that there are very few today who will openly defend the Soviet economic model. Meanwhile, mounting evidence of unparalleled ecological destruction in lands formerly under communist rule has finally begun to persuade even some environmentalists that too much government is as bad for nature as it is harmful to man.[3]

It is now considered acceptable in "politically correct" circles to talk of "market incentives" and "market solutions" to environmental problems. But, amazingly, many of those who use these terms envision a marketplace heavily or completely regulated and controlled by government. In other words, they have not really turned away from their government-is-the-only-answer mentality.

Competitive Enterprise Institute president Fred L. Smith was one of several who journeyed to Rio de Janeiro to bring a non-statist perspective to the Earth Summit. At an "Earth Summit Alternatives" conference held during the proceedings, he stated: "Economic central planning was a utopian dream, but it became a real world nightmare. Today, the international environmental establishment seems eager to repeat this experiment in the ecological sphere, increasing the power of the state, restricting individual and economic freedom." Thus, Smith warned, despite the horrendous record of human, economic and environmental destruction left as a legacy by these centrally planned governments, "the world is moving decisively toward central planning for ecological rather than economic purposes."[4] But the determined environmentalists in Rio were not interested in these warnings.

Decades of Persistent Globalist Planning

One of the noteworthy early calls for the creation of a global environmental agency appeared in an advertisement sponsored by the World Association of World Federalists (WAWF) in the January-

February 1972 issue of *The Humanist*, published by the American Humanist Association. It read:

> World Federalists believe that the environmental crisis facing planet earth is a global problem and therefore calls for a "global" solution — a worldwide United Nations Environmental Agency with the power to make its decisions stick. WAWF has submitted a proposal for just such an agency to be considered at the 1972 U.N. Environmental Conference to be held in Stockholm.

That first UN Environmental Conference, held in Stockholm, Sweden June 5-16, 1972, proved to be the launching pad for the worldwide campaign to establish a UN planetary environmental authority. One result of the conference was the establishment of a United Nations Environment Program (UNEP) intended as the overseer of a future monitoring system of the world's environment. The man selected to be the first executive director of the new agency was Maurice Strong, a Canadian, who had served as secretary-general of the Stockholm event and was at the time a trustee of the Rockefeller Foundation.

This same Maurice Strong was named 20 years later to serve as secretary-general of the United Nations Conference on Environment and Development (UNCED), the official name of the 1992 Earth Summit in Rio de Janeiro. A millionaire businessman with a passion for socialist, one-world causes, Strong is a radical environmentalist and New Age devotee (see Chapter 12). He is also a major player in such Insider circles as the Club of Rome and the Aspen Institute for Humanistic Studies.

In the months leading up to the major event in Rio, Strong grabbed headlines on several occasions with outlandish rantings against the United States and the middle class of the industrialized countries. Though a Canadian, Strong maintains his primary residence in the United States. During one ill-tempered fit, he declared that "the United States is clearly the greatest risk" to the world's ecological health. This was so, he said, because, "In effect, the United States is committing environmental aggression against the rest of the world." Including himself in the indictment, he said, "We didn't start doing this with any mal-intent. But we've lost our inno-cence now."[5]

In an UNCED report issued in August 1991, Strong wrote: "It is clear that current lifestyles and consumption patterns of the afflu-ent middle-class ... involving high meat intake, consumption of large amounts of frozen and 'convenience' foods, ownership of motor-vehicles, numerous electric household appliances, home and work-place air-conditioning ... expansive suburban housing ... are not sustainable."[6]

"A shift is therefore necessary," the UNCED chief insisted, "to-wards lifestyles ... less geared to ... environmentally damaging con-sumption patterns...."[7] Of course, when Strong talks about "damaging consumption patterns," he exempts his own globe-hop-ping, champagne-and-caviar lifestyle and that of good friends like David Rockefeller, pillar of international banking and the leading Insider of both the CFR and Trilateral Commission elites.

Rockefeller and Strong teamed up to write, respectively, the Fore-word and Introduction to the revealing 1991 Trilateral Commission book, *Beyond Interdependence: The Meshing of the World's Economy and the Earth's Ecology*, by Canada's Jim MacNeill, Holland's Pieter Winsemius, and Japan's Taizo Yakushiji. "... I have been privileged to work closely with the principal author, Jim MacNeill, for over two decades," wrote the UNCED chief. "He was one of my advisors when I was secretary general of the Stockholm Conference on the Human Environment in 1972. We were both members of the World Com-mission on Environment and Development and, as secretary gen-eral, he played a fundamental role in shaping and writing its landmark report, *Our Common Future* [a socialist/environmentalist manifesto also known as *The Brundtland Report*]." Moreover, re-vealed Strong, MacNeill "is now advising me on the road to Rio."[8]

Beyond Interdependence served as the Trilateral game plan for Rio, and it had Strong's full endorsement. "This book couldn't ap-pear at a better time, with the preparations for the Earth Summit moving into high gear," said Strong. To stress its importance, he said it would help guide "decisions that will literally determine the fate of the earth." According to this head summiteer, the Rio gath-ering would "have the political capacity to produce the basic changes needed in our national and international economic agendas and in our institutions of governance...." In his estimation, *"Beyond Interdependence* provides the most compelling economic as well as environmental case for such reform that I have read."[9]

MacNeill's "reform" proposals are summed up on page 128 of the book so enthusiastically endorsed by Strong. MacNeill and his co-authors advocated "a new global partnership expressed in a revitalized international system in which an Earth Council, perhaps the Security Council with a broader mandate, maintains the interlocked environmental and economic security of the planet." "The Earth Summit," wrote MacNeill and his cohorts "will likely be the last chance for the world, in this century at least, to seriously address and arrest the accelerating environmental threats to economic development, national security, and human survival."[10]

The same globalist-socialist vision was presented in *Global Economics and the Environment: Toward Sustainable Rural Development in the Third World*, another Earth Summit guide published just prior to the UNCED confab by the Council on Foreign Relations.[11] The common apocalyptic theme has been repeated innumerable times in environmental jeremiads coming from a bevy of one-worlders ranging from David Rockefeller, Henry Kissinger, and Helmut Kohl to Francois Mitterrand, Willy Brandt, and Mikhail Gorbachev, and even to Ted Turner, Jane Fonda, and Tom Hayden. It's not possible to study the environmental movement in any depth without repeatedly tripping over the recurring connection between the socialist/communist left and the corporate/banking elite personified by David Rockefeller and the organizations he has led.

A diligent survey of environmentalist activity also leads one to the conclusion that all of the official preparatory meetings and negotiations leading up to the Earth Summit were really just so much spectacle for public consumption. And the Rio gathering itself was additional "consensus" sideshow to provide an aura of planetary "democracy" for a program that was already worked out in detail by the one-worlders long ago.

Consider, for example, Lester R. Brown (CFR), the supposed anti-establishment ecofanatic who heads the very influential Worldwatch Institute, one of the driving forces behind UNCED. His best-selling

1972 book, *World Without Borders*, proposed a "world environmental agency" because "[a]rresting the deterioration of the environment does not seem possible within the existing framework of independent nation-states."[12] His superagency would first "assess the impact of man's various interventions in the environment."[13] But there's no doubt that the conclusions to be reached were already firmly cast in stone.

Brown then stated: "Once the necessary information and analysis is complete, tolerance levels can be established and translated into the necessary regulations of human economic activity."[14] His books and statist solutions are hyped by the CFR-dominated media and CFR academics, while the big CFR-controlled foundations shower his think tank with millions of dollars.

"Building an environmentally sustainable future," Brown later said of the Earth Summit's mission, "requires nothing short of a revolution." This would involve "restructuring the global economy, dramatically changing human reproductive behavior and altering values and lifestyles."[15] At least no one can accuse these guys of thinking small or hiding their ultimate goals!

In *State of The World 1991*, the annual doomsday report issued by the Worldwatch Institute, Brown predicted that "the battle to save the planet will replace the battle over ideology as the organizing theme of the new world order."[16] And, with "the end of the ideological conflict that dominated a generation of international affairs, a new world order, shaped by a new agenda, will emerge." The world's agenda, he wrote, will "be more ecological than ideological."[17]

Over and over while presuming to speak for the entire environmental movement, Brown indicated its intention to focus on the environment as the justification for establishing controls over mankind. "In the new age," he asserted, "diplomacy will be more concerned with environmental security than with military security."[18]

Pushing the Line

How prescient! How did Brown know that a few months later the *New York Times* would be reporting favorably in an editorial ("The New World Army," March 6, 1992) that the UN's "Security Council recently expanded the concept of threats to peace to include economic, social and ecological instability"? Of course, it's not difficult to seem to be prescient if you are hooked into the Insider party line. Ronald I. Spiers (CFR) was similarly prescient when he stated in the March 13, 1992 *New York Times*: "The [United Nations] Trusteeship Council should be changed from a body dealing with the vestiges of colonialism to one dealing with the environment, becoming in effect the trustee of the health of the planet."

An earlier purveyor of this line, CFR "wise man" George F. Kennan, the author of our nation's cold war policy of containment against communism, explained in a *Washington Post* column appearing on November 12, 1989 that we now live "in an age where the great enemy is not the Soviet Union but the rapid deterioration of our planet as a supporting structure for civilized life."[19]

Jessica Tuchman Mathews (CFR), vice president of the World Resources Institute, followed with an article in the July/August 1990 *EPA Journal* asserting that "environmental imperatives are changing the concept of national sovereignty," and "multipolarity [is] replacing the bipolar U.S.-U.S.S.R. axis around which nations used to array themselves." Moreover, she wrote, "it is likely that international problem-solving in the decades ahead will for the first time depend on collective management, not hegemony. And it is to precisely this form of governance that global environmental problems will yield."

In an opinion column in the *New York Times* of March 27, 1990, Michael Oppenheimer (CFR) warned darkly: "Global warming, ozone depletion, deforestation and overpopulation are the four horsemen of a looming 21st century apocalypse." He assured readers: "As the cold war recedes, the environment is becoming the No. 1 international security concern."

It is vitally important to understand that the particular environmental problems being addressed are either greatly overblown or non-existent. As we stated previously, responsible scientists in these fields are increasingly speaking out about the excessive and fraudulent claims of the ecocrats. Yet, the cry for increased government goes on and on, emanating from one Insider "expert" after another and being shoved down the throats of the American people by the Insider-dominated media.

Mikhail Gorbachev, who is the darling of new world order promoters, has learned the line well. Addressing the 1990 Global Forum in Moscow, he called for "ecologizing" society and said: "The ecological crisis we are experiencing today — from ozone depletion to deforestation and disastrous air pollution — is tragic but convincing proof that the world we all live in is interrelated and interdependent."[20]

"This means," Gorbachev continued, "that we need an appropriate international policy in the field of ecology. Only if we formulate such a policy shall we be able to avert catastrophe. True, the elaboration of such a policy poses unconventional and difficult problems that will affect the sovereignty of states."[21] In other words, we'll all have to get used to the idea of a global EPA under the UN dictating policies about spotted owls, wetlands, auto emissions, hair spray, barbecue lighter fluid, and anything else affecting "the environment." Which is virtually everybody and everything.

This is a theme to which Gorbachev has frequently returned, much to the approbation of the one-world Insiders. One of his greatest fans in this regard is *New York Times* columnist Flora Lewis (CFR), who has praised him for going "beyond accepted notions of the limits of national sovereignty and rules of behavior." She is thrilled by his "plan for a global code of environmental conduct," which "would have an aspect of *world government*, because it would provide for the World Court to judge states." This, she gushed with obvious delight, "is a breathtaking idea, beyond the current dreams of ecology militants.... And it is fitting that the environment be the topic for what amounts to *global policing*.... Even starting the effort would be a giant step for *international law*."[22] (Emphasis added)

Predictably, John Lawrence Hargrove (CFR), executive director of the American Society of International Law, was tickled pink over Gorbachev's support for compulsory jurisdiction of the International Court of Justice. "Before Gorbachev," said Hargrove, "this would have been regarded as astounding."[23]

To key Insider Richard N. Gardner (CFR), Gorbachev's proposals are "solid nuggets of policy that offer constructive opportunities for the West."[24] Gardner, co-chairman of a "Soviet-American working group on the future of the U.N.," is one of those globalists who, apparently, have been tutoring Gorbachev, Yeltsin, and other Kremlin "progressives" in new world order thinking and etiquette.[25]

It was Gardner, you may recall, who penned the now famous article, "The Hard Road To World Order," in the April 1974 issue of *Foreign Affairs*. One of the boldest calls for world government ever to appear in the CFR's journal, it called for building the "house of world order" through "an end run around national sovereignty, eroding it piece by piece." Moreover, it set out the CFR Insider plans for exploiting fears about environmental calamity as a vehicle for expanding the UN's power. In this 1974 article, Gardner wrote:

> The next few years should see a continued strengthening of the new global and regional agencies charged with protecting the world's *environment*. In addition to comprehensive monitoring of the earth's air, water and soil and of the effects of pollutants on human health, we can look forward to new procedures to implement the principle of state responsibility for national actions that have transnational environmental consequences, probably including some kind of "international environmental impact statement".... [Emphasis in original]

To any farmer, rancher, logger, miner, developer, businessman, or property owner who has had to wrestle with the ordeal of attempting to comply with local, state, or federal environmental impact statements, the idea of a planetary EPA demanding similar compliance must be a nightmare too horrible to contemplate. But to the one-world corporate statists who plan on running the show, it is a glorious vision of the future. Gardner was not indulging in idle speculation and wishful thinking here. As can be seen from currently unfolding events, he was merely reporting on actual developments that he and his fellow world order architects had initiated and were nurturing along.

The Report From Iron Mountain

There are many pieces of evidence to demonstrate that the entire environmentalist "movement" and all of its phony "crises" have been created, promoted, and sustained by the Insiders for the singular purpose of conjuring up a credibly terrifying menace to replace the fear of nuclear holocaust as the impetus for world government. Because of space limitations, we will focus on just one unique document and quote from it extensively. But before we do so, it is essential that we set it up by explaining briefly the Insiders' New Paradigm Shift.

The first try at "world order" came in the form of the League of Nations at the end of World War I. If only the nations of the world would come together in unity and begin the process of surrendering national sovereignty to a world body, went the siren song, the scourge of war would be vanquished. This type of propaganda almost produced its desired effect, but not quite. The United States was protected from armed invasion by ocean moats which made armed invasion unlikely. Moreover, the spirit of nationalism and independence still ran strong in American blood. A majority in the U.S. Senate decided, after all of the debate and wrangling, to stay out of the League of Nations. Our nation's refusal to go along doomed the League from its start.

The second try at world order followed World War II, and it culminated in the creation of the United Nations. The arrival of the atomic bomb and long-range delivery systems (bombers, missiles, etc.), together with CFR dominance of the White House and growing CFR influence in the media and the Senate,[26] provided the Insiders with the combination they needed to get the UN Charter ratified. But a UN with no real authority was still just half, or even less than half a loaf. Significant vestiges of national sovereignty still presented real barriers to full-blown world government.

For 40 years, the Insiders relied on fear of "the bomb" to keep America tied to the United Nations. If we dared quit the world body, went their argument, there would surely be nuclear war with the communists and global annihilation. Coexistence was our best available option, at least until such time as the UN became powerful enough to guarantee its version of peace. But, even while "the bomb" was serving its purpose well, long-range planning was underway to employ the threat of environmental cataclysm in future campaigns to build the world organization into a world government.

During the summer of 1963, it appears that Insiders in the Kennedy Administration convened a Special Study Group of 15 men who met at a secret facility at Iron Mountain, New York. Their mission: Come up with alternatives to war that would provide the same social and political "stabilizing" function.[27]

Two and a half years later the group produced its findings. They were not intended for public consumption. One member of the group, however, felt it should be made available for the American people. In 1967, therefore, it was published without identifying any of its authors under the title, *Report From Iron Mountain on the Possibility and Desirability of Peace*.[28] It proved to be an instant sensation and generated heated public debate. Was it an authentic report? A brilliant satire? A cruel hoax? Subsequent events, plus the release of other government studies (such as have been discussed in previous chapters) and the admissions by many of those at the center of the environmentalist movement concerning their true goals, argue for the report's authenticity. In addition, professor John Kenneth Galbraith later admitted he was "a member of the conspiracy" (the words are his) that produced the book.[29]

The Iron Mountain group found that "Credibility, in fact, lies at the heart of the problem of developing a political substitute for war." Such a substitute "would require 'alternate enemies,' some of which might seem ... farfetched in the context of the current war system." The participants considered a number of general social welfare programs as possible substitutes: health, transportation, education, housing, poverty, etc., but were not satisfied with any of them. "It is more probable, in our judgement," they opined, "that such a threat will have to be invented...."[30]

"When it comes to postulating a credible substitute for war capable of directing human behavior patterns in behalf of social organization," said the researchers, "few options suggest themselves. Like its political function, the motivational function of war requires the existence of a genuinely menacing social enemy." The "alternate enemy," they contended in the report, "must imply a more immediate, tangible, and directly felt threat of destruction. It must justify the need for taking and paying a 'blood price' in wide areas of human concern."[31] With this in mind, the group felt, the possible substitute enemies they were considering were insufficient.

According to the report, however, "One exception might be the environmental-pollution model, if the danger to society it posed was genuinely imminent. The fictive models would have to carry the weight of extraordinary conviction, underscored with a not inconsiderable actual sacrifice of life...."[32] These considerate experts even determined to provide for the spiritual needs of those they were "helping." They believed that "the construction of an up-to-date mythological or religious structure for this purpose would present difficulties in our era, but must certainly be considered."[33] Ecology seemed to be the best bet:

> It may be ... that gross pollution of the environment can eventually replace the possibility of mass destruction by nuclear weapons as the principal apparent threat to the survival of the species. Poisoning of the air, and of the principal sources of food and water supply, is already well advanced, and at first glance would seem promising in this respect; it constitutes a threat that can be dealt with only through social organization and political power. But from present indications it will be a generation to a generation and a half before environmental pollution, however severe, will be sufficiently menacing, on a global scale, to offer a possible basis for a solution.[34]

With respect to the time required to create widespread fear of a phony pollution crisis, that estimate seems to have been pretty accurate. The schemers even suggested "that the rate of pollution could be increased selectively for this purpose; in fact, the mere modifying of existing programs for the deterrence of pollution could speed up the process enough to make the threat credible much sooner. But the pollution problem has been so widely publicized in recent years that it seems highly improbable that a program of deliberate environmental poisoning could be implemented in a politically acceptable manner."[35]

"Economic surrogates for war," said the group's report, "must meet two principal criteria. They must be 'wasteful,' in the common sense of the word, and they must operate outside the normal supply-demand system. A corollary that should be obvious is that the magnitude of the waste must be sufficient to meet the needs of a particular society. An economy as advanced and complex as our own requires the planned average annual destruction of not less than 10 percent of gross national product if it is effectively to fulfill its stabilizing function."[36]

With this diabolical thought in mind, the seemingly insane EPA mandates requiring the expenditure of billions of dollars on minuscule or non-existent cancer risks, the sacrificing of thousands of jobs and businesses for a variety of "endangered species," and all of the other seemingly crazy governmental policies begin to make sense.

Pressure From Above and Below

Much more also begins to make sense. Like the long-standing symbiotic relationship between the Rockefeller Brothers Fund, Ford Foundation, Council on Foreign Relations, Exxon, IBM, Procter & Gamble, et al. on one hand, and Friends of the Earth, Nature Conservancy, Planned Parenthood, Sierra Club, Greenpeace, Environmental Defense Fund, et al. on the other. Pressure from above and pressure from below: the American people caught in a pincer attack.

At the Rio summit, this strategy was clearly discernible as the ecofanatics and the corporate collectivists linked arms and called on the United Nations to take charge of protecting the world's atmosphere, forests, oceans, fresh water, coastal areas, mountainous areas — virtually the entire planet. But that's not all. The new world order globalists want much more than just possession and control of the material environment. They want possession of your mind and soul as well.

Echoing the dire warnings of eco-destruction with which we've become familiar, the UNCED booklet *In Our Hands: Earth Summit '92* asserted in its closing paragraph: "The world community now faces together greater risks to our common security through our impacts on the environment than from traditional military conflicts with one another." Then, with a pagan hubris that would do credit to the Iron Mountain gang, it proclaimed: "We must now forge a new 'Earth Ethic' which will inspire all peoples and nations to join in a new global partnership of North, South, East and West."[37]

Fallout From Rio

The full meaning and significance of the Rio summit, hailed as history's largest gathering of world leaders, will not become known for months, or even years. No one has yet had a chance to read, let alone digest, all of the fine print in the voluminous agreements and documents hammered out during its two fractious weeks of negotiations. One thing is certain: What was produced at Rio will be the source of much future argument, negotiation, lobbying, and legislation. As Maurice Strong, secretary-general of the conference, put it, "This is a launching pad, not a quick fix."[38] The leaders of the huge environmental lobbying network in Washington, DC fully realize this and are gearing up for sustained warfare over the many issues addressed at the summit.

The summit, unfortunately, did produce some "accomplishments." We list some (both official and unofficial) that will be around to haunt, harass, and increasingly trouble us in the years ahead:

- *Agenda 21*, the 800-page blueprint for governmental action addressing everything from forests to deserts, oceans, rivers, women's rights, and health care, has set in motion a continuously evolving process of environmental policy formation.[39]
- A commitment was made to establish a new Commission on Sustainable Development to monitor national compliance with the environmental targets agreed upon at the summit.[40]
- This new commission will also review the development assistance contributions from the industrial countries to make sure they provide sufficient funds to implement the *Agenda 21* policies.[41]
- A new International Green Cross organization was formed to provide worldwide "emergency" environmental assistance. Mikhail Gorbachev was named to lead it.[42]
- President Bush called for an international conference on global warming by January 1, 1993 at which nations are to report on specific plans to reduce greenhouse gases.[43]
- President Bush pledged to double U.S. aid to international efforts aimed at the "protection" of forests.[44]
- The neo-pagan cult of nature worship, long prevalent in environmental and New Age circles, was formally launched as the new world religion (see Chapter 12).
- Environmentalism was elevated to new heights within the realm of international statecraft.

New Green World Order

One of the major organizational players (both out front and behind the scenes) at Rio and in the preparations leading up to the summit was the Washington-based Worldwatch Institute. An interview with Lester Brown (CFR), founder and president of Worldwatch, appeared in the June 3rd issue of *Terraviva*, a special daily newspaper distributed to participants during the Earth Summit. In it, Brown predicted that "ecological sustainability will become the new organising principle, the foundation of the 'new world order,' if you will."[45]

Brown actually admitted that the new world order he sought meant giving up national sovereignty. Here is how he put it:

> One hears from time to time from conservative columnists and others that we, as the United States, don't want to sign these treaties that would sacrifice our national sovereignty. But what they seem to overlook is that we've already lost a great deal of our sovereignty.
>
> We can no longer protect the stratospheric ozone layer over the United States. We can't stabilise the U.S. climate without the cooperation of countries throughout the world. If even one major developing country continues to use CFCs (chlorofluorocarbons), it will eventually deplete the ozone layer. We can't protect the biological diversity of the planet by ourselves. We've lost sovereignty; we've lost control.[46]

What it really gets down to, said Brown, is that "we can no longer separate the future habitability of the planet from the distribution of wealth."[47] No surprise there. With socialists like Brown advocating the extremes of social engineering, redistribution of the wealth is what it always gets down to — ultimately.

"But," suggested the *Terraviva* interviewer, "the current climate here in the U.S. seems very hostile to foreign aid." Acknowledging the dilemma, Brown responded: "It might take a few more scares to get this country energised."[48] No doubt the eco-saviors have "a few more scares" up their sleeves to "energize" those of us non-believers who value our freedom.

The influential Worldwatch Institute study, *After the Earth Summit: The Future of Environmental Governance* by Hilary F. French, has this to say on the subject:

> National sovereignty — the power of a country to control events within its territory — has lost much of its meaning in today's world, where borders are routinely breached by pollution, international trade, financial flows and refugees.... Because all of these forces can affect environmental trends, international treaties and institutions are proving ever more critical to addressing ecological threats. Nations are in effect ceding portions of their sovereignty to the international community, and beginning to create a new system of international environmental governance as a means of solving otherwise-unmanageable problems.[49]

What French then stated has a very strong bearing on what additional mischief may result from the summit:

> [T]he past twenty years' experience has yielded some instructive lessons in environmental negotiations — which the world community can now apply to the far larger challenges looming on the horizon. Paradoxically, one way to make environmental agreements more effective is in some cases to make them less enforceable — and therefore more palatable to the negotiators who may initially feel threatened by any loss of sovereignty. So-called 'soft law' — declarations, resolutions, and action plans that nations do not need to formally ratify and are not legally binding — *can help to create an international consensus, mobilize aid, and lay the groundwork for the negotiation of binding treaties later.*[50] [Emphasis added]

"*Agenda 21*," said French, "an action plan on nearly all aspects of sustainable development expected to emerge from UNCED, would fall into this category [of so-called 'soft law']."[51] She continued her explanation of how the environmental treaty process will work:

> When a binding treaty is necessary, the "convention-protocol" approach, which was used in both the transboundary air pollution and the ozone talks, is now the dominant model. Under this approach, a "framework" treaty is agreed to first that generally does not involve

any binding commitment, but represents a political commitment to take action at a later date. It also strengthens the joint research and monitoring programs needed to build enough scientific consensus and knowledge to convince countries to eventually commit to specific targets. The framework treaty is then followed by specific protocols on various aspects of the problem. [52]

Operators like French are not moaning because they didn't get everything they wanted in the Rio agreements and treaties. They got their feet in the door, and that's what matters most. *New York Times* writer William K. Stevens recognized this important lesson as well. In the June 14, 1992 *Times*, he noted that "blandness can sometimes prove a surprisingly effective bludgeon. The parcel of treaties signed here have been portrayed by disappointed advocates as pitiful gutless creatures with no bite. But they have hidden teeth that will develop in the right circumstances." That is why Richard E. Benedick, the former State Department official who helped negotiate the ozone layer treaty, has observed that the Earth Summit "should not be judged by the immediate results, but by the process it sets in motion." [53]

And the Rio Summit has set a great many processes in motion. In her aforementioned work, *After the Earth Summit*, Hilary French noted: "Events in Rio also may lay the groundwork for a more ambitious reform of the United Nations proposed for 1995. An independent group of current and past world leaders including Willy Brandt, Jimmy Carter, Václav Havel, Julius Nyerere, and Eduard Shevardnadze has recommended that a World Summit on Global Governance be held that year — the fiftieth anniversary of the founding of the United Nations." [54]

Pretext for Control

Every call to action, every solution offered by the green globalists, always leads to a loss of freedom and more power in government. The final goal is always centralization of that power in the United Nations. For those truly concerned with protecting the environment, that is exactly the wrong direction to be heading. As Dr. Fred Smith has explained and documented with many studies: "Wherever resources have been privately protected, they have done better than their politically managed counterparts — whether we are speaking of elephants in Africa, salmon streams in England, or the beaver in Canada. Where such rights have been absent or suppressed, or not creatively extended, the results have been less fortunate."[55]

The world should not be speeding toward a centrally-planned environment. That is precisely what has been proven so ecologically destructive throughout the world. Rather, we should be "extending property rights to the full array of ecological resources that have been left out in the cold"[56] and rolling back the socialist controls that are preventing people from finding solutions through voluntary arrangements and freedom of choice in the open marketplace.

It is becoming ever more obvious that the plans of the planet guardians and green globalists we have described have virtually nothing to do with saving endangered species, protecting the ozone layer, or whatever else they are using as cover for their real goal. Instead, their plans have everything to do with forging the chains for a UN-dominated world dictatorship.

PHOTOS BY WILLIAM F. JASPER

UN Earth Summit in Rio de Janeiro was a pagan, New Age, socialist love-in. Center: Senator Al Gore led Senate delegation, called for global environmental controls. Bottom right: former California governor Jerry Brown joins ecofanatics in Rio Earth Walk.

"Inside and outside the main conference hall, the biggest applause went for Fidel Castro," said the *New York Times* of Rio earth fest. "Castro drew cheers when [he] strode to the platform to denounce the industrialized countries as guilty of most of the world's environmental problems."

At Rio, Drs. Fred Smith and Dixy Lee Ray debunked eco-hysteria, offered rational science, free enterprise, and private property rights alternatives to statist "solutions" proposed by global ecofascists.

140

UN Earth Summit was the launchpad for many treaties on environment and economy that are being used to build a world socialist superstate.

UNCED chief Maurice Strong, a New Age devotee and Establishment Insider, accuses the U.S. of "committing environmental aggression against the rest of the world," denounces middle-class "lifestyles and consumption patterns."

Mikhail Gorbachev named head of new International Green Cross for "emergency" environmental aid.

Worldwatch head Lester Brown (CFR) says "new world order" will be dominated by "ecological" concerns.

Keynesian economist John Kenneth Galbraith (CFR) was a member of the secret Iron Mountain study group set up by the Kennedy Administration to devise means for the federal government to control the American people. The group concluded environmental concerns offered best opportunities.

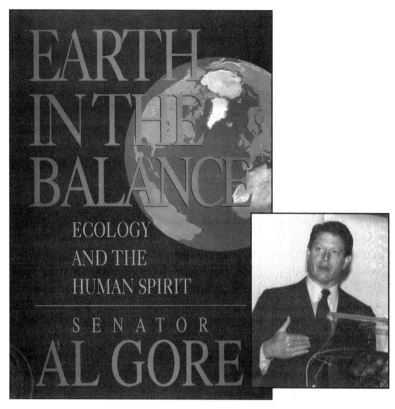

Bill Clinton chose environmental extremist Senator Al Gore (D-TN) for vice president. A member of GLOBE (Global Legislators Organization for a Balanced Environment) and leader of the U.S. Senate delegation to the Earth Summit, Gore is also author of eco-babble best-seller *Earth in the Balance.* In that volume Gore calls for a "Global Marshall Plan" under which UN envirocrats will dictate global energy and industrial policy, population control, and redistribution of world wealth. The price tag: a mere $100 billion per year for U.S. taxpayers. "With the original Marshall Plan serving as both a model and an inspiration," he wrote, "we can now begin to chart a course of action." His course calls for global intervention-ist policies "serving the central organizing principle of saving the global environment." It also calls for new taxes on oil, coal, minerals, and wood, and the phaseout of the earth's most dreaded enemy, the internal combustion engine. Gore frets over world population growth and cites as his authority Paul Ehrlich, the discredited dean of doomsayers. He refers to "the day the scientific community confirmed that the dangerous hole in the sky above Antarctica was caused by CFCs" — a day that exists only in his perfervid imagination. Similarly faulty "science" concerning "global warming," air and water pollution, and other environmental "crises" appears on almost every page, along with Gore's totalitarian "solutions."

CHAPTER 8

The UN Grab for Your Child

*I submit that this House has not taken the time to reflect upon
the implications of the Convention and will be in for a tremen-
dous shock when judges around the country start applying the
Convention as the supreme law of the land.* [1]
— Representative Thomas J. Bliley (R-VA)
September 17, 1990

The United Nations World Summit for Children, held in New
York during September 1990, was widely heralded as "the largest
gathering ever of world leaders." President Bush, in the midst of his
Persian Gulf military buildup, left Washington to join more than 70
other heads of state at the UN for the historic event. The poignant
photographs and news clippings of presidents and prime ministers
embracing adorable tykes while calling on the world to "save the
children" contrasted sharply with the grim forecasts of war and gave
a softer edge to the President's almost daily calls for a new world
order and a strengthened United Nations.

According to UN organizers, more than a million persons worldwide participated in candlelight vigils that week. [2] In New York, politicians and entertainment celebrities jostled with one another for
television and photo opportunities at the city's numerous summit
programs. Over and over again, summit participants and media
pundits parroted the litany of statistics compiled by the officials of
the Children's Defense Fund and other self-proclaimed guardians of
the world's children. Beneath all of these emotional appeals lay an
agenda full of ever-larger and ever-more-costly socialist programs.

Time magazine and its collectivist chorus of media allies cheered
the summit's support for what was termed "a bold 10-year plan to
reduce mortality rates and poverty among children and to improve
access to immunizations and education." [3]

Noble Sounding Rhetoric

But the real summit send-off was saved for the United Nations Convention on the Rights of the Child. The UN has hailed this treaty as "a landmark in international efforts to strengthen justice, peace, and freedom in the world," and "the most complete statement of children's rights ever made."[4] UNICEF Director James Grant called the treaty "the Magna Carta for children, an instrument of far-reaching significance for the needs of those who are humanity's most vulnerable."[5]

Who could find fault with such lofty aspirations? Almost no one, it seems. The Convention won world support like no previous treaty. According to the UN's *Fact Sheet No. 10, The Rights of the Child*:

> The Convention on the Rights of the Child was adopted — unanimously — by the United Nations General Assembly on 20 November, 1989....
>
> After its *adoption* by the General Assembly, the Convention was *opened for signature* on 26 January 1990. Sixty-one countries signed the document on that day — a record first-day response....
>
> The Convention entered into force on 2 September 1990 — one month after the twentieth State ratified it.... A little over seven months separated the opening for signature and the entry into force of the Convention; this is a very short period for an international treaty — generally it takes much longer — and it shows the world-wide interest and support for the child Convention. [Emphasis in original]

A Lone Voice in Congress

More truthfully, it shows the effectiveness of the worldwide propaganda campaign orchestrated by internationalists who are willing to exploit a natural concern for the plight of children to advance their agenda for a new world order. In the days before the summit, both Houses of the U.S. Congress hurriedly passed resolutions urging President Bush to sign the convention and send it to the Senate for ratification before attending the summit. Opposition to the Convention was virtually nonexistent. Only Representative Thomas J. Bliley (R-VA) rose to urge caution and restraint.[6]

Bliley did not merely nitpick about commas and whereases. His reading of the document left him convinced that "the convention represents a potential threat to our form of government."[7]

Was he reading the same document his colleagues were given? More than likely, he was the only member of Congress who actually did read what the Convention says. During his remarks in the House on September 17, 1990, Bliley asked, "Will the Convention really solve the problems our children face? Is it merely an article of good intentions to make us feel good about ourselves? Or, is it actually a potential threat to some of our most precious freedoms, civil liberties, and our form of government?"[8]

The congressman from Virginia reminded his colleagues that no hearings had been held on the treaty they were asking the President to sign. "I submit," said Bliley, "that this House has not taken the time to reflect upon the implications of the Convention and will be in for a tremendous shock when judges around the country start applying the Convention as the supreme law of the land."[9]

Bliley continued: "Have we determined the impact that this Convention will have on our system of federalism? No. Have we resolved in our minds its inherent conflicts with the U.S. Constitution? I think not. Do we realize the great new powers Congress is taking away from the sovereign States, as well as giving up itself, to the judiciary?"[10]

Dangerous Document

The Convention is a lengthy, complex document comprised of 54 articles dealing with adoption, education, child labor, child pornography, child abuse, prenatal and postnatal health care for women, family reunification, and many other issues. Although it is replete with rhetoric about "rights" and "freedom" and noble-sounding appeals for the protection of children, from the standpoint of American constitutional law it is fundamentally flawed. Like the UN Charter and many UN conventions addressing "rights," this Convention on the Rights of the Child is based on the philosophy that rights are granted by governments, and it is, therefore, completely at odds with the Declaration of Independence, and the Constitution and its Bill of Rights.

In an op-ed piece appearing in the *Washington Times*, Bliley's solitary voice again warned of the dangers presented by the Convention:

> As written, it places government in a superior position to its citizens by granting these rights to children. What is so bad about that? Such an interpretation is antithetical to our limitations on government. Most of these "rights" are not presently found in our Constitution, but rather, are considered to be among our inalienable rights endowed by our Creator.[11]

It can't be repeated too often that, in the Declaration of Independence, our Founding Fathers asserted the revolutionary and "self-evident" truth that "men ... are endowed by their Creator with certain unalienable Rights." The Founders went on to assert, "to secure these Rights, Governments are instituted among Men." Note the logical sequence: 1) God exists; 2) God creates man and endows him with rights; and 3) Man creates government to protect those rights. The individual precedes and is superior to government. Our Constitution is not a body of law to govern the people; it was formulated to govern the government, to make government the servant and not the master of the people.

The United Nations Convention on the Rights of the Child springs from a totally different philosophical foundation. Like the UN Charter and the Soviet Constitution, it views rights not as God-given and unalienable, but as government-given and conditional. This view of the origin of rights is completely incompatible with liberty. For, if one accepts the premise that rights come from government, then one must accept the corollary that government is entitled to circumscribe, withhold, or even cancel those rights. This concept of rights was stated by Andrei Vishinsky, Stalin's chief prosecutor and chairman of the Soviet Supreme Court, during debate on the Universal Declaration of Human Rights on December 10, 1948 at the United Nations. Said Vishinsky: "The rights of human beings cannot be considered outside the prerogatives of governments, and the very understanding of human rights is a governmental concept."[12]

A typical example of this philosophy can be found in Article 14, Section 1 of the Convention on the Rights of the Child: "States Parties shall respect the right of the child to freedom of thought, conscience and religion." Section 3 then proceeds to neuter that right with a Soviet-style clause: "Freedom to manifest one's religion or beliefs may be subject only to such limitations as are prescribed by law and are necessary to protect public safety, order, health or morals or the fundamental rights and freedoms of others." Similar words are used repeatedly in the Convention to legally wipe out all guarantees for the "rights" that are set forth in the document.

Article 10 says: "The right to leave any country shall be subject only to such restrictions as are prescribed by law...." This is the kind of pliable legalese beloved by all tyrants. And it stands in stark contrast to the absolute, unconditional nature of our Bill of Rights.

At Odds With Constitution

The U.S. Constitution and Bill of Rights are directed primarily at limiting the power and scope of the federal government and secondarily at providing the legal standing for the people and the states to assert themselves against any encroachments by the federal government. The First Amendment, for example, states: "Congress shall make no law...." The Convention on the Rights of the Child, on the other hand, supplies opportunity and authority for the United Nations — or the U.S. government acting under the UN Convention — to enforce its provisions against state and local governments, and even against parents.

Article 13 of the Convention mandates that the child "shall have the right to freedom of expression," including "freedom to seek, receive and impart information and ideas of all kinds, regardless of frontiers, either orally, in writing or in print, in the form of art, or through any other media of the child's choice."

Could this be construed to mean that parents who do not allow their child to "express" himself by wearing Satanic symbols or obscene T-shirts are violating the child's rights? Do children have the "right" to speak to their parents in any manner they choose? Could school authorities who impose dress codes or who prohibit the printing of obscene, racist, or other objectionable material in a school newspaper be prosecuted under the Convention? Would state laws and local ordinances restricting the access of minors to pornography and "mature" literature be struck down?

Could Article 16's provisions for the child's right to privacy be used to secure abortions for youngsters without parental knowledge or consent, or to prohibit parents from searching a child's room for drugs or other dangerous or illegal items? What about Article 31's guarantee of the child's right to "rest and leisure," "recreational activities," and "cultural life and the arts"? Would parents who make little Ricky do chores or practice the piano when he says he wants to play baseball be liable for prosecution? Might they be hauled before a judge or have their child removed from their custody because they didn't allow him to attend a "heavy metal" rock concert?

Blank Check for Judiciary

Are these unfounded, paranoid fears? Hardly. Anyone in the least familiar with similar litigation and court decisions of the past few years knows that cases like these are certain to arise. And then? "Hundreds of judges will be left to interpret the convention as they please," warns Representative Bliley, "and will possess all power to supersede state laws...."[13] Under the currently-prevailing jurisprudence, Article VI of the Constitution is badly misconstrued to hold that all treaties — regardless of their constitutionality — are the "supreme law of the land" (see Chapter 6). And there are plenty of revolutionaries in our state and federal judiciaries who would leap at the opportunity to use this UN Convention to launch judicial assaults against state and federal laws, state constitutions, and even the U.S. Constitution itself.

From the floor of the House of Representatives, Bliley asked his colleagues: "Who can explain to me the meaning of Article 24, Section 3 which provides that 'States parties shall take all effective and appropriate measures with a view to abolishing traditional practices prejudicial to the health of children.'"[14]

"Here," noted Mr. Bliley, "is a new standard for us to ponder: Something need not be hazardous or even pose a risk — it need be only prejudicial to be abolished by government. Who will define what is prejudicial as this Convention takes effect?"[15]

Who indeed, but the very state and federal judges who have already run roughshod over the Constitution. These same judges will define what the Convention means by "health" and by "traditional practices." Does "health" encompass physical, mental, emotional, and spiritual well-being, as some argue? If so, what about the situation of the confused teenager who has been convinced by the pro-homosexual "Project 10" program at school that he is "gay"? If his parents try to convince him otherwise, or take him to their pastor or a psychologist for counseling, are they engaging in illegal "traditional practices" prejudicial to his emotional health? Could requiring a child to participate in traditional practices, like family prayer and devotions, or to attend church services also be prejudicial? Without doubt, there are many lawyers who would so argue, and many judges who would so rule.

A Socialist Manifesto

There are many other pitfalls to be found in the Convention. The treaty recognizes a "right of the child to education" (Article 28), and in true Marxist fashion requires every nation that is a contracting party to "make primary education compulsory and available to all." Private education is not explicitly outlawed, but private schools, like government schools, must teach "the principles enshrined in the Charter of the United Nations" and must "conform to such minimum standards as may be laid down by the State." (Article 29)

Several other articles of this UN Convention would impose new, open-ended obligations on national and/or state governments. In addition to "free" education, the state would also be required to provide free child care, health care services, social security, family planning services, prenatal and postnatal care for mothers, and nutrition and housing "to the maximum extent of their available resources." (Article 4)

This amounts to a whole new socialist manifesto for America. Not only would it provide politicians and judges unprecedented opportunity to reach into the taxpayers' pockets for all "available resources," but the Convention would fundamentally alter the function of government from a protector of rights to a provider of services. This would make government a violator of rights, since government has no wealth of its own and must first take from one segment of society (violating its rights) to provide for another segment. And government's ability and propensity to violate rights and to control the people it cares for always increase as more and more people become dependent upon government for goods and services.

Look Who Has Signed

One hundred thirty-four countries have signed the Convention on the Rights of the Child, and 85 have ratified it. Although President Bush has voiced his support of the Convention, the United States has not yet signed or ratified the treaty — a situation that "liberals," internationalists, and Establishment Insiders find intolerable. After all, the argument goes, as the world's leading exemplar of freedom, our nation must show itself to be at least as "progressive" regarding children's rights as Convention signatories China, Zambia, Afghanistan, Albania, Yemen, Cuba, Bulgaria, and Algeria.

If we ratify this treaty, we will join the stellar company of ratifiers like the former USSR, Angola, Mongolia, Romania, Nepal, Uganda, Vietnam, Laos, Zaire, Zimbabwe, Nigeria, Ethiopia, Lebanon, Yugoslavia, and North Korea. Many of these signatory nations outdo one another as the worst child abusers in the history of mankind. Even as their heads of state signed the parchment, their troops and police forces were murdering, oppressing, and otherwise violating the rights of millions of children in Africa, Asia, Europe, and Latin America.

In an attempt to win pro-life support, the Convention's preamble feigns support for "appropriate legal protection, before as well as after birth." But the preamble is not legally binding, and every effort to include specific language in the treaty protecting the unborn has been rebuffed. This should surprise no one, since the UN, through its Population Fund, World Health Organization, and other agencies and programs, is one of the world's greatest promoters of abortion (see Chapter 9).

"A great many people," observes Bliley, "would probably be willing to sacrifice major portions of our Constitution if the ratification of this document could instantly end poverty and drug abuse, guarantee that not another child would be physically or sexually abused and shut down the pornography industry that has infected the cell of our society, the family. But it will not, and we will have exchanged our history as the oldest constitutional government for a new bureaucracy."[16]

Bliley concludes: "It finally becomes clear. Ratification is not about children; it is about power."[17] Like the many other UN treaties (addressing the environment, women's rights, animal rights, minority rights, drug trafficking, etc.), the Convention on the Rights of the Child is about power — the power to undermine and destroy our Constitution, our national sovereignty, and our God-given rights.

New York, September 1990: United Nations World Summit for Children draws more than 70 heads of state and results in propaganda bonanza for the dangerous UN Convention on Rights of the Child.

World leaders joined President Bush in UN assault on parents' rights and power grab for control of world's children. Signers of the misnamed Convention on Rights of Child include such paragons of virtue as China, USSR, Zambia, Afghanistan, Romania, Ethiopia, Yugoslavia, Cuba, Bulgaria, and North Korea.

154

UNICEF's James Grant claims treaty is a "Magna Carta for children."

Congressman Thomas J. Bliley (R-VA) calls treaty "a potential threat to our form of government."

President Bush supported UN Convention but to avoid offending conservative, pro-family vote did not send it to the Senate.

Nicaraguan President Violeta Chamorro signs Convention on Rights of Child.

Britain's Margaret Thatcher endorses UN child grab.

"Save the Children" slogans and warm, fuzzy rhetoric about children's rights do not alter fact that the proposed treaty will deed children over to the federal government and a UN world government.

CHAPTER 9

The UN War on Population

The battle to feed all of humanity is over. In the 1970's the world will undergo famines — hundreds of millions of people are going to starve to death in spite of any crash programs embarked upon now.[1]

— Paul Ehrlich
The Population Bomb (1968)

Central to the issues we are going to have to deal with are: ... the explosive increase in population.... We have been the most successful species ever; we are now a species out of control.[2]

— Maurice F. Strong
UNCED Secretary-General

Since its inception, the U.N. has advanced a world-wide program of population control, scientific human breeding, and Darwinism.[3]

— Claire Chambers
The SIECUS Circle: A Humanist Revolution

The United Nations Fund for Population Activities and the International Planned Parenthood Federation have the blood of millions of innocent babies worldwide on their hands.[4]

— Rev. Paul Marx, Founder
Human Life International

One of the greatest hoaxes of the 20th century, now accepted without question by much of the world's "educated" populace, is the fraudulent contention that the earth is terribly overpopulated with humans. So serious is the "overpopulation crisis," according to prevailing wisdom, that it threatens not only to outstrip food production and all other basic resources, but also to render our planet un-inhabitable for humans and other animal species because of pollution. Overpopulation is a crucial tenet underlying much of the collectivist One-World agenda. According to its theorists, this global "crisis," justifies the most far-reaching government controls imaginable: controls over the economy, the environment, and, of course, over the most private and intimate of areas, our reproductive lives.

The high oracle of the doctrine of overpopulation for more than two decades — and a leading advocate of totalitarian "remedy" for this supposed affliction — has been Paul Ehrlich. Since its publishing debut in 1968, more than 20 million copies of his book *The Population Bomb* have been sold, making it one of the best-selling books of all time. It remains on high school and college required reading lists, along with Professor Ehrlich's newest diatribe, *The Population Explosion*,[5] a 1990 update of his famous doomsday message of 1968. In the earlier work he warned:

> Our position requires that we take immediate action at home and promote effective action worldwide. We must have population control at home, hopefully through a system of incentives and penalties, *but by compulsion if voluntary methods fail....* We can no longer afford merely to treat the symptoms of *the cancer of population growth; the cancer itself must be cut out.*[6] [Emphasis added]

Although his radically pessimistic predictions of dying oceans and imminent global catastrophes were refuted at the time by many men of science (and the passing years have seen the refutations increase in number),[7] the biologist from Stanford University rocketed to stardom as a leading spokesman of the environment/population control movement. In *The Population Bomb*, Ehrlich praised abortion as "a highly effective weapon in the armory of population control," and suggested that "compulsory birth regulation" through the government-mandated addition of "temporary sterilants to water supplies or staple food" may become necessary.[8]

A few months earlier, in the Winter 1968 issue of *Stanford Today*, he was even more explicit. "It must be made clear to our population," he said, "that it is socially irresponsible to have large families." Then, completely disregarding parental rights, norms of morality, and the fact that our constitutional system grants the federal government absolutely no authority to meddle in such affairs, he called for "federal laws making instruction in birth-control methods mandatory in all public schools."[9]

Increasing the intensity of his totalitarian demands, he stated, "If these steps fail to reverse today's population growth, we shall then be faced with some form of compulsory birth regulation. We might institute a system whereby a *temporary sterilant would be added to a staple food or to the water supply*. An antidote would have to be taken to permit reproduction."[10] (Emphasis added)

Sound a bit authoritarian? Well, according to this anti-population crusader, we're facing a deadly serious situation, and the "operation will require many brutal and tough-minded decisions."[11]

Ehrlich's critical acclaim in the major media and his phenomenal book sales ushered in a doom boom that has fed, and in turn has been fed by, an ever-expanding proliferation of population control programs. They are funded by tax dollars funneled through national government agencies, the United Nations, and an international network of private anti-natalist organizations. Of the many ecological jeremiads following in the wake of *The Population Bomb*, two of the most influential were *The Limits to Growth* (1972),[12] a report produced for the Club of Rome, and the *Global 2000 Report to the President of the United States* (1980),[13] a federal government publication that gives legitimacy to the thoughts of a large assemblage of professional wailers from environmental/population control circles.

The Limits to Growth has sold over 10 million copies and has been translated into more than 30 languages. The prodigious *Global 2000*, whose physical size resembles a New York City telephone book, sold over one million copies. Both achieved an aura of importance with their reliance on sophisticated computer modeling to analyze massive banks of data, factor in various assumptions and variables, and then predict the future.

Like Ehrlich, these publications predicted a dismal future for both mankind and nature unless governments intervened on a massive scale. As the Club of Rome's researchers at the Massachusetts Institute of Technology reported in *The Limits to Growth*: "Entirely new approaches are required to redirect society toward goals of equilibrium rather than growth." And, "joint long-term planning will be necessary on a scale and scope without precedent." The ultimate goal of this "supreme effort" would be "to organize more equitable distribution of wealth and income worldwide."[14] Karl Marx could not have phrased it better. And, of course, the social engineers with their mighty computers would show the way.

Not everyone, however, was favorably impressed by their efforts or their results. Scientists and scholars from many disciplines, representing a broad cross-section of political thought, thoroughly discredited these studies with facts, logic, and sound analysis. Even socialist Gunnar Myrdal, certainly no opponent of heavy-handed government, remained unconvinced that the celebrated MIT researchers had made a worthwhile contribution to our knowledge of the world, how it works, or what to expect in the future. The Nobel Prize-winning economist said of the Club of Rome's vaunted "science":

> [T]he use of mathematical equations and a huge computer, which registers the alternatives of abstractly conceived policies by a "world simulation model," may impress the innocent general public but has little, if any, scientific validity. That this "sort of model is actually a new tool for mankind" is unfortunately not true. It represents quasi-learnedness of a type that we have, for a long time, had too much of...."[15]

Or, as another unimpressed scholar would aptly put it, the MIT team amounted to little more than a glorified "Malthus with a computer."[16]

The *Global 2000* team differed little from the MIT group in approach, methodology, assumptions, and conclusions. In its letter of transmittal to the President of the United States, its staff reported, as expected, that the world's future was indeed bleak:

> Environmental, resource, and population stresses are intensifying and will increasingly determine the quality of human life on our planet. These stresses are already severe enough to deny many millions of people basic needs for food, shelter, health, and jobs, or any hope for

betterment. At the same time, the earth's carrying capacity ... is eroding.[17]

But a different group of eminent scientists and academics, surveying precisely the same horizons, came away with a completely
opposite picture of what the future holds. In *The Resourceful Earth:
A Response to Global 2000*, these experts predicted:

> Environmental, resource, and population stresses are diminishing,
> and with the passage of time will have less influence than now upon
> the quality of human life on our planet. These stresses have in the past
> always caused many people to suffer from lack of food, shelter, health,
> and jobs, but the trend is toward less rather than more of such suffer-
> ing. Especially important and noteworthy is the dramatic trend toward
> longer and healthier life throughout all the world. Because of increases
> in knowledge, the earth's "carrying capacity" has been increasing
> throughout the decades and centuries and millennia to such an extent
> that the term "carrying capacity" has by now no useful meaning.[18]

The authors of *The Resourceful Earth* marshaled an avalanche of
scientific evidence to substantiate their optimistic projections and
to refute the dire prophesies of the *Global 2000* alarmists. Their authoritative refutations received scant media attention, however, and
were not successful in offsetting the harmful influence of the doomsday reports or in stanching the seemingly endless succession of imi-
tators.

What *The Resourceful Earth* scientists and many other scholars
have conclusively demonstrated is that the scientific credibility of
overpopulation alarmists is about as reliable as that of Chicken
Little. There is no evidence that the earth, or any region of it, is
overpopulated. China and India, two countries most often cited as
cases of extreme population density, in reality have population den-
sities similar to Pennsylvania and the United Kingdom, respectively.[19] These and other socialist nations suffer not from
overpopulation, but overregulation: not too many people, but too
many bureaucrats and too much government stifling productivity
and progress.

We do not have the space here to attempt to dispel the overpopulation myths that have been so assiduously promoted over the past two decades. For those with an interest in exploring this important issue, however, there are a number of excellent works that deserve attention: *The Myth of Overpopulation* by Rousas J. Rushdoony; *Grow or Die* by James A. Weber; *The War Against Population* by Jacqueline Kasun; *The Ultimate Resource* by Julian Simon; *Population Growth: The Advantages* by Colin Clark; *Handbook on Population* by Robert Sassone; and *The Birth Dearth* by Ben Wattenberg.

The globalists at the Club of Rome, Council on Foreign Relations, Zero Population Growth, Planned Parenthood, and the United Nations continue to hold to and support their doom-and-gloom worldview in the face of overwhelmingly contrary evidence. Doing so supplies the excuse for their continuing proposals for global "crisis management." Thus we have reports like *Changing Our Ways* (1992) from the Carnegie Endowment's National Commission on America and the New World, claiming population growth "threatens international stability," and "universal access to family planning services ... is the least costly and ... the most pragmatic means to address the issue."[20] The Carnegie Commission charged that "American leadership has been absent on the population crisis for too long," even though it admits in the next breath "the United States remains the largest donor (in 1990, $280 million)."[21]

"Since the 1980s," continued the report of this prestigious panel of Establishment Insiders, "the United States has abandoned the two major international organizations devoted to population control efforts: the International Planned Parenthood Federation ... and the United Nations Population Fund (UNFPA)."[22] The Carnegie collectivists were referring to the congressional cutoff of funding for these organizations, beginning in 1985, because of the support they were providing for coercive abortion policies and programs in China. But the cutoff of American-supplied funds for one UN agency did not kill the UN's efforts to force population control.

The UN Supplies the Funds

The barbarity of China's one-child policy was so repugnant that, as reports came out, even many liberals were repelled. In her book entitled *The War Against Population*, conservative Professor Jacqueline Kasun supplied a stunning summary of the shocking brutality directed against pregnant women by China's communist officials:

> Christopher Wren reported in the *New York Times* that thousands of Chinese women were being "rounded up and forced to have abortions." He described women "locked in detention cells or hauled before mass rallies and harangued into consenting to abortions." He told of "vigilantes [who] abducted pregnant women on the streets and hauled them off, sometimes handcuffed or trussed, to abortion clinics," and of "aborted babies which were ... crying when they were born." Michele Vink wrote in the *Wall Street Journal* of women who were "handcuffed, tied with ropes or placed in pig's baskets" for their forced trips to the abortion clinics. According to Steven Mosher, the *People's Republic Press* was openly speaking of the "butchering, drowning, and leaving to die of female infants and the maltreating of women who have given birth to girls."[23]

China scholar Steven Mosher, who personally witnessed the harshness of these policies in the rural Chinese village where he lived and worked on his doctoral studies during 1979-80, noted that U.S. "tax dollars were providing about 25 percent of the annual budget for the United Nations Fund for Population Activities. Monies from UNFPA's budget (which ran $136 million in 1985) have aided China's population control program."[24]

Long after China's atrocious policies were brought to light, UNFPA was still supporting the totalitarian measures. In July 1987, for example, the New China News Agency in Beijing reported the praise an UNFPA official had showered on the regime. "China is actively working to set up a model of how social and economic factors can be harnessed in a harmonious way," he said. "The government has shown its full commitment to a family planning program that has been internationally acknowledged as *one of the most successful efforts in the world today*."[25] (Emphasis added)

The Council on Foreign Relations chose to swallow the line put out by Chinese communist officials and UN bureaucrats rather than believe the independently corroborated stories of both Chinese and Western observers. In his article entitled "The Case for Practical Internationalism" in the Spring 1988 issue of *Foreign Affairs*, top CFR strategist Richard N. Gardner reiterated earlier calls for programs to meet the "population challenge" and asserted:

> A major challenge to the next president will be to restore U.S. support for the U.N. Fund for Population Activities, which we have cut off over charges that China's population program uses coercive abortion, something both China and UNFPA deny.

The U.S. Agency for International Development (AID) denied any direct role in supplying funds for China's population program.[26] According to Jacqueline Kasun, AID may not have done so directly, but "it was a major contributor to the International Planned Parenthood Federation and the UN Fund for Population Activities, both of which supplied funds to the Chinese program. China and the United States also exchanged researchers to study population policy."[27]

But, if the UNFPA received U.S. funds *indirectly* through other U.S.-funded organizations, isn't it still accurate to state that the citizens of this nation are helping to fund the population control activities of the UN? Also, the denial by Chinese and UNFPA officials that coercive abortion is being practiced in China is a bald-faced lie.

AID officials could hardly back up their disavowal; AID records plainly show the agency's funding of IPPF and UNFPA, both of which have been open advocates of coercive population measures. For example, the outspoken president of Planned Parenthood, Alan Guttmacher, who was also a top official of IPPF, bluntly stated in 1969: "Each country will have to decide its own form of coercion, determining when and how it should be employed.... The means presently available are compulsory sterilization and compulsory abortion."[28]

The taxpayer-funded IPPF, says Fr. Paul Marx, the founder of Human Life International, "is the world's largest purveyor of abortion on demand. IPPF's model of 'safe motherhood' is a sterile woman with a dead baby, preferably a baby killed at one of their numerous abortion mills."[29]

Author Claire Chambers, who has done extensive research on the history of the population control movement, charged in 1977: "Since its inception, the U.N. has advanced a world-wide program of population control, scientific human breeding, and Darwinism."[30] Evidence to support that contention is plentiful. Jacqueline Kasun made the same point in her *The War Against Population*:

> Since 1965 the United States has contributed more to foreign population-control programs than all other countries combined and has pressured other countries and international agencies to back the programs. In addition to more than 2 billion dollars in explicit AID "population assistance" appropriations to various countries and international organizations such as the United Nations Fund for Population Activities, the United States has made donations to the World Bank and to United Nations organizations — including the World Health Organization, the Food and Agriculture Organization, UNESCO, UNICEF, and the International Labor Organization — that have been used for population control, with a degree of enthusiasm and dedication equal to that of the AID bureaucracy.[31]

UN Pushes War on Population

From the UN's very beginning, key UN figures such as Brock Chisholm, Julian Huxley, and Paul Hoffman were promoting anti-natalist policies.[32] The first director general of the United Nations Educational, Scientific and Cultural Organization (UNESCO) was humanist leader Julian Huxley, who in 1947 wrote in *UNESCO: Its Purpose and Its Philosophy*:

> Thus even though it is quite true that any radical eugenic [controlled human breeding] policy will be for many years politically and psychologically impossible, it will be important for Unesco to see that the eugenic problem is examined with the greatest care, and that the public mind is informed of the issues at stake *so that much that now is unthinkable may at least become thinkable*.[33] [Emphasis added]

UNESCO's quarterly journal, *Impact of Science on Society*, served as a regular platform for anti-natalist propaganda. In the fall of 1968, almost the entire issue of this publication was devoted to population control themes. The UN's formal acceptance of the world leadership role for population control can be traced back at least to 1954 when a UN Population Commission recommended that every country should "have a population policy."[34]

"Human Rights Day," December 11, 1967, proved to be a landmark date. On that occasion, UN Secretary-General U Thant, President of the United States Lyndon B. Johnson, and 29 other heads of state issued a Declaration on Population. "This Declaration proclaimed 'fertility control' to be a new, so-called basic human right," notes author Claire Chambers. "During the same period, various specialized agencies of the U.N. acted in concert with this edict, developing their own corresponding mandates."[35]

That same year saw the establishment of the UN Fund for Population Activities by Secretary-General U Thant, a Marxist, and the subsequent organization and management of the Fund under the administration of Paul Hoffman (CFR) was another major advance for the population planners. UNFPA, says Professor Kasun, "excellently illustrates the labyrinthine financial connections of the world population network." She explained:

> Deriving its income from the United States and other governments, it provides support to numerous "nongovernmental organizations," including the Population Council, the Population Action Council, Worldwatch, the Population Crisis Committee and Draper Fund, and the Centre for Population Activities. These organizations in turn make grants to each other and to still other organizations.[36]

On November 12, 1971, the UN Population Commission adopted a resolution urging, among other things, that all member states:

> ... cooperate in achieving a substantial reduction of the rate of population growth [in the countries where it was needed].
>
> ... ensure that information and education about family planning, as well as the means to effectively practice family planning, are made available to all individuals by the end of the Second United Nations

Development Decade [1980].[37]

This Commission further designated 1974 as World Population Year, invited all member states to participate in the event, and requested the UN Secretary-General, among other things, to:

... study the possibilities of developing a global population strategy, including population movements, for promoting and co-coordinating population policies in Member States with the objective of achieving a balance between population and other natural resources....[38]

The year 1972 saw the convening of the UN's Conference on the Human Environment, which met in Stockholm, June 5-16. Just prior to the conference, UN Secretary-General Kurt Waldheim expressed the opinion that the conference's leaders "must surely link the increasing pollution of the planet with the increasing population of the planet."[39] The Stockholm conference urged that "special attention be given to population concerns as they relate to the environment during the 1974 observance of World Population Year."[40] The population conference was held in Bucharest, where, notes Professor Kasun, "The dean of the American activists, John D. Rockefeller III, addressed the assembled delegates to stress that 'population planning' should be incorporated into all plans for economic development." Rockefeller added: "Population planning must be a fundamental and integral part of any modern development program, recognized as such by national leadership and supported fully."[41]

The year 1994 will mark the 20th anniversary of that event. Accordingly, plans are being laid for a Population Summit in 1994, along the lines of the 1992 UNCED Earth Summit in Rio de Janeiro.

Not that population issues were ignored at Rio. Far from it. Underlying all of the issues dear to the hearts of "environmentalists" is the matter of population, or rather, population control. In spite of disagreement on many other issues, the one thing that finds the greens in greatest unanimity is the belief that there are too many people in this world and that something drastic must be done to address the situation.

Many UNCED speakers worked population themes into their speeches. UNCED chief Maurice Strong deplored the world's "explosive increase in population," and warned, "[w]e have been the most successful species ever; we are now a species out of control." He thundered: "Population must be stabilized, and rapidly."[42]

Jacques Cousteau, one of the most venerated attractions at the Rio summit, issued a dire warning that "the fuse connected to a demographic explosion is already burning." At most, he said, humanity has ten years to put it out. Parroting the new Paul Ehrlich population scare stories, the famed oceanographer urged "drastic, unconventional decisions" if the world is to avoid reaching the "unacceptable" and "absurd figure of 16 billion human beings" by the year 2070.[43]

The same theme was echoed by Norwegian Prime Minister Gro Harlem Brundtland, who is a member of the Socialist International and chair of the World Commission on Environment and Development; by Mostafa Tolba, executive director of the United Nations Environment Program; and by many others.[44] *Agenda 21*, one of the main documents to come out of the UN's Rio conference, asserts that $4.5 billion per year is needed for demographic policies in developing countries and says some $7 billion per year is needed until the year 2000 to implement "intensive programmes" necessary for population stabilization.[45] What that means, in plain English, is that the UN wants a lot more money to expand its population control programs of sterilization, abortion, and universal access to sex education and contraceptives.

"Safe Motherhood" Scam

Much of the UN's activity in support of its war on population comes from its World Bank. At the Rio Earth Summit, Bank president Lewis Preston (CFR) pledged to increase greatly his institution's support for population control programs.[46] He had already begun those efforts earlier in 1992 with the launching of the so-called "Safe Motherhood Initiative" that opponents were denouncing as "a policy that puts a bounty on the lives of unborn children."

At the International Safe Motherhood Initiative conference held March 9-11, 1992 in Washington DC, Preston promised the 120 delegates from 20 developing countries a doubling of World Bank support for anti-population programs.[47] Ostensibly initiated to improve the general health needs of women in Third World nations, the core of the program is population control. The initiative is a joint project of the World Bank, International Planned Parenthood Federation (IPPF), Family Care International, the U.S. AID-funded Population Council, and several other agencies — including the supposedly pro-child United Nations Children's Fund (UNICEF), the UN's World Health Organization (WHO), and UNFPA.

According to Jean M. Guilfoyle, director of the pro-family, Washington-based Population Research Institute, the Safe Motherhood program involves "the legalization of abortion surgeries and the imposition of restrictive population control policies." She noted that there are "those among the targeted nations who dare to call this 'economic blackmail with genocidal intent.'"[48] In the May/June 1992 issue of *Population Research Institute Review*, Guilfoyle stated: "Within the partnership, the World Bank is intended to provide economic compulsion and guaranteed funds to carry out the agenda forcefully."[49]

Population Research Institute Review reported that, in addition to the Safe Motherhood strategy session held in March 1992 at World Bank headquarters in Washington, there had also been an earlier conference in January in Guatemala. At this gathering, a World Bank official proposed that Latin American countries make the legalization of abortion the centerpiece of their maternal and infant health programs. Speakers at the conference claimed that large monetary savings would accrue if maternal and child health programs in both the public and the private sector were oriented toward "safe abortion" and contraception.[50]

World Bank officials at the conference actually pressured Latin American governments to legalize abortion and make it the center of the maternal-infant health programs. Mexican officials promptly fell in line. According to Human Life International, World Bank official Anne G. Tinker demanded that governments provide "safe abortion" in all maternal-infant health programs. Legislative changes needed to legalize abortion must be undertaken immediately, she told the gathering.[51] Abortion currently is illegal in all

Latin American countries except Uruguay and communist Cuba.

World Bank president Preston said the Bank will integrate the full "Safe Motherhood" agenda into its "policy dialogue" with developing countries.[52] This means that developing countries must meet World Bank requirements in the area of population control in order to qualify for Bank loans. By including the "Safe Motherhood" agenda in its "policy dialogue," the Bank is extending its tremendous financial clout into the political arena of sovereign nations, compelling those nations to legalize abortion and initiate or expand heavy-handed population control programs.

Human Life International president Father Marx has charged: "The bank is misusing its enormous worldwide economic and political clout to ordain and bankroll a misanthropic effort to 'assist humanity' by destroying pre-born human beings, by introducing unsafe, intrusive and culturally repugnant, often abortifacient, methods of birth control and by mutilating healthy people with wholesale neutering programs."[53]

"Through such initiatives," Father Marx said, "women in the Third World are being used for medical experimentation and their offspring are the target of a massive, well-financed eugenics campaign aimed at the poorest and most defenseless members of the human family.... Here you have an array of some of the major enemies of unborn children, women and families gathered to discuss 'safe motherhood.'"[54]

And the leader of those "major enemies of unborn children, women and families" is the United Nations, supported by major funding from the U.S. government.

In his 1968 best-seller, *The Population Bomb,* prophet of doom Paul Ehrlich said hundreds of millions would starve to death in the 1970s "in spite of any crash programs embarked upon now." His 1990 diatribe offers the same bad science and totalitarian "solutions."

President Carter's *Global 2000 Report* echoes Ehrlich's false alarm.

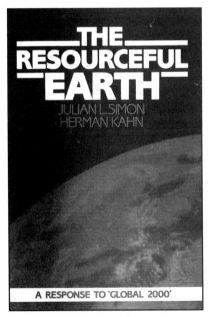

Science and reason refute overpopulation fright peddlers in *The Resourceful Earth.*

Professor Jacqueline Kasun's book, *The War Against Population,* demolishes the faulty arguments of the population controllers and exposes their collectivist political agenda.

Human Life International's Fr. Paul Marx condemns UN lead role in promoting abortion worldwide.

Julian Huxley, humanist, first head of UNESCO, supported radical eugenics and abortion.

Norway's Gro Harlem Brundtland chaired UN World Commission on Environment and Development.

John D. Rockefeller III, avid advocate of statist population control.

Mostafa Tolba, head of UN Environment Program, warned Earth Summit of overpopulation dangers.

World Bank President Lewis Preston (CFR) funds coercive population control programs.

CHAPTER 10

The New World Money System

What I really think is at stake here globally is the future of free institutions.... It really is an open question in my mind of whether we can cope with these chronic problems — problems that you don't need to solve tomorrow in order to survive — within the context of freedom....[1]

— William D. Ruckelshaus
Business Council for Sustainable Development

A Real Mover and Shaker

Early in 1990, journalist Daniel Wood was riding along Highway 17 through the arid and sagebrush-filled terrain of southern Colorado. He had just spent a week visiting a sprawling ranch where a 60-year-old Canadian millionaire, oil tycoon, environmentalist, UN official, and New Age devotee was constructing a controversial global village and ecumenical ashram. Although the tycoon had risen into the rarefied atmosphere of international finance where he dined with Rockefellers and Rothschilds, his name had not yet become a household word as each of theirs had. Soon that would change, as orchestrated world events would thrust him into the international limelight.

As the highway through the desert slid by, Wood's driver, the tycoon-environmentalist himself, told him of a novel he had been planning to write. It was about a group of world leaders who decided the only way to save the world was to cause the economies of the industrialized countries to collapse. The journalist sat transfixed as his host explained how his fictional leaders had formed a secret society and engineered a worldwide financial panic and, ultimately, the economic collapse they sought. While the tycoon drove and talked about the proposed novel, the increasingly astonished reporter took copious notes. His account of that conversation appeared in the May

174

1990 issue of *West* magazine:

> Each year, he [the tycoon] explains as background to the telling of
> the novel's plot, the World Economic Forum convenes in Davos, Swit-
> zerland. Over a thousand CEO's, prime ministers, finance ministers,
> and leading academics gather in February to attend meetings and set
> economic agendas for the year ahead. With this as a setting, he then
> says: "What if a small group of these world leaders were to conclude
> that the principal risk to the earth comes from the actions of the rich
> countries? And if the world is to survive, those rich countries would
> have to sign an agreement reducing their impact on the environment.
> Will they do it?... The group's conclusion is 'no.' The rich countries won't
> do it. They won't change. So, in order to save the planet, the group de-
> cides: Isn't the *only* hope for the planet that the industrialized civiliza-
> tions collapse? Isn't it our responsibility to bring that about?"[2]
> [Emphasis in original]

"This group of world leaders," the driver-tycoon continued, "form
a secret society to bring about an economic collapse." It was becoming obvious to Wood that this unfolding "novel" was a thinly-veiled
roman à clef starring the tycoon and his power-elite comrades. The
millionaire storyteller went on:

> It's February. They're all at Davos. These aren't terrorists. They're
> *world leaders*. They have positioned themselves in the world's commod-
> ity and stock markets. They've engineered, using their access to stock
> exchanges and computers and gold supplies, a panic. Then, they pre-
> vent the world's stock markets from closing. They jam the gears. They
> hire mercenaries who hold the rest of the world leaders at Davos as
> hostages. The markets *can't close*. The rich countries.... [Emphasis in
> original]

Wood wrote that at that point the tycoon "makes a slight motion
with his fingers as if he were flicking a cigarette butt out the window." Pffffft! The fates of hundreds of millions, even billions, of
people callously sealed with the flick of a finger — their livelihoods,
life savings, jobs, businesses, homes, dreams — tossed out like a

cigarette butt, "to save the planet."

"I probably shouldn't be saying things like this," the tycoon confessed to the reporter. No, he should not even have been thinking things like that. For some reason, however, the millionaire insider felt compelled to tell the outsider his story, somewhat like Colonel House did when revealing his megalomaniacal nature in *Philip Dru: Administrator.*[3]

Wood wrote: "I sit there spellbound. This is not *any* storyteller talking. This is Maurice Strong. He knows these world leaders. He is, in fact, co-chairman of the Council of the World Economic Forum. He sits at the fulcrum of power. He is in a position to *do it.*" (Emphasis in original)

Most of the world was first introduced to Maurice Strong in 1992 while he was serving as secretary-general of the United Nations Conference on Environment and Development (UNCED), the so-called Earth Summit held in Rio de Janeiro. Before, during, and after the summit, the Canadian activist made headlines more than once with environmental tirades against the life-styles of "the rich countries" that sounded uncomfortably similar to the story line of the "novel" he related to Wood. The fact that he was the top executive of the privately owned Dome Petroleum of Canada, president of Power Corporation of Canada, and later head of Petro Canada, the giant government oil company, is fairly well known from the many profiles about him appearing in the major media. Many of these articles mention that he was head of the 1972 United Nations Conference on the Human Environment in Stockholm and the first secretary-general of the United Nations Environmental Program (UNEP).

We were unable, however, to uncover any articles even suggesting the range of Strong's Insider connections. Yet, this man is president of the World Federation of United Nations Associations, co-chairman of the World Economic Forum, member of the Club of Rome, trustee of the Aspen Institute, a director of the World Future Society, director of finance of the Lindisfarne Association, a founding endorser of Planetary Citizens, convener of the 4th World Wilderness Congress, organizer of the international Business Council for Sustainable Development, and builder of "The Valley of the Refuge of World Truths," a spiritual center on his controversial Baca

Grande ranch in Colorado.

Strong, it turns out, may also be the planet's richest eco-warrior. His Colorado ranch sits atop one of the largest aquifers in the world. Together with his wife, Hanne, and his former partners in the American Water Development company, Strong may control water worth, by some estimates, as much as $600 *billion!*[4]

Whether or not the Davos conspiracy scenario laid out by Strong for journalist Wood is (or was) an actual game plan, it is clear that in the new world order economic system envisioned by Strong and his fellow Insiders, the United Nations and its financial institutions would be able to wield the kind of world-economy-collapsing power he described in his "fictional" story.

The 20th century has seen the creation of fractional reserve banking controlled by national central banks in most of the nations of the world. Its effect has been an explosion of spending accompanied by massive deficits, oppressive taxation, and a mushrooming of administrative bureaucracy. With the founding of the United Nations and its affiliated financial institutions, these problems grew worse.

In his 1977 book *The War on Gold*, Dr. Antony C. Sutton surveyed the incredible turnabout of America's economic fortunes in the short period from 1945 to 1975:

> At the end of World War II the United States was in a unique and seemingly unassailable monetary position. The world's largest gold stock was secure in the vaults of Fort Knox and the Federal Reserve Banks. The American dollar was everywhere in short supply, facing an apparently insatiable demand. American technology and the standard of living it made possible were the envy of the world.
>
> Three decades later the United States is wracked by internal political and moral problems, inflation, and self doubts. The world's most powerful nation had been defeated by a third-rate country in a wasteful no-win war. Half of its gold stock had been lost, and it had short-term liabilities to foreigners totalling almost ten times the value of what gold it still owned.[5]

Two years later, surveying the same post-war phenomena as had Dr. Sutton, political analyst Dan Smoot asked, "What earthquake of history has occurred?" To which he answered: "None. All of it was planned."[6]

Betrayal at Bretton Woods

The planning had been formulated by the Economic and Finance Group of the Council on Foreign Relations during the early years of the war,[7] and the plans were put into effect at the Bretton Woods Conference in July 1944. Sitting as the leader of the conference and the head of the U.S. delegation was Assistant Secretary of the Treasury Harry Dexter White, a secret member of a Soviet espionage ring.[8] Serving as the technical secretary for the conference was Virginius Frank Coe, a director of monetary research for the Treasury Department. Coe became the first secretary of the new International Monetary Fund (IMF), a post he held until 1952 when it was revealed in congressional testimony that he was a member of the same communist ring White had joined.[9] From 1958, until his death in 1980, Coe lived in Communist China.

Working hand-in-hand with communists White and Coe were numerous Establishment Insiders among whom was Secretary of the Treasury Henry Morgenthau, Jr. It was he who declared at the time: "It has been proved ... that people in the international banking business cannot run successfully foreign exchange markets. It is up to the Governments to do it. We propose to do this if and when the legislative bodies approve Bretton Woods."[10]

The incredible deceit now evident here is that Morgenthau personally represented the very "international banking" establishment he was criticizing, and the system he was helping construct would place the world economy more firmly in its grasp than ever before. The two primary institutions to come out of the conference, the International Monetary Fund and the World Bank, have been run by certified members of the Insider banking fraternity ever since.

Dan Smoot observed in his 1979 article:

> White's Bretton Woods Conference set policies which our government has followed, without deviation, under all Presidents, since the end of World War II. These policies were intended to accomplish four major objectives:

(1) Strip the United States of its monetary gold reserve by giving the gold to other nations;

(2) Build the industrial capacity of other nations, at our expense, to eliminate American productive superiority;

(3) Take world markets — and much of the American domestic market — away from American producers to stop American domination of world trade;

(4) Entwine American affairs with those of other nations until the United States could not have an independent policy, but would become an interdependent link in a worldwide socialist chain. [11]

The Bretton Woods participants, of course, did not state their resolves as bluntly or succinctly. It makes little sense to dispute the fact, however, that the policies and institutions they established have indeed produced the tragic results enumerated by Smoot. Bretton Woods opened the floodgates of government spending worldwide. As free-market economists warned, it has led to massive growth of government, mountains of debt, and global inflation.

At the time the Bretton Woods agreements were being hammered out, the near-solitary voice in the major American media opposing the one-world economic scheme and warning of its dire consequences was Henry Hazlitt, then the financial editor of the *Wall Street Journal*. In one article after another, he soundly refuted the sophistry put forward for the new global economic plan. Unfortunately, his arguments were ignored.

Hazlitt was always a strong opponent of inflation. But, unlike many others, he employed a proper definition of the often mis-defined term. Inflation is an increase in the quantity of currency. Its effect is a lessening of the value of all existing currency. When merchants and others ask for more of it in return for their goods and services, they are responding — even if they are unaware of the process that has been forced on them — to the fact that the currency has lost value. That value, stolen from all existing currency through the introduction of more currency, was actually stolen from currency holders by the issuer. In virtually all cases, the issuer is either government or a privately-run central bank.

The path to inflation begins with the removal of precious metal backing for the currency. Once the requirement for gold or silver in the issuer's vault (in this nation, the U.S. Treasury formerly served this purpose) is removed, inflation is possible, even inevitable.

In his 1984 book, *From Bretton Woods to World Inflation*, Henry Hazlitt reviewed the tragic worldwide devastation and upheaval that he insisted are

> ... the consequences of the decisions made by the representatives of the forty five nations at Bretton Woods, New Hampshire, forty years ago. These decisions, and the institutions set up to carry them out, have led us to the present world monetary chaos. For the first time in history, every nation is on an inconvertible paper money basis. As a result, every nation is inflating, some at an appalling rate. This has brought economic disruption, chronic unemployment, and anxiety, destitution, and despair to untold millions of families.[12]

Of course there had been inflations before Bretton Woods. But it was at that conference, primarily under the leadership of White and Fabian Socialist John Maynard Keynes of England, that, as Hazlitt noted, "inflation was institutionalized." Many nations are now saddled with impossible debt burdens and oppressive bureaucracies because, claims this dean of free market thinkers, "the IMF, in effect encourages them to continue their socialist and inflationist course."[13]

Hazlitt, who has called the shots correctly during all of these many years, does not mince words when it comes to solutions. "The world cannot get back to economic sanity," he has warned, "until the IMF is abolished.... We will not stop the growth of world inflation and world socialism until the institutions and policies adopted to promote them have been abolished."[14] Unfortunately, our elected leaders have continued along the course set by communists, socialists, and globalist Insiders decades ago.

Again, we turn to Hazlitt:

> Yet the supreme irony is that the Bretton Woods institutions that have failed so completely in their announced purpose, and led to only

monetary chaos instead, are still there, still operating, still draining the countries with lower inflations to subsidize the higher inflation of others.[15]

In fact, the internationalist Insiders have stepped up the pace of these suicidal policies. In his Spring 1988 *Foreign Affairs* article entitled "The Case for Practical Internationalism," CFR strategist Richard N. Gardner stated bluntly:

> But most of all, the world needs to enlarge the flows of private and official capital to developing countries in order to stimulate an adequate level of global growth. *A near-doubling of World Bank capital and International Monetary Fund quotas should be a high priority for American leadership....* [Emphasis added]

A World Central Bank

Even worse, the one-worlders are working to expand their scheme in order eventually to achieve complete global economic control by transforming the International Monetary Fund and World Bank combine into a central Federal Reserve system for the planet. One of the first in-depth presentations of this plan to CFR membership came in 1981 with the publication of *Collective Management: The Reform of Global Economic Organizations*. Written by Miriam Camps (CFR) in collaboration with Catherine Gwin (CFR), it was the 21st volume in the Council's 1980s Project series.

Collective Management's proposals for "restructuring" United Nations institutions included designing a new global trade organization to supersede the General Agreement on Tariffs and Trade (GATT) and the United Nations Conference on Trade and Development (UNCTAD), merging several United Nations aid programs in order to create in their places a new "United Nations Basic Support Program," and taking additional steps that would aid in "the continuing evolution of the IMF in the direction of a world central bank."[16]

Expanding further on this topic in the Fall 1984 edition of *Foreign Affairs*, Harvard University Professor Richard N. Cooper (CFR, TC) proposed "A Monetary System for the Future" that would mean the end of America as we know it. He wrote:

> A new Bretton Woods conference is wholly premature. But it is not premature to begin thinking about how we would like international monetary arrangements to evolve in the remainder of this century. With this in mind, I suggest a radical alternative scheme for the next century: *the creation of a common currency for all of the industrial democracies, with a common monetary policy and a joint Bank of Issue to determine that monetary policy.* [Emphasis in original]

"The currency of the Bank of Issue could be practically anything," the Harvard economist continued. "*... The key point is that monetary control — the issuance of currency and of reserve credit — would be in the hands of the new Bank of Issue, not in the hands of any national government....*" (Emphasis added) The problem, however, is that "a single currency is possible only if there is in effect a single monetary policy, and a single authority issuing the currency and directing the monetary policy. *How can independent states accomplish that? They need to turn over the determination of monetary policy to a supranational body.*" (Emphasis added)

Insider Cooper realized the challenge involved in selling this totalitarian idea to the public. "This one-currency regime is much too radical to envisage in the near future," he said. "But it is not too radical to envisage 25 years from now.... [I]t will require many years of consideration before people become accustomed to the idea." Getting people in the West, and particularly in the United States, warm to the idea of "a pooling of monetary sovereignty" — especially with communist countries — would be difficult. Cooper wrote:

> First, it is highly doubtful whether the American public, to take just one example, could ever accept that countries with oppressive autocratic regimes should vote on the monetary policy that would affect monetary conditions in the United States.... For such a bold step to work at all, it presupposes a certain convergence of political values....

Convergence with Totalitarian Regimes

That requisite "convergence" is already underway and well-ahead of Professor Cooper's 25-year estimate, thanks to the high-powered sales job his fellow CFR members have conducted on behalf of the "former" communist states. The Establishment policy line has been repeated again and again in the Insiders' elite journals (*Foreign Affairs, Foreign Policy, World Policy Journal*), as well as in the CFR-dominated popular media. It holds that the United States must provide Russia and all the nations of her former satellite empire with billions of dollars in credits and aid to help them make the transition to "a market economy."

Writing in the Summer 1990 *Foreign Policy*, Thomas G. Weiss (CFR) and Meryl A. Kessler set out the globalist line:

> As for the economic realm, there is little hope for cooperation between the superpowers until the United States allows the Soviet Union to become a full-fledged actor in global economic affairs.... The United States should follow up by supporting immediate Soviet observer status in the IMF and the World Bank, leading toward full membership....
>
> American interests and the credibility of the United States as a leader in world affairs would be enhanced by joining the Soviet Union in taking the lead at the United Nations.[17]

Those steps were adopted in toto by the Bush Administration. The 12 "republics" of the new Commonwealth of Independent States, the former Warsaw Pact countries of Eastern Europe, and the three Baltic states have either become members of the World Bank and International Monetary Fund or are in the process of joining. The IMF is now in the process of transferring billions of tax dollars from the West to socialist regimes in the East still run by communists and former communists. Not surprisingly, these regimes have shown little evidence of any serious intent to make the leap from collectivist to free-market economies.[18]

The Insider line, in fact, is that we must *slow down* the transition of the communist/socialist countries to free markets. Writing in the Summer 1992 *World Policy Journal* (published by the World Policy Institute — a CFR-dominated think tank — and the Fabian socialist New School for Social Research), Sherle R. Schwenninger asserted in an article entitled "The United States in the New World

Order" that "the United States should use its weight within the IMF and the World Bank to encourage a slower transition to an open market economy in Eastern Europe and the former Soviet Union."

Moreover, said Schwenninger, a senior fellow at the WPI-NSSR think tank, "If the industrialized nations gave up their SDRs [special drawing rights] to the developing countries and the former republics of the Soviet Union, these countries would be able to borrow more money from the IMF."

UN Taxing Authority

What is even more alarming, however, is Schwenninger's assertion further along in the article that due to "needs ranging from the global environment to U.N. peacekeeping, we can no longer afford to rely on 'voluntary' national contributions...." As you might expect, in the next breath, he proposes granting taxing authority to the United Nations: "If international agencies are to have the resources they need to address critical transnational problems, then we will need to move to a system of value-added taxes that would be collected automatically when goods and services cross national borders."

Proposals along these lines are cropping up everywhere. Complaining of the UN's "present mendicancy," in his June 1992 *An Agenda for Peace* report to the UN Security Council, Secretary-General Boutros-Ghali called for the following: "the establishment of a United Nations Peace Fund"; "a levy on international air travel"; "[a]uthorization to the Secretary-General to borrow commercially"; "[s]uspending certain financial regulations of the United Nations"; and "general tax exemption for contributions made to the United Nations."[19]

Boutros-Ghali's proposals were given a boost in *Changing Our Ways*, the 1992 report issued by the Carnegie Endowment's National Commission on America and the New World. The Carnegie report, which was released amid great media fanfare, declared: "Any plausible vision for America's future role in the world must include a renewed financial commitment to the United Nations." It referred to the Boutros-Ghali package as a "bold but pragmatic set of financing proposals," and urged "policymakers to study them carefully."[20]

This Carnegie Commission, made up of a panel of 21 prominent Americans from the fields of politics, business, finance, and higher education, offered many proposals to collectivize and internationalize the American economy. This is hardly surprising since all but three of the panelists are members of the Council on Foreign Relations. Several are also members of the Trilateral Commission. The group's chairman is Winston Lord, a former president of the CFR who is still a proud member. Other Establishment heavyweights on the panel include: C. Fred Bergsten, director of the Institute for International Economics and former Assistant Secretary of the Treasury; Morton Abramowitz, president of the Carnegie Endowment for International Peace and former Assistant Secretary of State; Barber B. Conable, former president of the World Bank; David Gergen, editor-at-large for *U.S. News and World Report*; and Jessica T. Mathews, vice president of the World Resources Institute and columnist for the *Washington Post*.

The Carnegie panel believes we must "reduce our defense spending," but we must also "[s]trengthen the peacekeeping capacities of the United Nations and regional organizations."[21] Its *Changing Our Ways* report advocates taxing Americans an additional $1.00 per gallon for "gasoline ... and other petroleum products," calls for a "weight tax" on automobiles, and proposes a "substantial" tax on "carbon content."[22]

More and More Power in Government

Consonant with the plans of the one-worlders at the United Nations and environmental extremists everywhere, these CFR elitists propose "swift ratification of the global warming treaty" and advancement of protocols "for the management of greenhouse gases." The Carnegie report recommends *Agenda 21*, the massive program adopted at the UN's Earth Summit that calls for government regulation and control of virtually every aspect of life in the name of protecting the environment.[23]

Other Insider-created organizations have come forward with similar proposals. One of the newest groups to enter the chorus is the Business Council for Sustainable Development (BCSD), an international group of globalist business executives. Launched in 1990 by

Maurice Strong, it is chaired by Stephan Schmidheiny, chairman of UNOTEC, a Swiss investment company. Its U.S. members include William D. Ruckelshaus (CFR), chairman of Browning-Ferris Industries; Frank Popoff (CFR), president and CEO of Dow Chemical; and Paul H. O'Neill, chief executive officer of ALCOA.

In a perfectly timed publicity coup, the BCSD released its 1992 book, *Changing Course: A Global Perspective on Development and the Environment*, just before the opening of the Rio Earth Summit.[24] While paying lip service to "market incentives," it quickly became apparent that, like the Carnegic panel's recommendations, everything offered by the BCSD will increase the size, cost, and power of government.

This Business Council calls for "[n]ew forms of cooperation between government, business and society" to achieve "sustainable development." According to these business leaders, "the prices of goods and services must increasingly recognize and reflect the environmental costs of their production, use, recycling, and disposal." This, they say "is best achieved by a synthesis of economic instruments designed to correct [market] distortions" and "regulatory standards" to help the market "give the right signals."[25]

The real philosophy behind the BCSD's statist nostrums was revealed (most likely unintentionally) by BCSD member William Ruckelshaus, the first head of the U.S. Environmental Protection Agency. Just prior to the 1992 Earth Summit, he stated: "What I really think is at stake here globally is the future of free institutions.... It really is an open question in my mind of whether we can cope with these chronic problems — problems that you don't need to solve tomorrow in order to survive — within the context of freedom...."[26]

Still more propaganda for UN intervention in and control of the world economy came from the influential Club of Rome. Founded in 1968 by Italy's Aurelio Peccei, a former top executive with the Olivetti Company and Fiat Motors, the Club of Rome boasts an elite membership of some 200 members worldwide who have backgrounds in business, science, politics, higher education, and religion.

In its celebrated 1991 report, *The First Global Revolution*, the group called for the implementation of "energy accounting," which it announced "is becoming increasingly necessary in measuring, for example, the carrying capacity of countries for human and animal populations.... It is urgent that a *Worldwide Campaign of Energy Conservation and Efficiency* be launched."[27] (Emphasis in original) Moreover, the Club of Rome document proposed:

> It would be appropriate that the scheme be launched by the United Nations in association with the United Nations Environment Programme, the World Meteorological Organization and UNESCO. A corollary would be the setting up in each country of an *Energy Efficiency Council* to supervise the operation on the national scale.[28]

Because of the "global nature as well as the seriousness of the environmental threats," the Club called for "the creation of a *UN Environmental* Security Council parallel to the existing Security Council on military matters." Also, the United Nations "should convene an intergovernmental scientific meeting to plan a comprehensive *World Alternative Energy Project.*"[29]

Like the Club's 17 previous reports, *The First Global Revolution* sees more government as the solution to every real or imagined problem. And because its members hold that all of mankind's problems today are global, it only makes sense to favor global government. "The market is ill-adapted to deal with long-term effects," says the Club's report. "... The system of the market economy countries based on competition is motivated by self-interest and ultimately on greed."[30]

Echoing the socialist slogans of the environmental left, these globe-trotting, champagne-and-caviar-consuming elitists hypocritically state: "Our efforts to create a sustainable world society and economy demands that we diminish the profligate life-styles in the industrialized countries through a slow-down in consumption...."[31]

Appropriately, *The First Global Revolution* opens with the following excerpt from *The Rubayat* of Omar Khayyam:

> Ah love! Could thou and I with fate conspire,
> to grasp this sorry scheme of things entire,
> would not we shatter it to bits and then,
> remould it nearer to the heart's desire.

Students of political history will recognize this as the same quatrain adopted by the Britain's Fabian Socialist Society in their "open conspiracy" to create a socialist world. This verse was represented pictorially in the famous stained glass window at the Beatrice Webb House, a world-renowned socialist shrine in Surrey, England. The window shows socialist leaders Sidney Webb and George Bernard Shaw smashing the world with hammers and, above their heads appears the last line of the quatrain, "remould it nearer to the heart's desire." [32]

Is it mere coincidence that the socialist-elitist-internationalist Club of Rome chose this favored Fabian verse? Don't the proposals they and their fellow globalists offer lead inexorably to the creation of an all-powerful socialist superstate ruled by the United Nations?

With each passing day, the words and actions of the CFR, Trilateralist, Club of Rome, World Federalist one-worlders make plain that they intend to shatter freedom to bits and, then, remould the world to their collectivist heart's desire.

Harry Dexter White (left) with Fred M. Vinson and Dean Acheson. White, a secret Soviet agent in the Silvermaster spy network, became Assistant Secretary of the Treasury and headed the Bretton Woods conference.

Soviet agent White and British Fabian Socialist John Maynard Keynes were the two dominating forces at Bretton Woods, where the world economic system was transformed. Aiding them was Soviet agent Virginius Frank Coe, technical secretary of the conference.

189

Was Maurice Strong revealing real plans to cause worldwide "economic collapse" in *West* magazine interview?

Treasury Secretary Henry Morgenthau put Soviet agent White in charge at Bretton Woods.

Constitutional scholar Dan Smoot said of Bretton Woods' economic destruction: "All of it was planned."

Antony Sutton's *War On Gold* detailed the destructive economic policies of the World Bank and IMF.

Henry Hazlitt was lone voice in American media opposing one-world Bretton Woods scheme.

William Ruckelshaus (CFR) doubts "chronic problems" of environment can be solved "within the context of freedom."

Richard N. Gardner (CFR,TC), a leading Insider strategist, called for "an end run around national sovereignty, eroding it piece by piece." Gardner is UN adviser to Bill Clinton.

Aurelio Peccei is the founder of the Club of Rome, a coterie of elite one-worlders promoting population control and a global socialist regulatory state. Inset: Club of Rome symbol.

REMOULD IT NEARER TO THE HEARTS DESIRE

Fabian Socialist stained-glass window commissioned by George Bernard Shaw shows Fabians Shaw and Sidney Webb reshaping world with hammers while their followers worship stack of socialist propaganda. Fabian crest shows wolf in sheep's clothing while line from *The Rubayat* graces top of window.

CHAPTER 11

The Compassion Con

One day I should like to understand how the U.N.'s highest representative in Ethiopia could be unable to see the murderous nature of these deportations, thereby lending a blessing to one of the world's bloodiest and most tyrannical governments. [1]
— Dr. Rony Brauman, director of Doctors Without Borders
Reader's Digest, October 1986

Ethiopia's awful tragedy is but one reason a growing number of economists, from left to right, are beginning to realize that the World Bank and its "good intentions" have become the chief paving agent for the road to hell.... [T]he World Bank's financing of major governmental agricultural restructuring and resettlement projects had been the main cause of the famine-deaths of millions, and of the denuding of the environment.
— Warren Brookes, syndicated columnist
December 16, 1987

The World Bank is helping Third World governments cripple their economies, maul their environments, and oppress their people. Although the bank started with the highest ideals some 40 years ago, it now consistently does more harm than good for the world's poorest. [2]
— James Bovard
The World Bank vs. the World's Poor, September 28, 1987

"The UN has its glaring faults," many people readily acknowledge, "but it also is responsible for so many important humanitarian efforts around the world." This vision of selfless UN servants distributing food to famine victims, providing emergency relief to refugees, and immunizing "Third World" children against killer diseases is a powerful image that has, no doubt, saved the United Nations from mass defections among its supporters. It is difficult to think ill of an organization involved in such noble endeavors. Unfortunately, this image too is largely a myth, one of the UN's cruelest hoaxes as well as one of its most tightly guarded secrets.

This is not to say that *no* famine victims, refugees, or children have been helped through UN programs; indeed, many have. Many of these UN aid recipients, however, were actually placed in their dire predicaments by harmful actions and wrong-headed policies of the UN and its agencies. Moreover, in stark contrast to the portrait of saintly benevolence bestowed on UN relief programs, the record clearly shows that UN aid personnel, particularly at the higher levels, are guilty of some of the most crass, heartless, and unethical behavior imaginable. The UN propagandists have cynically and persistently exploited the world's compassion as a protective cover to advance their sinister global agenda. Before we venture any further down this dangerous path we would do well to examine the real results of the UN's "humanitarian" programs.

Ethiopian "Relief"

In December 1985, the medical personnel of Doctors Without Borders (Médecins Sans Frontières) were expelled from Ethiopia. Dr. Rony Brauman, a French physician and director of the international, nonprofit, humanitarian group, described their experience:

> Armed militiamen burst into our compounds, seized our equipment and menaced our volunteers. Some of our employees were beaten, and our trucks, medicines and food stores confiscated. We left Ethiopia branded as enemies of the revolution. The regime spoke the truth. The atrocities committed in the name of Mengistu's master plan *did* make us enemies of the revolution.[3] [Emphasis in original]

Unfortunately, it took a great deal more time before the governments and press of the Free World decided to declare themselves "enemies of the revolution."

The major Western news media "discovered" the Ethiopian famine in October 1984. Then, for months, the haunting images of masses of starving refugees and vacant-eyed, dying children huddled in pathetic make-shift camps dominated the newspaper front-pages and nightly newscasts. Our hearts were touched, even devastated. How could they not be, in the face of such suffering and carnage? People responded worldwide with a phenomenal outpouring of financial and material aid.

What most of the people of the world did not find out until much later was that the tragic drama they had been witnessing was not the result of a natural drought; it was a *planned* famine, the result of conscious, inhuman policies of the communist regime of "President" Mengistu Haile Mariam. It was an extension of the communist textbook-style terror program Mengistu had unleashed on the populace in 1977. Copying the "successful" starvation campaigns employed by Lenin against the Russian peasants, Stalin against the Ukrainian kulaks, and Mao against the rural Chinese, the central government in Addis Ababa initiated forced "collectivization" of agriculture and began massive "resettlement" programs that guaranteed large-scale starvation.

The famine had already been in progress for several years and many tens of thousands had already perished when NBC's broadcast of October 23, 1984 brought the shocking reality of Ethiopia's anguish into American homes for the first time. But not until May 21, 1991, when the Soviet-backed Mengistu regime was overthrown, did it become politically acceptable in the CFR-Establishment media to denounce the brutal policies and expose the Marxist central planning responsible for the famine. By then, this "news" was too late to be of any help in speeding Mengistu's removal or in averting the agony of his millions of hapless victims.

What most Americans — and most people of goodwill the world over who contributed generously to the famine relief effort — still have not been told, however, is that the United Nations and its specialized agencies bear an enormous share of the responsibility for promoting and prolonging the Ethiopian nightmare.

Soon after seizing power, Colonel Mengistu did what all Marxist dictators do: He asked for aid from America and the United Nations "lending" institutions — the World Bank and International Monetary Fund. He was met with open arms and open wallets, courtesy of the taxpayers of the United States, Western Europe, and other reviled "capitalist" countries. "Between 1978 and 1982," Robert W. Lee reported in *The New American* for March 23, 1992, "Ethiopia received $1 billion in aid from the West, most of it channelled through the IMF and other multilateral lending agencies."[4]

During this time, the aid officials could not have been unaware of Mengistu's diabolical record. Did his well-documented atrocities and disastrous, openly-Marxist economic policies endanger his credit-worthiness or raise eyebrows at the UN? To the contrary, these excesses made him a *preferred customer* with the World Bank/IMF pinstripes and a hero to an array of UN-backed petty tyrants throughout the Third World. On October 16, 1984, the UN's Administrative and Budgetary Committee voted 83 to 3 to provide $73.5 million in UN funds to Ethiopia. But these funds were *not* intended for the starving famine victims; *the money was specified for improvements on the conference facilities of the UN's Economic Commission for Africa (ECA) in Addis Ababa!* While entire Ethiopian villages and provinces were succumbing to unimaginable privation, the pampered and sanctimonius UN "humanitarians" were whining that the ECA facilities were "wholly inadequate" and "sorely" in need of upgrading. By a vote of 122 to 5, the UN General Assembly, "the conscience of the world," backed the committee and approved the appropriation.

Richard Nygard, U.S. Representative to the UN, noted that the $73.5 million could have inoculated one million Ethiopian children, built 25,000 wells and pumps for 12.5 million people, and fed 125,000 Ethiopian families for a year with enough left over to supply all 1985 cereal imports for drought-stricken Chad.[5] The $73.5 million for improving the conference facilities, however, was a pittance compared to the big-time sums Mengistu customarily obtained from the World Bank.

The World Bank, wrote author/researcher James Bovard in 1987, "helped to lay the groundwork for the Ethiopian government's current murderous resettlement program." In *The World Bank vs. the World's Poor,* a scorching indictment of bank's lending record, published by the Washington DC-based Cato Institute, Bovard noted that because of government policies, thousands of Ethiopians "are being kept in concentration-camp-type facilities, where death rates are reported to be quite high."[6] In 1986, human rights groups began to point to UN backing of the murderous regime. The influential British *Economist* "cited Ethiopia for the worst human rights record in the world." Yet, said Bovard, "Throughout this period, the bank has provided large amounts of aid to the Mengistu regime."[7]

Other UN agencies and officials performed in the same criminally callous manner. Perhaps one of the worst examples involves Edouard Saouma, Director General of the UN's Food and Agriculture Organization (FAO) since the late 1960s. According to other FAO officials and the former commissioner of the Ethiopian Relief and Rehabilitation agency, Saouma held up emergency food aid for 20 days in 1984, at the height of the famine, because of a personal dislike for Tessema Negash, an Ethiopian FAO official.

Ethiopian Relief and Rehabilitation Commissioner Dawit Wolde-Giorgis has described his meeting in 1984 with the intractable Saouma:

> I went [to FAO headquarters in Rome] and tried to brief [Saouma] on what was going on in Ethiopia.... He interrupted the discussion and told me that our representative was not a very likeable person ... that it would be very difficult for him to co-operate ... as long as we had Tessema Negash as our FAO representative.... There I was trying to brief a senior UN official about the impending disaster and the number of people dying every day and I was confronted with personal problems ... that was sickening.[8]

This was not the only indictment of UN official Saouma. Throughout the famine years, it is charged, Saouma also carried on a long-running battle with the Director of the UN World Food Program (WFP) over which of them had authority over food aid shipments.[9] Was Mr. Saouma disciplined, reprimanded, or even investigated as a result of these serious charges? To the contrary, in 1987 he was given another six-year claim on his posh post, along with the usual automatic UN pay raise.

Occasionally, embarrassing publicity will result in a modicum of justice. As, for instance, in the case of UN High Commissioner for

Refugees Jean-Pierre Hocké. Hocké, a Swiss citizen, resigned in October 1989 after a scandal erupted over his misuse of tens of thousands of dollars annually for personal expenses from a fund established to educate refugees. According to the *New York Times*, Hocké misappropriated the money from

> ... a fund set up by Nordic countries for refugee education to pay for entertainment and first-class air travel, sometimes aboard the Concorde, for himself and his wife.... Mr. Hocké spent between $32,000 and $96,000 a year from Denmark's contribution on his entertainment and travel without informing the Danish government or asking its permission. Mr. Hocké has never denied this. [10]

Again and again, the UN's pious platitudes and noble rhetoric prove to be cynical devices exploited by the organization's professional plutocrats, who are too preoccupied with personal empire-building to be bothered with "the world's poor" they claim to serve.

This point was driven home to Dr. Brauman time after time in Ethiopia. "Even the famous drought proved to be something of a false issue," he learned. The physician recounted that his group had dispatched a hydrogeologist to the northern Sek'ot'a area, where "he discovered an enormous deposit of readily accessible underground water. At relatively low cost — only a small fraction of what was being raised for famine aid — there could have been water for everyone." [11] But UN officials and government officials weren't interested. Neither were the UN officials interested in hearing about the atrocities and genocidal policies of their "host," Colonel Mengistu. Brauman was outraged:

> I was particularly shocked by the U.N.'s resident representative, an assistant secretary-general installed in Addis, who invariably dismissed our protests with a few condescending phrases. Even when I told him point-blank that the resettlement program which the West's aid had made possible was killing more Ethiopians than the famine was, he answered, "I have no reason to believe that these people left the camps against their own free will." One day I should like to understand how the U.N.'s highest representative in Ethiopia could be unable to see

the murderous nature of these deportations, thereby lending a blessing to one of the world's bloodiest and most tyrannical governments. [12]

Ethiopia is, however, far from being the only victim of the UN's "compassion" and "largesse." Through its myriad agencies and ever-multiplying programs the United Nations and its adjuncts have wreaked havoc world wide; few corners of the globe have escaped their "benevolence." The World Bank, for instance, said Bovard in 1987, "is a major cause of the Tanzanian people's current misery." [13] The bank underwrote the communist regime of former President Julius Nyerere, who implemented his *ujamaa* or villagization program to

> ... drive the peasants off their land, burn their huts, load them onto trucks, and take them where the government thought they should live.... with the result that hunger has increased in Tanzania....
>
> The bank also helped finance the brutal policies of the Vietnamese government in the late 1970s that contributed to the deaths of tens of thousands of boat people in the South China Sea. [14]

After surveying the economic destructiveness of the World Bank's policies in many countries, James Bovard concluded:

> [T]he bank exists largely to maximize the transfer of resources to Third World governments. And by so doing, the bank has greatly promoted the nationalization of Third World economies and has increased political and bureaucratic control over the lives of the poorest of the poor.
>
> Bank officials are now leading a rhetorical crusade in favor of the private sector. Yet every time the bank loudly praises the private sector, it silently damns its own record. More than any other international institution, the bank is responsible for the rush to socialism in the Third World — the rise of political power over the private sector — and the economic collapse of Africa. [15]

The Debt Profiteers

Likewise, the World Bank's sister institution, the International Monetary Fund, has been subsidizing the global socialist revolution for decades. Columnist Doug Bandow pointed out in March 1992:

> Six nations — Chile, Egypt, India, Sudan, Turkey and Yugoslavia
> — relied or have relied on I.M.F. aid for more than 30 years; 23 na-
> tions have been borrowers for 20 to 29 years. And 48 have been using
> fund credit for 10 to 19 years.
>
> Since 1957 Egypt has never been off the I.M.F. dole. Yugoslavia,
> which got its first loan in 1949, was not a borrower in only three of the
> last 40 years. Bangladesh, Barbados, Gambia, Guinea-Bissau, Paki-
> stan, Uganda, Zaire and Zambia started borrowing in the early 70's
> and haven't stopped. [16]

Like domestic welfare drones, once these parasites attach themselves to the taxpayers, they never let loose. With the admission in
1992 of virtually all of the "former communist" countries into both
the IMF and World Bank, UN officials and their international welfare lobbyists launched a sustained campaign for massive new infusions of capital (to come primarily from U.S. taxpayers, of course)
that they could lend to the tottering socialist regimes. Bandow
warned against succumbing to the IMF sirens:

> [T]he West provided some $44 billion to Russia last year without ob-
> vious results. Moreover, once the I.M.F. begins lending to Moscow it
> will be under enormous pressure to maintain its lending, irrespective
> of Russia's compliance with its conditions. And the fund's record sug-
> gests that it is likely to give in to such pressure....
>
> For years, foreign money has helped delay the day of reckoning for
> many economies. Today the borrowers are left with huge debts *and* low
> growth. They need economic reform, not more loans. Once reforms are
> in place, private credit and investment will follow naturally....
> [I]ncreased lending, whether in the former Soviet Union or the third
> world, is only likely to waste more money. [17] [Emphasis in original]

While these "development" and "restructuring" loans further im-
poverish the so-called Third World peoples under crushing debt pay-
ments, they enrich certain Insider bankers. U.S. Senator Jesse Helms
exposed and denounced the shameful racket in 1987 in these words:

[I]t is no secret that the international bankers profiteer from sovereign state debt. The New York banks have found important profit centers in the lending to countries plunged into debt by Socialist regimes....

The New York banks find the profit from the interest on this sovereign debt to be critical to their balance sheets. Up until very recently, this has been an essentially riskless game for the banks because the IMF and the World Bank have stood ready to bail the banks out with our taxpayers' money.[18]

To which banks was Senator Helms referring? That is not difficult to deduce; their loan sheets are filled with socialist client states, their boards of directors are filled with members of the Council on Foreign Relations and Trilateral Commission, and they are closely identified with the Rockefeller-Morgan banking interests. The CFR-Rockefeller-Morgan Establishment has had a monopoly hold on the World Bank presidency since the institution was created: Eugene Meyer (CFR), 1946; John J. McCloy (CFR), 1947-49; Eugene R. Black (CFR), 1949-62; George D. Woods, 1963-68; Robert S. McNamara (CFR), 1968-81; A. W. Clausen, 1981-86; Barber Conable (CFR), 1986-1991.

Lewis T. Preston (CFR), the current president of the World Bank, sports a career path typical of his predecessors. After joining J. P. Morgan in 1951, he rose to become chairman of the board and president of both J. P. Morgan & Co. and Morgan Guaranty.[19] In 1991, he stepped down from those prestigious offices to take over the World Bank, where he now transfers money from taxpayers in both the rich and poor countries to his fellow bankers in the rich countries and the privileged dictators and plutocrats in the poor countries.

"Success," then, as defined by the World Bank and other multilateral institutions, is measured by the amount of increase of their annual budgets, appropriations, and loans, rather than by an objective assessment of the performance of their projects. Thus, in 1987, World Bank President Barber Conable was able to boast: "The 1986-7 fiscal year, which ended on 30 June, was a *success*; our commitments represented $14.2 billion as against $13 billion in the previous year."[20] (Emphasis in original)

At the same time, the Bank's own Operations Evaluation Department was warning that "the drive to reach lending targets" is "potentially damaging" and is "a major cause of poor project performance."[21]

In his important 1989 book, *Lords of Poverty: The Power, Prestige, and Corruption of the International Aid Business*, experienced African correspondent Graham Hancock reported:

> It is thus probably not entirely coincidental that, out of a representative sample of 189 of its projects audited worldwide, no less than 106 — almost 60 per cent — were found in 1987 either to have "serious shortcomings" or to be "complete failures." A similar proportion of these projects — including many judged in other senses to be "successes" — were thought unlikely to be sustainable after completion. Furthermore, it is in the poorest countries of the world, and amongst the poorest segments of the populations of these countries, that the Bank does worst. In sub-Saharan Africa, for example, 75 per cent of all agricultural projects audited were found to have failed.[22]

Hancock catalogs numerous misguided projects of UN "aid" programs worldwide. Among the multitude of fiascos, he found:

> [S]everal fish-farms in Egypt financed and managed by FAO during the 1980s have been unmitigated disasters: to date more than $50 *million* has been wasted. The farms owe their existence to a single FAO expert who made a very brief field visit and then proposed the establishment in the delta region "of deepwater ponds rearing several species of fish." [Emphasis in original]

Proper field studies would have shown that the area's soil was not suitable for these grandiose, large-scale schemes. The UN "experts" could have learned something from local wisdom. Hancock reported:

> Meanwhile, not far away, a group of "un-aided" smallholders who had established their own much less ambitious ponds in the wetlands of the Lake Manzalah area were in no need of any expensive high-tech "solutions"; far from having problems they were successfully harvesting 27,000 tonnes of fish annually at no cost to Western tax-payers.[23]

Bankrolling Tyranny, Socialism

There is scarcely a tyrant anywhere in the world who hasn't benefited handsomely from UN handouts. Graham Hancock lists many examples, including Mobutu Sese Seku of Zaire and Jean-Claude "Baby Doc" Duvalier of Haiti.

According to the 1987 *World Bank Atlas*, Zaire was ranked as the eighth poorest country in the world.[24] The main reason this is so is dictator Mobutu, whose brutal police state discourages private investment and entrepreneurial activity. Mobutu himself, however, has become one of the richest men in the world, with an estimated personal net worth of over $3 billion, which he has stolen from his own people and the taxpayers of the West.[25]

Since launching this world-class grand larceny spree in 1965, the "Butcher of Zaire" has been showered with UN aid and IMF loans. In the 1986-87 period alone, Mobutu was the recipient of $570 million in new IMF loans, despite having defaulted on previous loans.

Next to Mobutu, Haiti's Duvaliers were pikers but still managed to expropriate tens of millions of dollars of public funds for their personal use while the vast majority of their subjects lived in abject poverty. All the while, they were developing a horrible record on human rights that matched the performance of some of the world's more infamous despots. Graham Hancock noted:

> Interestingly enough, however, Haiti was a major recipient of foreign aid throughout the Duvalier era — with the United States, Canada, West Germany and France prominent amongst the bilateral donors and with the World Bank, FAO, WHO, UNDP, and UNICEF the most notable of the multilaterals. With all these "assisters" on the scene, a question has to be asked: Did the ruin of the Haitian poor occur *in spite* of foreign aid, or *because* of it?[26] [Emphasis in original]

Indeed, the same question has to be asked regarding the ruin of scores of countries. The answer is not pleasant. Moreover, when one sees in this ruination a recurring pattern of foreign aid-caused calamities and crises, always leading to more loss of freedom and ever greater concentration of power in government, and when one observes the same individuals again and again implementing the same disastrous policies with the same tragic results in one country after another and with these same individuals and institutions benefiting from the misery they are inflicting, then a whole host of questions beg to be asked. The foremost of which is: Is it possible that the UN foreign aid officials and the bankers who have been involved in these repeated and colossal catastrophes are so incompetent and incapable of learning from their numerous mistakes that they continue to make the same blunders out of sheer ignorance?

To believe that simple incompetence is responsible for these disasters is to stretch credulity beyond all reason. These are some of the brightest men in the world, with all the advantages of the best education money can buy. They have armies of advisors and technicians — "the best and the brightest" — to plot and plan each move they make. They have had, additionally, the benefit of the warnings of a host of independent expert analysts, from all political and ideological stripes, who have repeatedly condemned these programs for the fraudulent schemes they are.

One individual who has researched this issue very extensively over many years and who has argued very trenchantly against multilateral and bilateral "aid" programs is British economist Peter T. Bauer. After two decades of critical examination of Third World economies, Lord Bauer, one of the world's most distinguished development economists, concluded:

> The central argument for foreign aid has remained that without it Third World countries cannot progress at a reasonable rate, if at all. But not only is such aid patently not required for development: it has tended to obstruct development more than it has promoted it.
>
> External donations have never been necessary for the development of any society anywhere. Economic achievement depends on personal, cultural, social and political factors, that is people's own faculties, motivations and mores, their institutions and the policies of rulers. In short, economic achievement depends on the conduct of people and their governments.
>
> It diminishes the people of the Third World to suggest that, although they crave for material progress, unlike the West they cannot achieve it without external doles. [27]

American philosopher-economist-theologian David Chilton, in *Productive Christians in an Age of Guilt-Manipulators*, his powerful riposte to Ronald J. Sider's redistributionist economics, cogently observed:

> The government-to-government transfer of tax receipts is not conducive to the development of a market-oriented society; indeed, it is a denial of it. Moreover, it positively encourages the growth of statism and the politicization of life in recipient countries. *Foreign aid simply turns the recipients into "little Soviets."* ...
>
> Like other bureaucracies, multinational aid organizations and their staffs have two main goals in life: spend the money, and increase the budget (as much as two-thirds of an aid organization's budget will be spent on "administrative costs").[28] [Emphasis in original]

On the left too, we have very devastating critiques of the aid fiascos by reputable scholars. The September 1987 issue of Britain's Keynesian-socialist *Economic Journal*, for instance, carried a withering blast at the World Bank authored by three British economists: Paul Mosley, John Hudson, and Sara Horrell. After exhaustive statistical analyses of Bank projects around the globe, they concluded, "empirically we have found it impossible to establish any statistically significant correlation between aid and the growth rate of GNP in developing countries."

Moreover, the economists said:

> The apparent inability of development aid over more than 20 years to provide a net increment to overall growth in the Third World must give the donor community, as it gives us, cause for grave concern.

Even "liberal" *Newsweek* (a principal CFR transmission belt) admitted in a 1990 survey of foreign aid programs that aid ultimately hurts Third World countries because it "tends to prop up incompetent governments or subsidize economies so they can never stand on their own."[29]

Perhaps the most damning indictment of the UN's so-called aid programs has come from author Graham Hancock, who would prob-

ably describe himself politically as a liberal. After examining repeated cases of the most destructive and unconscionable policies, he
wrote in *Lords of Poverty*: "UNICEF, UNHCR, and the World Food
Programme et al. do indeed deliver relief supplies during emergen-
cies; the quality, timeliness and relevance of these items, however,
as we have seen ... often leave a great deal to be desired."[30] The to-
tality of the record of these multilateral agencies led him to the following very negative and bitter conclusion:

> Of course, the ugly reality is that most poor people in most poor
> countries most of the time *never* receive or even make contact with aid
> in any tangible shape or form: whether it is present or absent, in-
> creased or decreased, are thus issues that are simply irrelevant to the
> ways in which they conduct their daily lives. After the multi-billion-
> dollar "financial flows" involved have been shaken through the sieve of
> over-priced and irrelevant goods that must be bought in the donor
> countries, filtered again in the deep pockets of hundreds of thousands
> of foreign experts and aid agency staff, skimmed off by dishonest com-
> mission agents, and stolen by corrupt Ministers and Presidents, there
> is really very little left to go around. This little, furthermore, is then
> used thoughtlessly, or maliciously, or irresponsibly by those in power
> — who have no mandate from the poor, who do not consult with them
> and who are utterly indifferent to their fate. Small wonder, then, that
> the effects of aid are so often vicious and destructive for the most vul-
> nerable members of human society.[31] [Emphasis in original]

Even if the UN's aid agencies and programs were as wonderfully
effective as they would have us believe, our continued membership
in, and support of, an institution dedicated to our destruction would
remain unconscionable. The new global superstate rising behind the
facade of UN beneficence presents a mortal danger to the independence and liberty of people in all lands, regardless of whatever appeals to compassion and claims to charity its public relations
wizards can concoct. We need not jeopardize our freedom in order to
assist those around the world who are truly in need.

Private charitable organizations such as Save the Children Fund,
International Christian Aid, World Vision, Catholic Relief Services,

International Red Cross, Oxfam, Africare, Doctors Without Borders, Project Hope, and many, many others are actively providing aid daily to the destitute and disaster victims in all four corners of the globe. They offer adequate alternatives for channeling our charity to those in need. In most cases, they do so far more effectively and with far lower overhead and corruption than their governmental counterparts, either national or international. Private charitable groups must rely on persuasion for their funding; governmental agencies — including the UN's — depend on coercion. Under the guise of compassion, will we allow the UN to acquire the means for global coercion?

Communist dictators Julius Nyerere of Tanzania (left) and Mengistu Haile Mariam of Ethiopia were recipients of massive IMF and World Bank aid, even while they carried out brutal, genocidal policies against their own people. The UN General Assembly voted millions of dollars for a new luxury convention center in Ethiopia while hundreds of thousands of Ethiopians were perishing from the famine (below). Nyerere now heads the UN South Commission and demands more aid from the North.

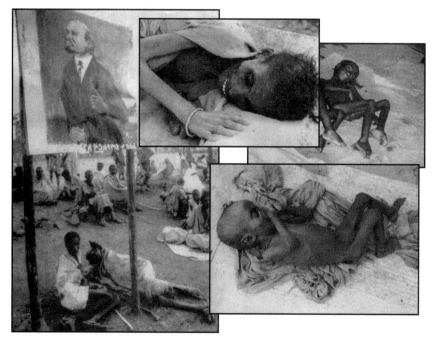

While the UN makes great pretense over concern for "human rights," the United Nations Development Program, IMF, and World Bank have poured hundreds of millions of dollars into communist Vietnam where human rights are non-existant and thousands of boat people have died trying to escape.

Insider bankers profiteer by "lending to countries plunged into debt by socialist regimes," charged Senator Jesse Helms. It's a "riskless game for the banks because the IMF and World Bank have stood ready to bail the banks out with our taxpayers' money."

Left: World Bank logo. Right: Former World Bank President Barber Conable (CFR) defines "success" as increased funding for his institutuion, even as his own auditors were warning of widespread failure of socialist projects funded by the Bank.

British journalist Graham Hancock's book *Lords of Poverty* is a devastating exposé of waste, corruption, and fraud in the international aid programs, including IMF, World Bank, UNDP, UNICEF, WHO, FAO, and UNHCR.

"Butcher of Zaire," Mobutu Sese Seku has become a billionaire, thanks to the World Bank and IMF. Meanwhile his people starve.

Brutal dictator Jean-Claude Duvalier of Haiti lived millionaire life-style with UN aid.

British economist P.T. Bauer and American political-economic-religious writer David Chilton have produced devastating critques of the tax-supported international aid programs. These programs "have been damaging both to the West and to the peoples of the less developed world," says Bauer. "Foreign aid simply turns the recipients into little Soviets," notes Chilton.

CHAPTER 12

The New World Religion

We have meditations at the United Nations a couple of times a week. The meditation leader is Sri Chinmoy, and this is what he said about this situation: "... The United Nations is the chosen instrument of God; to be a chosen instrument means to be a divine messenger carrying the banner of God's inner vision and outer manifestation. One day, the world will ... treasure and cherish the soul of the United Nations as its very own with enormous pride, for this soul is all-loving, all-nourishing, and all-fulfilling."[1]

— Donald Keys, president of Planetary Citizens
and author of *Earth At Omega*

In times past, when critics of the United Nations described the organization as a modern Tower of Babel, most were making reference to man's act of spiritual arrogance that the book of Genesis tells us earned God's displeasure. To back up such an unflattering characterization today, they could point to the confusing and combustible melange of tongues, cultures, ideologies, and politics for which the "house of peace" has become justly famous. The UN, along with its programs and policies, is becoming ever more worthy of comparison to the Tower of Babel, as rampant idolatry and militant paganism thoroughly permeate the organization.

The United Nations is steadily becoming the center of a syncretic new world religion, a weird and diabolical convergence of New Age mysticism, pantheism, aboriginal animism, atheism, communism, socialism, Luciferian occultism, apostate Christianity, Islam, Taoism, Buddhism, and Hinduism. The devotees and apostles of this new faith include the kind of strange admixture of crystal worshipers, astrologers, radical feminists, environmentalists, cabalists, human potentialists, Eastern mystics, pop psychologists, and "liberal" clergymen one would normally tend to associate with the off-beat, sandals-and-beads counterculture of the 1960s. But today's worshipers in this rapidly expanding movement are as likely to be scientists, diplomats, corporate presidents, heads of state, international bankers, and leaders of mainstream Christian churches.

Go East, Young Man

During the 1960s and '70s, droves of disenchanted intellectuals and alienated youth from Europe and America trekked to India and other points East seeking "enlightenment," "wisdom," and "truth" from an endless array of gurus, swamis, yogis, and other "illuminated masters." Most never realized as they began their search that they were following in the footsteps of one who a century earlier had laid the groundwork for the present cult explosion, and whose work is central to the spiritual character of the United Nations today.

That person is Helena Petrovna Blavatsky (1831-1891), widely revered as the high priestess of the New Age movement, who founded the Theosophical Society in New York in 1875. In her scrapbook for that year she wrote:

> The Christians and scientists must be made to respect their Indian betters. The Wisdom of India, her philosophy and achievement, *must* be made known in Europe and America....[2] [Emphasis in original]

Madame Blavatsky's theosophy taught esoteric "wisdom," the universal brotherhood of mankind, and unity among all religions, except the monotheistic religions — Christianity, Islam, Judaism — which could not be reconciled with individual "enlightenment." An early Theosophical Society statement left no mistake about the organization's special mission:

> To oppose ... every form of dogmatic theology, especially the Christian, which the Chiefs of the Society regard as particularly pernicious ... to counteract, as far as possible, the effects of missionaries to delude the so-called "Heathen" and "Pagans" as to the real origin and dogmas of Christianity and the practical effects of the latter upon public and private character in so-called Christian countries.[3]

"Esoteric Philosophy has never rejected God in Nature, nor Deity as the absolute and abstract [End]," Blavatsky wrote. *"It only refuses to accept any of the gods of the so-called monotheistic religions, gods created by man in his own image and likeness, a blasphemous and sorry caricature of the ever unknowable."* [4] (Emphasis in original)

The Wrong God

The high priestess of theosophy cursed the God of the Bible as "capricious and unjust." He was merely "a tribal God and no more," she maintained. [5] In Madame Blavatsky's twisted mind, the Bible had it all backwards; *it was really Satan who was the victim of Jehovah:*

> The appellation Sa'tan, in Hebrew Satan, and Adversary ... belongs by right to the first and cruelest "Adversary" of all other Gods — Jehovah; not to the serpent which spoke only words of sympathy and wisdom. [6]

According to Blavatsky's biblical hermeneutics:

> Once the key to Genesis is in our hands, the scientific and symbolical Kabbala unveils the secret. The Great Serpent of the Garden of Eden and the "Lord God" are identical. [7]

In the Blavatsky scheme of things, Satan is God the Creator, the Savior, the Father; and Jesus Christ is "the first born brother of Satan." She explains it thus:

> Satan, the Serpent of Genesis, is the real creator and benefactor, the Father of Spiritual mankind. For it is he ... who opened the eyes of the automaton (Adam) created by Jehovah, as alleged.... An adversary to Jehovah ... he still remains in Esoteric Truth the ever loving messenger ... who conferred on us spiritual instead of physical immortality. [8]

Blavatsky, who had spent several years in India and Tibet, claimed to have experience with astral projection and the ability to communicate with the spirit world. She claimed to have written *Isis*

Unveiled and her three-volume magnum opus *The Secret Doctrine* under the direction of the "Masters of Wisdom," Tibetan holy men who communicated telepathically with her in England from the Himalayas.

After she passed away in 1891, the mantle of leadership for the worldwide theosophical movement fell to Annie Besant, a militant feminist and a member of the Fabian Socialist Society of England. A close friend of George Bernard Shaw, H. G. Wells, and other leading Fabians, Besant was well-placed to spread theosophical thought in very influential circles. An indefatigable revolutionist and prolific writer, she enthusiastically joined in revolutionary street riots and penned numerous volumes of occultic writings to add to those of Blavatsky.

Besant was followed by Alice Bailey, who together with her husband, Foster Bailey, constructed much of the foundation of what is now known as New Age religion. Unabashedly acknowledging their demonic sympathies, they launched Lucifer Publishing Company, which published the theosophical periodical *Lucifer*. Realizing later that perhaps the Christian world was not yet ready for their open preference for Satanic religion, they changed the name to Lucis Publishing Company. The Lucis Trust, established by the Baileys in 1922, continues to serve as the umbrella organization for a profusion of globalist/New Age/occult organizations and programs that are key catalysts of the emerging new world religion. These include the Arcane School, World Goodwill, Triangles, Lucis Publishing, Lucis Productions, Lucis Trust Libraries, and the New Group of World Servers.

UN New Age Network

According to the Lucis Trust, "World Goodwill is recognised ... at the United Nations as a Non-governmental Organisation" and is "represented at regular briefing sessions at the United Nations in New York and Geneva."[9] The "regular weekly broadcasts of talks given at World Goodwill Forum meetings and programs produced by Lucis Productions" in London and New York are beamed by Radio For Peace International in English, Spanish, German, and French, on shortwave, to a "worldwide audience" from the UN University for Peace in Costa Rica. According to spokesmen at the Lucis Trust, all people of good will, whether they realize it or not, belong to the New Group of World Servers (NGWS) who will bring about "spiritual unfoldment" and "lead humanity into a new age of peace and plenty."[10]

"Humanity is not following a haphazard or uncharted course — there is a Plan," say the Lucis theosophists. And, "Men of goodwill who co-operate form part of the New Group of World Servers which is working to implement the Plan." The "Plan" involves a "spiritual Hierarchy of the planet" and the building of a "synthetic unity" that will be manifested in an "inner centre or subjective world government, whose members are responsible for the spread of those ideals and ideas which have led humanity onwards from age to age." The leaders of the New Group of World Servers "provide the vision and mould public opinion." But there is yet a higher class of adepts. "Behind these leaders and the co-operating men of goodwill," we learn, "are the Custodians of the Plan, 'the inner spiritual Government of the Planet.'"[11]

According to these possessors of esoteric wisdom, "People in the world at this time can be divided into four groups":

> First the uninformed masses.... They are, however, enough developed to respond to the mental suggestion and control of more advanced people.
>
> Second, the middle classes — both higher and lower.... [B]ecause they can read and discuss and are beginning to think, they form the most powerful element in any nation.
>
> Third, the thinkers everywhere.... They are steadily influencing world affairs — sometimes for good and sometimes for selfish ends.
>
> Fourth, the New Group of World Servers. *These are the people who are building the new world order....* They own to no creed, save the creed of Brotherhood, based on the One Life. They recognise no authority save that of their own souls.[12] [Emphasis added]

The "Enlightened Ones"

Ah, yes. But if one progresses through these circles-within-circles of higher planetary consciousness, one eventually may reach the exalted plane of "the Hierarchy." Examining the works of these individuals, we discover:

> Behind this four-fold division of humanity stand those Enlightened Ones whose right and privilege it is to watch over human evolution and to guide the destinies of men. In the West we call them Christ and His disciples.... They are also known as the Agents of God, or the Hierarchy of liberated souls, who seek ceaselessly to aid and help humanity. [13]

No doubt you will now rest easier knowing that your "destiny" and "evolution" have been entrusted to the providential care of the planet's "Enlightened Ones."

But surely, you ask, no one actually believes this arcane gibberish? Would that this were true. The NGWS boasts that its followers "will be able to swing into activity at any moment such a weight of thought and such a momentous public opinion that they will eventually be in a position definitely to affect world affairs." [14] To be sure, that represents more an aspiration than a true representation of their present level of influence.

But one cannot survey the New Age, occult, satanist, wicca, and hedonist phenomena all around us without recognizing that if these trends continue, the day will not be far off when occult forces will be able to make good on some of those claims. As G. K. Chesterton once observed, "If man will not believe in God, the danger is not that he will believe in nothing, but that he will believe in anything."

Messiahs and Megalomaniacs

On April 25, 1982, all across the planet, millions of pairs of eyes blinked in disbelief at the headlines they saw on full-page advertisements in their daily newspapers. "THE CHRIST IS NOW HERE," trumpeted the massive ad campaign in major newspapers around the world. "Throughout history," proclaimed the announcement, "humanity's evolution has been guided by a group of enlightened men, the Masters of Wisdom," a "Spiritual Hierarchy" at the center of which "stands the World Teacher, Lord Maitreya, known by Christians as the Christ." [15] This same individual, said the ad, is awaited also by Jews, Moslems, Buddhists, and Hindus, though he is known by these believers respectively as the Messiah, Imam Mahdi, the Fifth Buddha, or Krishna.

According to the ad proclamation, "the Christ" was at that moment living in the world and would "within the next two months" reveal his identity to all mankind. The advertising campaign coincided with the beginning of a worldwide speaking tour by one Benjamin Creme, a British theosophist and a spokesman for "the Christ." In various interviews and speeches, Creme explained that in speaking of "the Christ," he did not mean Jesus Christ but the "Master of Wisdom," of whom Jesus, Buddha, Krishna, and others are disciples. Creme's messianic campaign was coordinated by his New Age religious organization, the Tara Center, from its offices in Los Angeles, New York, and London.

In his 1980 book, *The Reappearance of the Christ and the Masters of Wisdom*, Creme left no doubt about his spiritual debt to Blavatsky and Bailey. In its pages, he prophesied:

> When the physical structures of human living are reconstructed ... the Christ will reveal to man an entirely new aspect of Reality.... The Ancient Mysteries will be restored, the Mystery Schools reopened, and a great expansion of man's awareness of himself and his purpose and destiny will become possible....
>
> Eventually a new world religion will be inaugurated, which will be a fusion and synthesis of the approach of the East and the approach of the West. The Christ will bring together, not simply Christianity and Buddhism, but the concept of God transcendent — outside of His creation in man and all creation.
>
> It will be seen to be possible to hold both approaches at the same time, and they will be brought together in a new scientific religion based on the Mysteries; on Initiation; on Invocation....
>
> Gradually, Christianity, Buddhism and other religions will wither away-slowly, as the people die out of them, as the new religion gains its adherents and exponents, and is gradually built by humanity.[16]

"Christ" and the UN

According to Creme, "The new religion will manifest itself through organizations like Masonry"[17] and will inaugurate a "new world order" to be headed by the United Nations:

> At the head of several of the governments of the world and in the great world agencies, like the United Nations' agencies, there will be either a Master or at least a third degree Initiate. So the great international agencies will be under the direct control of a high member of the Hierarchy.... The Christ Himself will have a great deal to do — with the release of energies; the work of Initiation, as the Initiator, the Hierophant, at the first two Initiations; and stimulating and inspiring the formation of the New World Religion.[18]

In the Tara Center's *Network News* letter of October 1987, New Age devotees were told: "In the coming years the United Nations is destined to be the world's main focal point for the practical application of love, brotherhood, justice and sharing. We can help bring this about through our support." This support is essential because when "all the impossible solutions have been eliminated, it will become clear that *the only answer to our problems is the U.N.*" (Emphasis added)

This being the case, a cosmic prayer was offered for the revered institution:

> May the Peace and the Blessings of the Holy Ones pour forth over the worlds — rest upon the United Nations, on the work and the workers, protecting, purifying, energizing and strengthening.[19]

No-Show

But Creme's "Maitreya — the Christ" failed to materialize as promised. So it would be reasonable to expect that Creme, his messiah, and his UN propaganda were all discredited and labeled irrelevant. But we do not live in the age of reasonableness. Creme remains a leading light of the vast New Age network, and his occult gospel can be found emanating from numerous UN conferences and programs where the power elite of the Club of Rome, Aspen Institute, Council on Foreign Relations, World Federalists, World Bank, etc. mingle with New Agers of every description.

The Rio Earth Summit

A prime example of this dangerous lunacy could be found at the June 1992 UN Earth Summit in Brazil, where both the official United Nations Conference on Environment and Development (UNCED) program and the Global Forum "peoples summit" featured a melding of pagan aboriginal rites, eco-babble, and an ecumenical hodgepodge of spiritual tenets from East and West to form an incoherent universal "faith."

In his opening address to the UNCED plenary session, Earth Summit Secretary-General Maurice Strong directed the world's attention to the Declaration of the Sacred Earth Gathering, which was part of the pre-Summit ceremonies. "[T]he changes in behavior and direction called for here," said Strong, "must be rooted in our deepest spiritual, moral and ethical values."[20] According to the declaration, the ecological crisis "transcends all national, religious, cultural, social, political, and economic boundaries.... The responsibility of each human being today is to choose between the force of darkness and the force of light. We must therefore transform our attitudes and values, and adopt a renewed respect for the superior law of Divine Nature."[21]

Nutty Goings-On

Delegates and members of the news media were referring to the Rio Declaration and the 800-page blueprint for government action known as *Agenda 21* as "sacred" texts. Senator Al Gore, who led the U.S. Senate delegation to Rio, reiterated his call for a new spiritual relationship between man and earth. Shirley MacLaine dropped in to lend the nutty ramblings of her psychic spirituality to the conference. A centerpiece of the Global Forum opening ceremony was the Viking ship *Gaia*, named for the Greek goddess of earth.

At the culmination of that program, a group calling itself the "Sacred Drums of the Earth" struck up a solemn cadence. The ceremony program said that the drummers would "maintain a continuous heartbeat near the official site of the Earth Summit, as part of a ritual for the healing of our Earth to be felt by those who are deciding Earth's fate." The Forum ceremony closed, appropriately, with Jamaican reggae singer Jimmy Cliff performing the song, "The Rivers of Babylon."

On the eve of the opening of UNCED, a midnight-to-dawn homage to the "Female Planet" was held on Leme Beach. After dancing all night, the worshipers followed a Brazilian tribal high priestess to the water's edge where they offered flowers and fruits to "Iemanje, mae orixa, mother of the powers, queen of the seas," and then invoked the blessings of the sea goddess upon the summit's deliberations.

At the first plenary session, Uri Marinov, Israel's Minister of the Environment, issued a New Ten Commandments on Environment and Development.[22] No one bothered to ask him what was wrong with the original Ten Commandments. Was the Creator of this planet somehow negligent, or so ignorant of environmental concerns, that his original decalogue is ecologically deficient? As we recall, the first commandment states: "I am the Lord thy God.... Thou shalt have no other gods before Me." That, understandably, makes many environmentalists uncomfortable. "Thou shalt not steal," and "Thou shalt not covet thy neighbor's goods" can also be troublesome to those whose plans call for expropriating the property of others.

The Union for Natural Environment Protection, an environmental group based in Sao Leopoldo, Brazil, declared the following about the work of the summit: "A world-wide citizens' movement is born around the UN system and will be in the years ahead a central focal point for the New World Order which Alice Bailey wrote about many decades ago and which is going to be politically free, socially fair, economically efficient and environmentally sustainable."[23] That pretty well ties it all together: the UN, Alice Bailey's New Age religion, the new world order, and environmentalism.

True, there were also "Christian" participants in the summit celebrations. Ministers from the World Council of Churches and Catholic clerics such as Dom Helder Camarra (known as Brazil's Red Archbishop because of his blatantly pro-communist sympathies) could be found amidst the cymbal-clanging Hare Krishnas, diapered swamis, saffron-robed gurus, and witch doctors in loincloths. But they were there because of their affinity for an ecumenical "spirit" that promotes an anti-Christian and syncretistic blend of Christianity and paganism.

Bible Out, Lucifer In

Many militant environmentalists make no bones about their animus toward Christianity. Jose Lutzenberger, former Brazilian Minister of the Environment, decried the foundation of modern education which he argued was "based on the Judeo-Christian philosophy of an evil world which needs to be subdued by man." He insisted: "We have to teach our children to dialogue with their world." And, "We need a moral revolution, and should learn from indigenous people who have successfully integrated our species in to the entire symphony of nature."[24] This blaming of the biblical world outlook for the world's environmental problems and the romanticizing of aboriginal religions and life-styles were rife among the summit ecocrazies.

Bible bashing is another practice that has become common in environmental circles, and its tone has become increasingly shrill. Tom Hayden, for instance, that pillar of 1960s spiritual rectitude, has taken up the crusade by teaching a college course about "Environment and Spirituality." "He wants to convince people," reports the *Los Angeles Times*, "that Judeo-Christian ethics, which teach that man has the God-given right to 'subdue' the Earth, are the root of many of today's environmental problems."[25]

The environmental gospel according to "We are all Vietcong" Hayden holds that "organized religion has either ignored or rationalized the exploitation of the natural environment for 2,000 years." Reverend Tom's 16-week course is described by the *Times* as "a wide-ranging survey of New Age philosophies and Eastern spirituality."[26]

New Age philosopher William Irwin Thompson is even more emphatic. The former professor of humanities from MIT and Syracuse University, and founder of the influential Lindisfarne Association, has said:

> We have now a new spirituality, what has been called the New Age movement. The planetization of the esoteric has been going on for some time.... This is now beginning to influence concepts of politics and community in ecology.... This is the Gaia [Mother Earth] politique ... planetary culture.[27]

According to this illuminated master, the age of "the independent sovereign state, with the sovereign individual in his private property [is] over, just as the Christian fundamentalist days are about to be over."[28] A former trustee of the Aspen Institute for Humanistic Studies and a member of the advisory council of Planetary Citizens, Thompson is no lightweight in the movement. Maurice Strong sits on the board of directors and serves as director of finance of the Lindisfarne Center. The Lindisfarne Center is located in Manhattan's historic Episcopal Cathedral of St. John the Divine and its work is "made possible by grants from the Lilly Endowment, the Rockefeller Brothers Fund, and the Rockefeller Foundation."[29] The Lindisfarne Institute lists among its faculty members eco-radical Amory Lovins and Luciferian adept and New Age author David Spangler.

So, what great wisdom is imparted at this Rockefeller-funded institute of higher learning? We can gain some appreciation by reading Mr. Spangler's books, such as *Reflections on the Christ*, wherein we find:

> Lucifer, like Christ, stands at the door of man's consciousness and knocks. If man says, "Go away because I do not like what you represent, I am afraid of you," Lucifer will play tricks on that fellow. If man says, "Come in, and I will give to you the treat of my love and understanding and I will uplift you in the light and presence of the Christ, my outflow," then Lucifer becomes something else again. He becomes the being who carries that great treat, the ultimate treat, the light of wisdom.
>
> The reason man has come to fear Lucifer is not so much that he represents evil as because he represents experience which causes us to grow and to move beyond the levels where we have been.... Lucifer is literally the angel of experience.[30]

Many Groups, Same Goal

Spangler, Thompson, Strong, and a host of other notables (Queen Juliana of the Netherlands, Sir Edmund Hillary, Peter Ustinov, Linus Pauling, Kurt Vonnegut, Leonard Bernstein, John Updike, Isaac Asimov, Pete Seeger) are listed as original endorsers of the world-government-promoting Planetary Citizens. Founded by New Age luminary and former UN consultant Donald Keys, and presided over for many years by the late Norman Cousins (CFR), the Planetary Citizens organization has marshaled the prestige of many influential world figures to support expansion of UN power and institutions. Keys, openly a disciple of Alice Bailey, calls the United Nations "the nexus of emerging planetary values" and expresses the hope that it will establish a "planetary management system."[31] In order to help speed that day, Planetary Citizens is "in consultative status with the Economic and Social Council of the United Nations."[32]

Another original endorser of Planetary Citizens and its "Human Manifesto" (not to be confused with *The Humanist Manifesto*) was Aurelio Peccei, founder of the Club of Rome. Known more for its role in launching "no growth" environmentalism in the 1970s, the Club has turned increasingly "spiritual" in recent years. Its most recent report, *The First Global Revolution*, takes special pains to stress this new interest. "In these difficult and complex times," say the report's authors, "we begin to realize that the pursuit of wisdom is the essential challenge that faces humanity."[33]

And where do they go for wisdom? Sprinkled throughout the book are numerous quotations from sacred texts, philosophers, poets, psychologists, historians, and sages. Hindus, Buddhists, aborigines, Taoists, humanists, even Aztec cannibals are reverently represented. Their wisdom includes adherence to the Blavatsky mandate holding that monotheism, Christianity, Islam, and Judaism are either excluded or denigrated.

Typical of the quotations highlighted in special boxes in the book's text is this "hymn" from India placed alongside a discussion about mining:

> Whatever I dig from thee, Earth, may that have quick growth again.
> O purifier, may we not injure thy vitals or thy heart.[34]

And sounding very much in tune with current New Age thought is the Club of Rome's discovery that the "spiritual and ethical dimension is no longer an object of scorn or indifference; it is perceived as a necessity that should lead to *a new humanism.*[35] (Emphasis added) Moreover, we learn:

> The global society we are heading towards cannot emerge unless it drinks from the source of moral and spiritual values which stake out its dynamics. Beyond cultures, religions and philosophies, there is in human beings a thirst for freedom, aspirations to overcome one's limits, a quest for a beyond that seems ungraspable and is often unnamed.[36]

We are witnessing here a very important phenomenon, what the New Agers call a "paradigm shift." After several centuries of warring with religion in general and Christianity in particular, "science" is now being reconciled with faith. Increasingly, infidel scientists who once expressed supreme confidence in "reeking tube and iron shard" (as Kipling referred to their technological idolatry) are acknowledging the deficiency of their "dust that builds on dust...." They seek to supply gods of their own choosing. And Blavatsky's gods of the East are infinitely more compatible with their plans than the Judeo-Christian God. Which may explain the Club of Rome's heavy reliance on the "spiritual values" of India, as expressed in the following prayer:

> May the divine Spirit protect us all; may we work together with great energy; may our study be fruitful and thorough; may there be no hatred between us.[37]
>
> Aum, Peace, Peace, Peace, Peace
> — Vedic Prayer [3000 B.C.]

Temple of Understanding

One of the principal channels through which this tilt toward Oriental spiritualism has been spread is the Temple of Understanding, located at the same Cathedral of St. John the Divine that houses the Lindisfarne Luciferians. Launched in the early 1960s as the "spiritual counterpart of the United Nations," its founding sponsors included the following odd assortment of Establishment Insiders, socialists, humanists, communist fronters, religious figures, and entertainment celebrities: John D. Rockefeller IV; then-Secretary of Defense Robert S. McNamara; Planned Parenthood founder Margaret Sanger; IBM president Thomas J. Watson; Socialist Party leader Norman Thomas; Eleanor Roosevelt; Time-Life president James A. Linen; homosexual author Christopher Isherwood; columnist Max Lerner; and entertainer Jack Benny.

The Temple organization, which works closely with the UN Secretariat, the World Council of Churches, and the World Conference on Religion and Peace, is currently aiding and abetting Columbusbashers with its sponsorship of the UN's Year of the Indigenous People. In 1993, it will be promoting the syncretic "Interfaith Movement" with its centennial celebration of the World's Parliament of Religions.

This favor toward Eastern mysticism was given a big boost in UN circles during the 1970s and '80s by New Age VIP Robert Muller, who served as an assistant secretary-general at the United Nations. Muller, author of the influential book *New Genesis: Shaping a Global Spirituality*, believes, "If Christ came back to earth, his first visit would be to the United Nations to see if his dream of human oneness and brotherhood had come true. He would be happy to see representatives from all nations."[38]

Of course, when Muller talks about "Christ," he is not speaking in the Christian tradition, but in that of Bailey, Creme, and Spangler. Muller openly supports Creme and has delivered lectures at the Lucis Trust's Arcane School. And in typical animist fashion, he refers to "our brethren the animals, our sisters the flowers."[39]

Who Is Maurice Strong?

Undoubtedly one of the most influential hands guiding the UN's unfolding spirituality over the past two decades has been that of the grand poobah of environmentalism, Maurice Strong. An article from the May 1990 issue of *West* magazine[40] sheds considerable light on the man who has been reverently dubbed by some "the custodian of the planet." Journalist Daniel Wood's research for the article included spending a week with Strong and his wife Hanne at their Baca Grande spiritual center in Colorado's San Luis Valley. While there, he witnessed many strange and troubling things. According to Wood, the Strongs' goal at "the Baca," as they refer to their compound, "is nothing less than to alter, utterly, the history of the world." They see their mystic commune serving "as a model for the way the world should be — and, they say, *must* be — if humankind is to survive."

The idea for the strange venture at "the Baca" took root in 1978, reported Wood, "when a mysterious man visited Hanne bearing a prophesy of the coming apocalypse. The dream grew amid omens that defy belief. It has been nourished by the Strongs' friends, such people as Rockefeller, [former Canadian premier] Trudeau, the Dalai Lama, and Shirley MacLaine." Another of the Strongs' friends, Najeeb Halaby (CFR), former chairman of Pan American and father of the Queen of Jordan, has built an Islamic ziggurat at the Baca. The first groups to join the Strongs in setting up operations at the desert site were the Aspen Institute and the Lindisfarne Association.

Mrs. Strong is a remarkably curious individual. "Hanne knew from earliest childhood," said Wood, "that she was different, that she had mystical abilities.... She could recall past lives." On one occasion, Wood recounted: "Hanne invites me to join her in her daily ritual of singing the sun down.... She chants her mantra, an ancient Vedic text, she explains, that goes back to the dawn of civilization."

But even more disturbing than Hanne's occult mysticism are Maurice's spiritual experiences. Strong allegedly told Wood of a freakish omen he had experienced while walking with famed author and public television icon Bill Moyers: "We'd been walking, talking, heading back to my parked car. Suddenly, this bush — some sagebrush — erupted in flames in front of us! It just burst into flames."

Pagan Spiritualism

With individuals like these leading the charge, the UN's pagan spiritualism will grow ever more blatant. There will be many more documents like the UN report entitled *The New International Economic Order: A Spiritual Imperative*, which brazenly proclaims:

[T]oday a new understanding of spirituality is emerging which recognizes that all efforts to uplift humanity are spiritual in nature. Alice Bailey said, "That is spiritual which lies beyond the point of present achievement...." ... Given this new understanding of spirituality, the work of the United Nations can be ... seen within the entire evolutionary unfoldment of humanity. The work of the U.N. is indeed spiritual and holds profound import for the future of civilization.[41]

It would seem that predictions concerning religion made half a century ago in the *Rosicrucian Digest* are coming to pass. The June 1941 issue of that occult journal carried the following prophesy that, tragically, is being fulfilled before our eyes:

> What then does the future hold for religion? We predict a mystical-pantheism as the religion of tomorrow. The central doctrine of this religion will be that a Universal Intelligence as a series or concatenations of causes, creative and perfect in its whole, pervades everywhere and everything.

One major effect of this religious conversion, the Rosicrucian oracle predicted, is that "the multiplicity of social states, countries, or nations will cease to be." Nations would be replaced by "the one United World State." The occultists are correct in noting that the mystical-pantheism they advocate will, if widely accepted, lead to a collectivist world state. And there are far too few Americans who understand the direct cause-and-effect relationship between the two.

Pantheist Connection

"Pantheism is a favorite doctrine of collectivists," notes one authority on occult deception, Father Clarence Kelly, "because ... it offers a concept of man which, on religious grounds, subordinates the individual to the collective."[42] Since "God" in this belief system is not the transcendent, personal God of the Bible, but an impersonal, immanent force that pervades all things, then all things — the universe, you, me, the rock, the tree — are "God." In this pagan world view, man is not a special creation of the one, true God, to whom, ultimately, he is accountable. Nor is he endowed by his Creator with intrinsic, unalienable rights — and responsibilities.

Thus pantheism "functions as an effective tool in the subversion of God-centered religion by making religion man-centered, and thereby giving a religious sanction to the doctrines and programs of political collectivism. At the same time, pantheism can be used as a stage in bringing people from theism to atheistic materialism. In religion, pantheism is most often expressed as Naturalism — 'the doctrine that religious truth is derived from nature, not revelation....' "[43]

It was just such neo-Paganism that paved the way for the totalitarian collectivism of the Third Reich. The Nazi high priesthood — Hitler, Himmler, Rahn, Rosenberg, Hess, Feder, Sebottendorf, et al. — were ardent theosophists, and their esoteric societies (the Thule, Vril, Seekers of the Grail) were steeped in the same occultism and pantheism so prevalent in today's New Age and environmental movements.[44] Hitler's paganism sought to create a nationalist-socialist new world order. And even though it was militantly anti-Christian, numerous Christian churches succumbed to the Nazi scheme and most were captured through subversion and accommodation, not through outright persecution.

Today, all people of good will recognize the diabolically evil nature of the *Fuehrer's* failed regime. What is now desperately needed is a widespread recognition of the fact that the neo-pagan, internationalist-socialist new world order being promoted by and through the United Nations is as militantly anti-Christian, as malevolently totalitarian, and as satanically evil as that jackbooted tyranny of our recent past.

This time, its headquarters is not in Berlin, but in New York City.

The Meditation Room at UN headquarters reflects the bizarre, syncretic world religion the UN is promoting. New Age guru Sri Chinmoy, who leads weekly meditations there, says: "The United Nations is the chosen instrument of God ... a divine messenger.... One day the world will ... treasure and cherish the soul of the United Nations as its very own."

Madame Helena Blavatsky and the occult seal of her Theosophical Society. Blavatsky, patroness of New Age cults, denounced Jehovah as "capricious and unjust" and praised Satan as "the real creator and benefactor" of mankind.

Former UN assistant secretary-general and New Age leader Robert Muller says "If Christ came back to earth, his first visit would be to the United Nations to see if his dream of human oneness and brotherhood had come true."

231

Photograph purporting to be of one Rahmat Ahmad, whom British theosophist Benjamin Creme and other New Agers call "Lord Maitreya, the Christ." This Lord Maitreya, says Creme, will inaugurate a "new world order" and a "New World Religion."

CHAPTER 13

UN Regionalism — The European Community

We are experiencing an increasing abandonment of sovereignty within the European Community in favor of this Community and, as I hope, also in favor of [a] European parliament equipped with full rights.
— German Foreign Minister Hans-Dietrich Genscher
Der Spiegel, September 25, 1989

Twenty years ago, when the process began, there was no question of losing sovereignty. That was a lie, or at any rate, a dishonest obfuscation.
— Sir Peregrine Worsthorne
London *Sunday Telegraph*, August 4, 1991

We have here the recreation of the familiar 20th century bureaucratic nation state, but on a Leviathan scale.... A monolithic Europe would be the last great folly of the 20th century, hustled into existence at the very moment when such concepts are withering everywhere else ... repeating all the errors, the vanities and conceits, of the collectivist epoch.
— David Howell, chairman of the Select Committee
on Foreign Affairs, British House of Commons
Wall Street Journal, December 31, 1990

The idea of a unified European Community (EC) was sold to the peoples of Western Europe under the misleading rubric of "a Common Market," an arrangement that would supposedly free commerce and consumers from labyrinthine national regulations and restrictions. The Single European Act of 1986, agreed to by the 12 member states that year, called for the establishment of "an area without internal frontiers, in which the free movement of goods, persons, services, and capital is ensured." With progress toward a single market, "... European industry will be able to achieve greater economies of scale," said U.S. Deputy Secretary of the Treasury M. Peter McPherson (CFR). He made this remark in an address in 1988 to the Institute for International Economics, a group led by fellow one-worlder C. Fred Bergsten (CFR, TC). McPherson continued:

> The demands of competition will spur technological innovation and greater productivity. The program can help stimulate growth and employment, reduce consumer prices, and raise standards of living throughout Europe.
>
> The force that will drive this transformation is opportunity — the opportunity to compete in a larger and freer marketplace.[1]

Economic analyst and former Republican Congressman from Texas Dr. Ron Paul saw the same developments in a completely different light. Long an ardent champion of free-market policies, he warned that the movement toward European "union" and "integration" is a statist scheme cloaked in free-market rhetoric that is likely to "produce a monster." "International statists have long dreamed of a world currency and a world central bank," wrote Dr. Paul in the October 1988 issue of *The Free Market*, published by the Ludwig von Mises Institute. "Now it looks as if their dream may come true." Ron Paul's essay, entitled "The Coming World Central Bank," went on to say:

> European governments have targeted 1992 for abolishing individual European currencies and replacing them with the European Currency Unit, the Ecu. Next they plan to set up a European central bank. The next step is the merger of the Federal Reserve, the European central bank and the Bank of Japan into a one world central bank....
>
> The European central bank (ECB) will be modeled after the Federal Reserve. Like the Fed in 1913, it will have the institutional appearance of decentralization, but also like the Fed it will be run by a cartel of big bankers in collusion with politicians at the expense of the public.

Time and events have proven Dr. Paul's assessment, not McPherson's, to have been correct. The much-touted "free trade/free market reforms" were merely bait laid out to entice Europeans into the trap of what is designed eventually to become an all-powerful, supranational government. This European regional government would later be merged into a world government under the United Nations. The agreements reached by the leaders of the European Community who met in Maastricht, Netherlands in December 1991 are now taking them down this road. Major concessions of national sovereignty given by the 12 member states (Belgium, Denmark, France, Germany, Great Britain, Greece, Ireland, Italy, Luxembourg, Netherlands, Portugal, and Spain) to the socialist-dominated European Parliament and to the Eurocrats in Brussels are underway. Foremost among these are the commitments to establish a single currency, the ECU, and a European Central Bank. The members also agreed to yield more defense and foreign policy control to the Western European Union.

The Socialist parties, which control a majority (260) of the 518 votes in the European Parliament, are certainly not going to promote free-market reforms. Nor are those reforms likely to come from the European Community Commission or the Council of Ministers, the institutions holding the EC's real legislative and executive powers. Those institutions have been dominated by socialists such as Commission President Jacques Delors, who is leading the push for a European central bank, and by members of David Rockefeller's world-government-promoting Trilateral Commission.

The EC Trilateralists include such influential Eurocrats as Willy De Clercq, Karl-Heinz Narjes, Carlo Ripa di Meana, Viscount Etienne Davignon, Raymond Barre, Rene Foch, Jorge Braga de Macedo, Francisco Lucas Pires, Gaston Thorn, Michael O'Kennedy, Henri Simonet, Simone Veil, and Edmund Wellenstein. These one-worlders are leading the nations of Western Europe — their own nations — not only into surrendering national sovereignty to Brussels, but into merging with the "former communist" regimes of Eastern Europe.

A study of the evolution of the European Community reveals ominous parallels with the campaign currently underway for the North

American Free Trade Agreement (NAFTA), signed by President George Bush on August 12, 1992. The EC is the model for this and other "common market" arrangements for Latin America, Asia, and Africa now being promoted by CFR Establishment figures and their globalist colleagues.

EC Emerges From Shadows of World War I

On November 9, 1988, European heads of state and government gathered in solemn ceremony at the Pantheon in Paris to inter the remains of Jean Monnet, the French internationalist who is often called "the Father of Europe." The celebration marking the centennial of his birth was the crowning highlight of numerous tributes in honor of the principal architect of the Common Market.

Jean Omar Marie Gabriel Monnet was born in Cognac, the son of a brandy merchant. In 1910, at the age of 20, he was sent to Canada by his father to open new markets for the family business. Hooking up with the Hudson Bay Company and the Lazard Brothers banking house, two of the Western Hemisphere's most eminent Establishment companies, the parvenu Frenchman was given entree into high British circles of power and soon became the protege of the Anglo-American Insiders. Thus began the mercurial rise of Jean Monnet, who — though lacking even the equivalent of a high school diploma — was to become a renowned wizard of high finance, a political mastermind, and a confidant and advisor to presidents and prime ministers.

Through the influence of French Foreign Minister Etienne Clementel, Monnet gained an exclusive and very lucrative contract for shipping vital materiel from Canada to France during World War I. Following that war, he won an appointment to the Allied Supreme Economic Council, was made an advisor to the committee preparing the Treaty of Versailles, and was introduced to that closed group of one-worlders around Colonel House that was preparing the way for the creation of the League of Nations. In 1919, he became an international figure at the age of 29 through his appointment as deputy secretary-general of the League.

Monnet, the committed internationalist, also became a steadfast socialist. Monnet biographers Merry and Serge Bromberger wrote:

"Behind the scenes he helped to arrange the appointment of the French Socialist Albert Thomas as head of the International Labor Office."[2] They also record Monnet's boast: "I've always voted Socialist, except on one occasion."[3] That single exception occurred during the 1965 French presidential election when he publicly supported Jean Lecanuet, a champion of a federated Europe.

In 1925, Monnet moved to America to accept a partnership with the Blair Foreign Corporation, a New York bank that had done a bonanza business in the "war effort." From there he went on to become vice president of Transamerica, the giant San Francisco-based holding company that owned Bank of America.

At that time there were many campaigns underway to create a United States of Europe. In 1923, Count Richard N. Coudenhove-Kalergi of Austria authored his book *Pan Europa*; three years later, he organized his first Pan European Congress in Vienna.[4] By the end of the 1920s, branches of the Pan European Union were operating throughout the continent and Britain.

In *How Can Europe Survive*, a piercing critique of Coudenhove's Pan European idea, the eminent free-market economist Hans F. Sennholz observed that there is no getting around "the fact that his plan is *a scheme for the attainment of wholesale socialism in Europe.*"[5] (Emphasis in original) Nevertheless, Coudenhove's plan received the support and patronage of many of Europe's leading statesmen and men of letters, not to mention that of the Anglo-American Establishment.

One of Count Coudenhove's most important disciples was Aristide Briand, who between 1909 and 1930 was the Socialist Premier of France 11 times and Minister of Foreign Affairs 12 times. In 1930, Briand unveiled a plan for "European Union" that provided for a regional supranational union within the League of Nations.[6] It failed not because of antipathy to the idea but largely because of differences of opinion among the various socialist and integrationist factions over the best means to accomplish the shared goal. That same year, another important apostle of Coudenhove's Pan Europa, Sir Winston Churchill, wrote an essay entitled "The United States of Europe" aimed at winning support for the idea from the American public. It was published in the February 15, 1930 issue of the *Sat-*

urday Evening Post, one of America's most popular periodicals at that time.

Coudenhove spent the devastating years of World War II in the United States propagating his Pan Europa idea. "In seeking to persuade America, once she became a belligerent, to adopt European unity as one of her war aims," said the Count's colleague and hagiographer Arnold J. Zurcher in *The Struggle to Unite Europe, 1940-1958*, "Count Coudenhove enlisted the cooperation of certain leading American citizens whom he had interested in his movement some years prior to his enforced wartime sojourn."[7] These "leading citizens" — all Establishment heavyweights — were: Nicholas Murray Butler, president of both Columbia University and the Carnegie Endowment for International Peace; Dr. Stephen Duggan, founder and first president of the International Institute of Education, a completely CFR-dominated internationalist propaganda operation; and William C. Bullitt, alternately U.S. ambassador to the Soviet Union and to France.

With the help of these high-powered patrons, Coudenhove and Zurcher obtained positions at New York University where, for the remainder of the war years, they conducted graduate seminars devoted exclusively to the need for European federation. Their CFR contacts aided them greatly in obtaining favorable media coverage. "The New York press, for example, was wholly sympathetic," wrote Zurcher, "both major morning dailies, *The New York Times* and the *New York Herald Tribune*, having given generous space to reporting the Count's occasional public utterances and to the efforts of the New York University seminar on federation."[8] With the academic respectability conferred by the NYU seminars and the popular dissemination of their ideas by a friendly press, said Zurcher, "For the first time in the twentieth century, the slogan 'United States of Europe' had become something more than a label for hortatory idealism."[9]

While Coudenhove-Kalergi and his sidekick Zurcher labored among the intelligentsia and the captains of industry in New York, Citizen Monnet was shuttling back and forth between Washington, Paris, and London on trans-Atlantic diplomatic missions for French Premier Edouard Daladier, President Roosevelt, Prime Minister

Churchill, and General de Gaulle. It was Monnet who gave Roosevelt the slogan "America will be the great arsenal of democracy" that the President would later use in one of his fireside chats.[10] "Monnet was above all a public relations man," claimed biographers Merry and Serge Bromberger. "He was particularly close to Harry Hopkins, Roosevelt's right-hand man. Through Hopkins he became the President's personal advisor on Europe."[11]

The close Roosevelt-Hopkins relationship has often been compared to the relationship between Wilson and House. In each case, there was almost total dependence of the president on a mysterious, shadowy advisor. Hopkins, like House, admired communism and played a key role in formulating many of the pro-Soviet policies of the Roosevelt Administration that proved so disastrous for the United States and the Free World. He and Monnet got along famously.

M. Bloch-Morhange, writing in the authoritative *Information Et Conjectures* for March 1957, summed up the French internationalist's pro-communist record this way: "Never in his long career has Jean Monnet a single time criticized the Soviet Union publicly." According to the Brombergers, "behind the scenes Monnet played an important role in the negotiations that prepared the ground for lend-lease,"[12] the operation that funneled to the USSR massive infusions of war materiel and money, even the blueprints and nuclear materials that enabled the Soviets to develop the atomic bomb.[13] The lend-lease program was supervised by Harry Hopkins.

In 1939 as World War II was about to begin, Clarence Streit, a Rhodes scholar and correspondent for the *New York Times*, authored *Union Now*.[14] In it, he advocated an immediate political union involving the U.S., Britain, Canada, and other Atlantic "democracies," and then, finally, world union. The book was lavishly praised in the CFR-dominated press and by 1949 had been translated into several languages, selling more than 300,000 copies.

Union Now and *Union Now With Britain*, published in 1941, gave rise to a sizable Federal Union movement (which later changed its name to Atlantic Union Committee and still later to the Atlantic Council of the United States), the leadership of which has always been top-heavy with CFR members. During the late 1970s, George

Bush sat on the Council's board of directors, along with Henry Kissinger, Winston Lord, and a long line-up of CFR-TC cronies. In 1942, Streit's Federal Union proposed the adoption of a joint resolution by Congress favoring immediate union with the aforementioned Atlantic states. The resolution had been written by John Foster Dulles (CFR), who was later to become Eisenhower's Secretary of State and a key player in the formation of Monnet's United Europe.[15]

One of the most ambitious and visionary schemes of this period was put forth in a book entitled *Plan for Permanent Peace* by Hans Heymann, a German economist and refugee who held a research and teaching post at Rutgers University. Funded by the Carnegie Endowment for International Peace, a perpetual font of world order schemes, *Plan for Permanent Peace* asserted:

> Nations have created international disharmony in the vain belief that harmony in our society can be achieved on a national basis.... This narrow-minded attitude has left us one strong hope, namely, that this fallacious concept may hold only during a transitional period.... After the debacle [World War II] an international organization will be imperative for the well-being of society as a whole.[16]

Heymann then detailed his scheme for a global superstate headed by a Federal World Authority, a Bank of Nations (with three branches: the Hemisphere Bank, Europa Bank, and the Oriental Bank), and a World Army, Navy, and Air Force.[17] *Plan for Permanent Peace* includes several ambitious fold-out maps and diagrams detailing the monstrous bureaucracy needed to regiment the hapless citizens of the proposed planetary union.

At the conclusion of World War II, the myriad of organizations, individuals, movements, and publications advocating various models of global governance all coalesced behind a concerted crusade to insure U.S. adoption of the United Nations Charter. Once that was accomplished, they returned to campaigning for what U.S. national security adviser Walt W. Rostow (CFR) would later term "an end to nationhood as it has been historically defined."[18] All of these individuals knew that the UN could never become a genuine world government as long as member nations retained any vestige of sovereignty and autonomy.

Winston Churchill and his son-in-law, Duncan Sandys, led the United Europe Movement, which convened a Congress of Europe at The Hague in May of 1948.[19] While world attention was focused on the glittering assembly of current and former heads of state — Churchill, Léon Blum, Alcide de Gasperi, Paul-Henri Spaak, et al. — it was Jean Monnet and the mysterious Polish Socialist, Joseph Retinger, the *bon vivant* and globe-trotting master of political intrigue, who ran the show.[20] One of the accomplishments of The Hague Congress was the adoption of seven Resolutions on Political Union. Resolution number seven stated: "The creation of a United Europe must be regarded as an essential step towards the creation of a United World."

Marshaling a United Socialist Europe

On June 5, 1947, General George C. Marshall, then Truman's Secretary of State, delivered a speech at Harvard University detailing the suffering and privation of war-ravaged Europe and calling for an American response.[21] Thus was launched the European Recovery Program (ERP) — better known as the Marshall Plan — a massive foreign aid program designed to restructure Europe along "cooperative," i.e., internationalist and socialist lines.

The ERP, however, did not originate with General Marshall, but rather with Jean Monnet and the Council on Foreign Relations. The Brombergers noted that prior to the Harvard speech, Marshall sent his assistant H. G. Clayton to confer with Monnet, and that Marshall himself conferred at length with Monnet at the Paris Peace Conference.[22] Laurence Shoup and William Minter, in their study of the CFR entitled *Imperial Brain Trust*, reported: "In 1946-1947 lawyer Charles M. Spofford headed a [CFR study] group, with banker David Rockefeller as secretary, on Reconstruction in Western Europe; in 1947-1948 that body was retitled the Marshall Plan."[23] David Rockefeller would later lead the Chase Manhattan Bank, serve as chairman of the board of the CFR from 1970-1985, launch the Trilateral Commission in 1973, and do everything he could to further the cause of global "interdependence."

The immediate problem faced by the Marshall Planners was selling the idea to Congress. There was considerable opposition to the scheme, led principally by Senator Robert Taft of Ohio, former President Herbert Hoover, and free-market economist and *Newsweek* commentator Henry Hazlitt. Taft and others argued that the proposed program would force U.S. taxpayers to subsidize the socialist policies of European governments — nationalization of industries, central planning, wage and price controls, excessive taxation, trade restrictions, burdensome regulation, currency devaluation — just the opposite of what was needed to help Europe recover from the war's devastation. They argued instead for a program that would unleash private enterprise to solve Europe's economic problems.

The Establishment responded by organizing an impressive assemblage of notables to campaign for the ERP. "The leadership of this group," said Michael J. Hogan, professor of history at Ohio State University and editor of *Diplomatic History*, "came largely from academic circles, from the major American trade unions, and from such business organizations as the Council on Foreign Relations (CFR), the Business Advisory Council (BAC), the Committee for Economic Development (CED) and the National Planning Association (NPA)."[24]

Strong promoters of the "New Deal synthesis," members of these groups "accepted the need for greater economic planning and for Keynesian strategies of fiscal and monetary management." These four organizations, said Professor Hogan, "played an important role in shaping and promoting the ERP," and in disarming the opposition.[25] "During the congressional hearings," Hogan wrote in his comprehensive study entitled *The Marshall Plan*, "these private leaders joined their government partners in a formidable defense of the ERP." Hogan explained:

> They published briefs on behalf of the program. Their spokesmen testified before the relevant congressional committees. They served on the President's Committee on Foreign Aid, or Harriman Committee, and on the Committee for the Marshall Plan to Aid European Recovery, a private, nonpartisan organization composed of labor, farm, and business leaders who worked closely with government officials to mobilize support behind the ERP. The result was something like a coordi-

nated campaign mounted by an interlocking directorate of public and private figures. Of the nineteen people on the executive board of the Marshall Plan Committee, eight were members of the CFR and two of these eight were also members of the BAC, CED, or NPA. Included in this list were Allen W. Dulles, president of the CFR, and Philip Reed, chairman of the board of General Electric. Former Secretaries of War Henry L. Stimson and Robert P. Patterson, along with former Under Secretary of State Dean Acheson, also served on the executive board.[26]

However, even with this massive and well-orchestrated campaign, the ERP advocates did not have it easy. They had originally packaged the plan as a humanitarian operation to alleviate the suffering, starvation, and devastation caused by the war. But Congress was not so willing to accept that Europe's economic woes could or should be solved by the American taxpayers.

So the Establishment one-worlders changed to a different tack: They said U.S. aid was urgently needed to protect Western Europe from the threat of communism. "People sat up and listened when the Soviet threat was mentioned" said John J. McCloy, the Insiders' Insider who was chairman of the CFR from 1953-1970. McCloy, who served as U.S. High Commissioner to Germany after the war, said his assignment there taught him a valuable lesson — that a good way to assure a viewpoint gets noticed is to cast it in terms of resisting the spread of Communism.[27]

The "chairman of the American establishment," McCloy, and his globalist CFR colleagues would master the lesson well. The "resisting communism" tactic was developed to such a fine degree that virtually any *pro-communist* policy could be sold to the American public if the *anti-communist* label was applied to it. That McCloy's "anticommunism" was a cynical charade is evident not only from statements like those above, but from the critical role he played in the many decisions and policies that proved so helpful to the communists and so harmful to America and the Free World over the course of his half century of "public service."[28]

McCloy's actions had not gone unnoticed by security agencies. Max Holland, contributing editor to *The Wilson Quarterly,* reported in the Autumn 1991 issue of that journal that the FBI had become concerned over McCloy's "leanings." Holland wrote:

> In a May [1946] memo, FBI head J. Edgar Hoover warned the Truman Administration of an "enormous Soviet espionage ring in Washington ... with reference to atomic energy," and identified McCloy along with Dean Acheson and Alger Hiss, as worrisome for "their pro-Soviet leanings."[29]

It was McCloy, who two years earlier, as Assistant Secretary of War, approved an order permitting Communist Party members to become officers in the U.S. Army. He defended identified Communist John Carter Vincent and supported J. Robert Oppenheimer after the scientist was denied a top security clearance. It was McCloy who organized the U.S. Arms Control and Disarmament Agency for President Kennedy and who, together with Soviet counterpart Valerian Zorin, drew up the 1961 *Freedom From War* surrender plan we have cited in previous chapters.[30]

President Truman also admitted paying lip service to anti-communism in order to win support for his European aid plan. His so-called Truman Doctrine — the policy of providing U.S. support to "democracies" around the globe supposedly to combat the spread of communism — was completely disingenuous. According to authors Walter Isaacson and Evan Thomas, when Secretary of State Marshall expressed concern that the President's "Truman Doctrine" speech was *too* anti-communist in tone, "The reply came back from Truman: without the rhetoric, Congress would not approve the money."[31]

The deception worked, and Congress did indeed approve the funding: some $13 billion dollars for the Marshall Plan, and tens of billions more through various other reconstruction programs. From the close of World War II through 1953, the United States government poured more than $43 billion into Europe. Professor Hans Sennholz described it as a "windfall for socialism," and in his *How Can Europe Survive* detailed the myriad of destructive government programs and wasteful state-owned monopolies that swallowed up these enormous funds while thwarting real economic growth and progress.

With the ERP, European socialists and one-worlders had hit on a veritable bonanza, and American Establishment Insiders had hit on a scheme that gave them the leverage they needed to push independent-minded European governments in a "cooperative" direction. "American officials interfered with foreign governments which endeavored to abolish controls and return to sounder principles of government," said Dr. Sennholz. "American Fair-Deal officials repeatedly exerted pressure on the Belgian and German governments to inflate their national currencies at a greater degree and create more credit through simple expansion. Fortunately for these nations, their governments usually resisted this Fair-Deal pressure."[32]

"Through American aid," said Professor Hogan, "and particularly through the use of counterpart funds, Marshall Planners tried to underwrite industrial modernization projects, promote Keynesian strategies of aggregate economic management, [and] ... encourage progressive tax policies, low-cost housing programs, and other measures of economic and social reform."[33] From its very inception, the ERP's main purpose was to destroy the European nation-states by merging them into a regional government. The early planning for the program was carried out by a special agency called the State-War-Navy Coordinating Committee (SWNCC) under the direction of George Kennan. One of the concerns of the agency, wrote Hogan, was *"to consider how national sovereignties might be transcended.* As Joseph Jones, who attended the meetings, recalled, the State Department's economic officers encouraged committee members to think of Europe as a whole and to administer aid in ways that would foster economic unification."[34] (Emphasis added)

Of course, not everyone advocating the abolition of Europe's sovereign governments was so subtle. Some pursued an open frontal approach. On March 21, 1947, before Marshall had made his Harvard speech, Senators William Fulbright and Elbert D. Thomas submitted to Congress the following concurrent resolution: "Resolved by the Senate (the House of Representatives concurring) that the Congress favors the creation of a United States of Europe."

The CFR-Insider press sprang forth to champion the incredibly arrogant Fulbright resolution. According to the March 17, 1947 issue of *Life* magazine (whose publisher, Henry Luce, was a leading

CFR member), "our policy should be to help the nations of Europe federate as our states federated in 1787." "Europe desperately needs some effective form of political and economic federation," wrote Sumner Welles (CFR) in the *Washington Post*, owned by CFR member Eugene Meyer. The *Christian Science Monitor* (long a CFR mouthpiece) advised on April 28, 1947: "For its part, the U.S. could hardly impose federation on Europe, but it could counsel.... It could mold its leading and occupation policies toward upbuilding a single continental economy." The *New York Times*, the Establishment's most influential organ, editorialized on April 18, 1947: "But it is only too true ... that Europe must federate or perish." The *St. Louis Post Dispatch* of March 16, 1947 declared that "for Europe it is a case of join — or die."[35]

Cooler heads among the "brain trust" realized, however, that any attempt at openly forcing a European federation would stir nationalist resistance and resentment in Europe, and would rightly be viewed as American imperialism. *They had to make it appear that the call for a United States of Europe was coming from "the people" of Europe themselves.*

The most informative account of the role of America's Insider Establishment in organizing the movement for a United Europe can be found in a six-part report about the Common Market appearing in the authoritative *H. du B. Reports* during 1972 and 1973. Written by geo-political analyst Hilaire du Berrier, an American who has been publishing his highly respected intelligence reports from Europe for more than 30 years, the "Story of the Common Market" series details the intrigues of the American CFR-Atlantic Council-Bilderberger-Trilateral Commission combine and its European accomplices in their joint campaign for a supra-national European government. In part five of his series, du Berrier relates a story from the diary of Joseph Retinger that illustrates how the CFR's agents built the movement for European merger. Retinger was seeking more funds for the European Movement headed at the time by Belgian Prime Minister Paul-Henri Spaak, who was affectionately known in Europe as "Mr. Socialist." Du Berrier wrote:

Retinger and Duncan Sandys, the British Eurocrat, went to see John

J. McCloy, who in 1947 was American High Commissioner to Germany. McCloy, we learn from Retinger's diary, embraced the idea at once. Sheppard Stone, who was on McCloy's staff, and Robert Murphy, the U.S. ambassador to Belgium, whom Retinger called one of the European Movement's best supporters, joined McCloy in raiding the huge reserve of European currencies called 'counterpart funds' which had piled up as a result of Marshall Plan aid.... McCloy, Stone and Murphy "promptly and unhesitatingly put ample funds at the disposal of Paul Henri Spaak," Retinger recorded.[36]

It was this same Joseph Retinger who recruited Prince Bernhard of the Netherlands to host the meeting at the Hotel Bilderberg in Oosterbeek, Holland in May 1954 that launched the annual secretive Bilderberger conclaves where the international ruling elite meet to scheme and palaver. McCloy would become a member of the Bilderberger steering committee.[37]

The Merger Begins

The first concrete step toward the abolition of the European nation-states was taken in 1951 with the signing of the treaty creating the European Coal and Steel Community (ECSC). "This was a truly revolutionary organization," wrote Professor Carroll Quigley, the Insiders' own *inside* historian, "since it had sovereign powers, including the authority to raise funds outside any existing state's power."[38]

The ECSC treaty, which went into force in July 1952, merged the coal and steel industries of six countries (West Germany, France, Italy, Belgium, the Netherlands, and Luxembourg) under a single High Authority. Professor Quigley wrote in his 1966 history of the world, *Tragedy and Hope:*

> This "supranational" body had the right to control prices, channel investment, raise funds, allocate coal and steel.... Its powers to raise funds for its own use by taxing each ton produced made it independent of governments. Moreover, its decisions were binding, and could be reached by majority vote without the unanimity required in most international organizations of sovereign states.[39]

The proposal for the ECSC was introduced, amidst great fanfare, in May 1950 as the "Schuman Plan." Although Monsieur Monnet, then head of France's General Planning Commission, was the real author of the plan, he thought it expedient to name it for his comrade Robert Schuman, the Socialist French Foreign Minister who later became Prime Minister.[40]

The American Insiders leapt to praise the Schuman Plan. John Foster Dulles called it "brilliantly creative."[41] Dean Acheson termed it a "major contribution toward the resolution of the pressing political and economic problems of Europe."[42] And President Truman called it "an act of constructive statesmanship."[43] The Carnegie Foundation awarded Monnet its Wateler Peace Prize of two million francs "in recognition of the international spirit which he had shown in conceiving the Coal and Steel Community...."[44]

Monnet, whom columnist Joseph Alsop (CFR) called the "good, gray wizard of Western European union,"[45] was appointed the first president of the powerful new ECSC. Monnet knew full well just how powerful and revolutionary his new creation was. Merry and Serge Bromberger reported in *Jean Monnet and the United States of Europe* that when Monnet and his "brain trust" had outlined the basics of the ECSC proposal, they called in legal expert Maurice Lagrange to take care of the detail work. The Brombergers wrote:

> Lagrange was stunned. An idea of revolutionary daring had been launched and was being acclaimed by the Six and the United States — a minerals and metals superstate.... "I hope the structure will stand up," Monnet said dubiously.
>
> The brain trust worked feverishly from ten o'clock in the morning until midnight, without taking Sundays or holidays off, not even Christmas day. Even the secretaries and the office boys were infected by the general excitement, by the feeling that they were part of a fantastic undertaking.[46]

The Brombergers, who are ardent admirers of Monnet, then admit the conspiratorial and totalitarian mind-set of their hero:

> Gradually, it was thought, the supranational authorities, supervised

by the European Council of Ministers at Brussels and the Assembly in Strasbourg, would administer all the activities of the Continent. A day would come when governments would be forced to admit that an integrated Europe was an accomplished fact, without their having had a say in the establishment of its underlying principles. All they would have to do was to merge all these autonomous institutions into a single federal administration and then proclaim a United States of Europe....

Actually, the founders of the Coal and Steel Community would have to obtain from the various national governments — justifiably reputed to be incapable of making sacrifices for the sake of a federation — a whole series of concessions in regard to their sovereign rights until, having been finally stripped, they committed hara-kiri by accepting the merger.[47]

Realizing that some nations might at some point rebel against the "new order," the "good gray wizard" and his Eurocrats sought to establish their own army, which they dubbed the European Defense Community (EDC). After clamoring for national disarmament, the Eurocrat pacifists were now demanding that an independent armed forces complete with nuclear weapons be put under their command.[48] The EDC treaty was signed by the six ECSC nations in 1952, but plans for the supranational army fell apart when, after two years of bitter debate, the treaty was rejected by the French Parliament.

The next nail in the coffin of European national sovereignty came on March 25, 1957 with the signing by the six ECSC nations of the two Treaties of Rome. These created the European Economic Community (EEC or Common Market) and the European Atomic Energy Community (Euratom), which greatly furthered the process of merging the economic and energy sectors of the member states. (The ECSC, Euratom, and EEC are now collectively referred to as the European Community or EC.)

"The EEC Treaty," said Carroll Quigley, "with 572 articles over almost 400 pages ... looked forward to eventual political union in Europe, and sought economic integration as an essential step on the way."[49] But the merger architects settled on an approach of patient gradualism; what Richard N. Gardner (CFR) would later call "an end run around national sovereignty, eroding it piece by piece."[50] According to the late Professor Quigley, "This whole process was to be achieved by stages over many years."[51]

The next stage involved bringing the rest of Western Europe into the fold. In 1973 the United Kingdom, after more than two decades of resisting, came in, as did Ireland and Denmark. Greece joined in 1981, bringing the number of member states to ten. Spain and Portugal became the 11th and 12th members in 1986.

"The CFR," wrote du Berrier in January 1973, "saw the Common Market from the first as a regional government to which more and more nations would be added until the world government which the UN had failed to bring about would be realized. At a favorable point in the Common Market's development, America would be brought in. But the American public had to be softened first and leaders groomed for the change-over."

The CFR spared no expense or effort in aiding its European co-conspirators, especially Jean Monnet, to establish their dreamed-of Brave New World. A very enlightening source on this phenomenon is Insider Ernst H. van der Beugel, honorary secretary general of the Bilderberger Group, vice chairman of the Netherlands Institute for Foreign Affairs (a CFR affiliate), Harvard lecturer, etc. In his book *From Marshall Aid to Atlantic Partnership* — which contains a foreword by "my friend Henry Kissinger" — Trilateralist-Bilderberger van der Beugel explained:

> Not only has Monnet been the auctor intellectualis of many steps on the road to European unification, he has also been a driving force in the execution of existing plans.
>
> His most remarkable capacity has been his great influence on the formulation of United States policy towards Europe.
>
> He exercised this influence through a network of close friendships and relationships, some of them going back to the pre-war period.[52]

Explaining further the workings of the Monnet-CFR symbiosis, van der Beugel cited examples of the diplomatic bludgeoning of those officials who balked at administering national "hara-kiri." For instance, he reported how Monnet's Action Committee, which was "supported by funds from United States foundations," ramrodded the negotiations for the Rome Treaties:

> Monnet and his Action Committee were unofficially supervising the negotiations and as soon as obstacles appeared, the United States diplomatic machinery was alerted, mostly through Ambassador Bruce ... who had immediate access to the top echelon of the State Department....
>
> At that time, it was usual that if Monnet thought that a particular country made difficulties in the negotiations, the American diplomatic representative in that country approached the Foreign Ministry in order to communicate the opinion of the American Government which, in practically all cases, coincided with Monnet's point of view.[53]

Monnet's high-level friends, who assisted him in these strong-arm tactics, included President Eisenhower, John Foster Dulles, John J. McCloy, David Bruce, Averell Harriman, George Ball, and C. Douglas Dillon.[54]

Monnet's diabolical designs are coming to fruition at a frightening pace. The Single European Act (SEA) and the Maastricht Accords are intended to make political and economic union irreversible. Citizens of the EC countries are finding their lives and livelihoods increasingly controlled by Eurocrats in Brussels, even as national governments find their sovereign rights sacrificed under such deliberately vague and ambiguous rubrics as "cooperation," "union," "integration," "convergence," and "harmonization." Soon it will be impossible for member states to block policies that are clearly harmful to their national interests. EC Commissioner Willy De Clercq, in a 1987 speech, boasted that the SEA should make it possible for two-thirds of the EC decisions to be made by a qualified majority, in contrast to the 90 percent of decisions that previously required unanimous consent.[55]

In his prophetic book *New Lies for Old*, published appropriately in 1984, KGB defector Anatoliy Golitsyn warned of the coming "false liberalization" in the Soviet Union and Eastern Europe. This deception, he predicted with uncanny accuracy, would be embraced by the West and would lead to "a merger between the EEC [European Economic Community, now referred to simply as the European Community, EC] and Comecon," the Council of Mutual Economic Assistance of Communist States. Once that occurred, Golitsyn stated, the "European Parliament might become an all-European socialist parliament with representation from the Soviet Union and Eastern Europe. 'Europe from the Atlantic to the Urals' would turn out to be a neutral, socialist Europe."[56] It is happening as he predicted.

This "Finlandization" of Europe does not seem to bother the new world order ruling elite, however. In 1990 the Council on Foreign Relations and the Royal Institute of International Affairs jointly published a study entitled *The Transformation of Western Europe*. Written by RIIA Deputy Director William Wallace, it triumphantly proclaimed:

> We face, as Pierre Hassner has remarked, "not the Finlandization of Western Europe which Americans feared, but the Brusselization of Eastern Europe."[57]

To which the obvious response should be, "What is the difference?" More and more, the plans of the CFR-Trilateral-Bilderberg elite converge with and become indistinguishable from those of the Kremlin. Stalin's 1936 official program of the Communist International declared:

> This world dictatorship can be established only when the victory of socialism has been achieved in certain countries or groups of countries, when the newly established proletarian republics enter into a federative union with the already existing proletarian republics ... [and] when these federations of republics have finally grown into a World Union of Soviet Socialist Republics uniting the whole of mankind under the hegemony of the international proletariat organized as a state.[58]

Is the Stalin formula essentially different from the globalist vision announced by former German Foreign Minister Hans-Dietrich Genscher, one of the most outspoken proponents of full-tilt European unification? Speaking about "The Future of Europe" in Lisbon, Portugal on July 12, 1991, he declared: "The road points not backward to the nation-state of the past.... *Basically, it is a matter of constructing a world order of peace in which the United Nations must at last play the central role assigned it in its Charter.*[59] (Emphasis added)

And there we have a clear admission that the economic and political union of European nations is not the final goal of these socialist and internationalist manipulators. What they have always sought ultimately is control of the entire planet by the United Nations.

The upside-down pentagram, often superimposed on a goat's head, is a common symbol in occult and satanic ritual. The circle of upside-down stars in the poster on the opposing page, ostensibly representing the nations of the European Community, would appear to be a conscious attempt by the artist to convey an occultic message.

Famous painting of the Tower of Babel by 16th century Flemish artist Bruegel (above) depicts the well-known event described in the Book of Genesis. For their arrogant actions, the Bible says, God divided and confused them with different languages.

254

The Council of Europe's decision to employ the Tower of Babel in this poster as the central motif symbolizing their efforts to build the European suprastate is a telling choice. It would appear to be an open statement of defiance to God, particularly considering that the stars have been intentionally inverted to form occult pentagrams.

The European Parliament in Strasbourg, France. The 518-member body, dominated by the Socialist parties, is taking the EC further in the socialist direction and gradually overriding national legislatures.

The EC Commission, which wields most of the power in the EC governing agreement, is top heavy with socialist one-worlders, members of the Trilateral Commission pushing surrender of national sovereignty to supranational EC government.

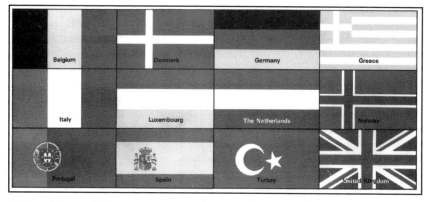

National flags of European countries have not been totally displaced by the EC flag, but if the Maastricht Treaty is adopted, the nations of Europe will be submerged in a socialist bureaucratic state, their flags merely hollow symbols.

Berlaymont Building where EC Commission is headquartered in Brussels. Europeans are finding that more and more aspects of their lives are being dictated by the Eurocrats in Brussels, the EC Court of Justice in Luxembourg, and the EC Parliament in Strasbourg.

EC Commission President Jacques Delors leads Insiders' assault against European national sovereignty.

Insider Jean Monnet, "Father of the Common Market," was adviser to presidents and prime ministers.

Soviet agent Harry Hopkins was FDR's closest confidant and Monnet's key connection to the White House.

The Marshall Plan, named after George Marshall, originated with the CFR and Jean Monnet.

Jean Monnet (left) and French Foreign Minister (later Prime Minister) Robert Schuman, architects of the EC. With U.S. funds from the Marshall Plan and tax-exempt foundations, and strong-arm help from CFR's Eisenhower, McCloy, Dulles, et al, they built "support" for the EC idea.

For more than three decades, Monte Carlo-based foreign affairs analyst Hilaire du Berrier has provided the most detailed exposés of the conspiratorial designs of the EC schemers in his intelligence newsletter, *H. du B. Reports.*

President Truman (left) and "Chairman of the Establishment" John J. McCloy. As U.S. High Commissioner in Germany, McCloy (CFR) used Marshall Plan funds to support socialism and the United Europe movement. J. Edgar Hoover warned Truman about McCloy's "pro-Soviet leanings."

McCloy supported pro-communist atom bomb scientist J. Robert Oppenheimer after he was denied a security clearance.

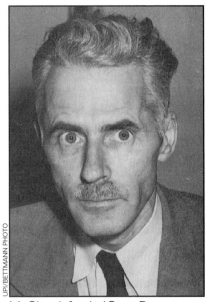

McCloy defended State Department Communist John Carter Vincent, a key player in our betrayal of China to the Reds.

CHAPTER 14

Get US out!

The U.N. has become a trap. Let's go it alone.[1]
— U.S. Senator Robert Taft

Until my dying day, I will regret signing the United Nations Charter.[2]
— U.S. Senator Patrick McCarran

[T]he time has come to recognize the United Nations for the anti-American, anti-freedom organization that it has become. The time has come for us to cut off all financial help, withdraw as a member, and ask the United Nations to find a headquarters location outside the United States that is more in keeping with the philosophy of the majority of voting members, someplace like Moscow or Peking.[3]
— U.S. Senator Barry Goldwater

Unless the U.N. is completely reorganized without the Communist nations in it, we should get out of it.[4]
— former President Herbert Hoover

More than at any time in its history, the United Nations should indeed be recognizable as a terrible trap. Yet the nations of the world continue marching forward, step by step, into a UN-led global tyranny. Like sleep-walking automatons, oblivious to approaching peril, millions of normally intelligent individuals pass by the danger signs each day without paying the slightest notice. The world's peoples seem incapable of comprehending the looming danger, even though it is so plainly evident.

Ours is the age of omnipotent government. Because it is, we have had ample exposure to the lessons of totalitarianism; we have no excuse if we close our eyes and minds to the danger. We can take no refuge behind a plea of "ignorance." It has been well observed that the "increasing quantity of government, in all nations, has constituted the greatest tragedy of the twentieth century."[5] This tragedy, however, is but the manifestation of an even deeper spiritual tragedy: the decreasing quantity and quality of the Christian faith in all nations.

The century now drawing to a close has witnessed man's greatest achievements in science, engineering, and technological progress. Our monumental advances in medicine, agriculture, communications, transportation, space exploration, and virtually every field of learning have far eclipsed the most ambitious hopes of those who lived only a generation ago. So sweeping and breathtakingly rapid have these advances come that peoples everywhere have been seduced by the "gospel of progress," the beguiling doctrine of salvation through the all-powerful cognitive powers of man. "Science" and "reason," this secular faith contends, will ultimately triumph over religious "superstition" and then usher in a new age of enlightenment, peace, prosperity, and continuous progress.

The adherents of this "new" faith come in many stripes. Their "spiritual" lineage may be traced to Rousseau, Bacon, Hume, Descartes, Kant, Weishaupt, Marx, Lenin, Asimov, or a myriad of other masters. Darwin is certainly one of the leading points of light in this glittering firmament.

Charles Darwin was not the originator of the ideas that have led to the abandonment of belief in the existence of objective, transcendent truth. "But Darwin's role was to dignify these ideas with 'scientific' backing and to make them accessible to the average man in terms he could understand," observed Jane H. Ingraham. "His shattering 'explanation' of the evolution of man from the lower animals through means excluding the supernatural delivered the *coup de grace* to man's idea of himself as a created being in a world of fixed truth. Confronted with the 'scientific proof' of his own animal origin and nature, Western man, set free at last from God, began the long trek through scientific rationalism, environmental determinism, cultural conditioning, perfectibility of human nature, behaviorism, and secular humanism to today's inverted morality and totalitarian man."[6] The rejection of Divine revelation and the sovereignty of God has resulted in the enthronement of man's "reason" as the ultimate source of truth and the apotheosis of the State as the supreme authority.

More recently, we have seen defections from the cult of science to the cult of nature. But, as was discussed in earlier chapters, this development has involved merely switching from one pagan "church" to another, while maintaining the same faith in the god of the State.

More Deadly Than War

The fruits of this "faith" have been horrific as totalitarianism (fascism, nazism, communism, socialism, etc.) and its various wars and revolutions have wrought death, suffering, and destruction on a scale undreamt of before. There are few who will argue the point that war is hell, and that a nation should go to great lengths to avoid it. *But is war the ultimate evil? Must we be willing to accept anything — even tyranny and slavery — in order to avoid war?* Before answering, the peace-at-any-price advocates would do well to consider the sobering research compiled by Professor R. J. Rummel about the human cost of 20th century totalitarianism. The results of Dr. Rummel's exhaustive investigation, published under the title *Lethal Politics: Soviet Genocide and Mass Murder Since 1917,* can be ignored only at the peril of every living being on this planet. The "shocking" (his own word) conclusion of the professor's meticulous research is mind-numbing. Rummel found that

... independent of war and other kinds of conflict — governments probably have murdered 119,400,000 people — Marxist governments about 95,200,000 of them. By comparison, the battle-killed in all foreign and domestic wars in this century total 35,700,000.

These monstrous statistics sharply reoriented my research. For more than thirty years as a political scientist and peace researcher, I had focused my research on the causes and conditions of war, conflict, and peace. I had believed that war was the greatest killer and that nuclear war would be a global holocaust. Now I have found that the total killed by government in cold blood was almost four times that of war. *It was as though a nuclear war had already occurred.*[7] [Emphasis in original]

The "Cold War" body count alone is at least 22.5 million. That's the number of human beings murdered by the Soviet Communists from the end of World War II until 1987. To describe this phenomenon of mass homicide, Dr. Rummel, a professor of political science at the University of Hawaii, coined the word "democide," which he defined as "a government's concentrated, systematic, and serial murder of a large part of its population."[8]

For Soviet democide alone, Rummel arrived at "the most probable estimate of 61,911,000 murdered." This, he pointed out, "is more than *four* times the battle dead (15,000,000) for all nations in the Second World War. Indeed, it exceeds the total deaths (35,654,000) from all this century's international, civil, guerrilla, and liberation wars, including the Russian Civil War itself."[9] (Emphasis in original)

For still another quantitative perspective, the professor reported that "from 1918 to 1953 [the Lenin-Stalin years], the Soviet government executed, slaughtered, starved, beat or tortured to death, or otherwise killed some 39.5 million of its own people.... In China, under Mao Tse-tung, the communist government eliminated ... 45 million people. The number killed in just these two nations is about 84.5 million, or a *lethality of 252% more than both world wars together.*" (Emphasis added) "Yet," asks Rummel, "have the world community and intellectuals generally shown anything like the same horror or outrage over these Soviet and Chinese megakillings as has been directed at the much less deadly world wars?"[10]

These figures, horrendous as they are, do not begin to tell the whole story. Quantitatively, it is very likely that they err on the low side and, says Rummel, "may underestimate the true total by 10 percent or more. Moreover, they do not even include the 1921-1922 Soviet famine and the 1958-1961 Chinese famine, which caused about four million and 27 million deaths, respectively."[11] Those deaths should certainly be included, since they were the direct, intended result of conscious, cold-blooded policies of the communist regimes.

The figures also do not include suicides, which by many accounts occurred in very significant numbers due to widespread fear, terror, shock, and despair under Soviet totalitarianism. From a qualitative perspective, it is impossible for the raw statistics to convey the immeasurable mental, physical, and spiritual agonies suffered by each of those millions of souls who were starved, tortured, executed, or otherwise disposed of as if they were nothing more than so much debris.[12]

Furthermore, says Rummel, "these figures do not measure the misery among those loved ones left alive, the mothers and fathers, the husbands or wives, or the children, friends, and lovers of those killed. No accounting is made of those who died of heartbreak, who gave up on life and succumbed to disease or privation, or whose remaining years were full of anguish and bitterness."[13]

All of this horrendous record of annihilation and desolation can be attributed, says Rummel, to *"utopia empowered,"* the "melding of an *idea* and *power*." (Emphasis in original) It is the natural and inevitable result of the implementation of Lenin's brutal dictum: "The scientific concept of dictatorship means nothing else but this: power without limit, resting directly upon force, restrained by no laws, absolutely unrestricted by rules."[14]

Anyone truly committed to the cause of peace must confront the terrible realities that are the ineluctable consequences of Lenin's unrestricted absolutism. They are: 1) Unrestrained government invariably results in the regime waging war against its own people, a development described by G. Edward Griffin as "more deadly than war [between nations]"[15]; and 2) governments not bound by strict constitutional limits and vigilant, moral citizens are those most likely to cause wars with other nations. In fact, notes Dr. Rummel:

> Absolutist governments ... are not only many times deadlier than war, but are themselves the major factor causing war and other forms of violent conflict. They are a major cause of militarism. Indeed, absolutism, not war, is mankind's deadliest scourge of all.[16]

Rummel observes that the essential wisdom to be gained from any study of utopian barbarism, empowered and unlimited, is that *the more freedom in a nation, the fewer people killed by government. Freedom serves as a brake on a governing elite's power over life and death.*"[17] (Emphasis added) And this salutary freedom is itself, of course, the result of keeping government small and strictly contained. No one who wants to be free should forget Lord Acton's famous axiom, "Power tends to corrupt and absolute power corrupts absolutely." From the Christian perspective, it could more accurately be said that power tends *further* to corrupt man (any man) because of his already fallen, sinful, corrupt nature.

This unfortunate but unassailable fact about government power was duly noted and amply illustrated decades before Rummel's revelations by Harvard University sociologist Pitirim A. Sorokin. In 1956 Professor Sorokin published the results of his own survey of the criminality of rulers. His study of various heads of state, in a selection large enough to constitute a very fair sample, demonstrated that there was an average of one murderer for every four of these rulers! "In other words," said Professor Sorokin, "the rulers of the states are the most criminal group in a respective population. With a limitation of their power their criminality tends to decrease; but it still remains exceptionally high in all nations."[18]

Commenting on Sorokin's findings, John Birch Society founder Robert Welch observed:

> An obvious reason for this is the greater temptation to criminality on the part of those who control or influence the police power of a nation, of which they would otherwise stand in more fear. Another is that ambitious men with criminal tendencies naturally gravitate into government because of this very prospect of doing, or helping to do, the policing over themselves. A third reason is that so many apologists can always be found, for criminal acts of governments, on the grounds that such acts ultimately contribute to the public good and that therefore the criminal means are justified by the righteous ends.[19]

Bind Them Down From Mischief

The framers of our constitutional system were hardly unaware of these truths. "Whoever would found a state and make proper laws for the government of it," said John Adams, "must presume that all men are bad by nature."[20]

"If men were angels," concurred James Madison, "no government would be necessary. If angels were to govern men, neither external nor internal controls on government would be necessary. In framing a government which is to be administered by men over men, the great difficulty lies in this: you must first enable the government to control the governed; and in the next place oblige it to control itself."[21] The difficulty referred to by these men should be readily appreciated by all who seriously ponder the perennial problems of governance.

Aldous Huxley, who was certainly neither a constitutionalist nor a conservative, grasped it well. Sounding remarkably like Adams and many other early Americans, he noted:

> In actual practice how many great men have ever fulfilled, or are ever likely to fulfill, the conditions which alone render power innocuous to the ruler as well as to the ruled? Obviously, very few. Except by saints, the problem of power is finally insoluble. But since genuine self-government is possible only in very small groups, societies on a national or supernational scale will always be ruled by oligarchical minorities whose members come to power because they have a lust for power.[22]

Unrestricted "democracy," that modern political idol, offers no solution to the dilemma. For as John Adams again accurately observed, "We may appeal to every page of history we have hitherto turned over, for proofs irrefragable, that the people, when they have been unchecked, have been as unjust, tyrannical, brutal, barbarous and cruel as any king or senate possessed of uncontrollable power."[23]

Adams fully comprehended the fundamental truth of George Washington's maxim, "Government is not reason; it is not eloquence; it is force! Like fire, it is a dangerous servant and a fearful master."[24] In order that it remain the servant and not become the master, it is incumbent upon the citizenry to keep governmental force small, fragmented and decentralized, allowing it only those powers necessary to perform its essential functions, and scrupulously guarding against the temptation to rely on government to do for them what they ought to do for themselves. It was this philosophy of strictly limited government that Thomas Jefferson endorsed in his first inaugural address when he stated:

> [A] wise and frugal Government, which shall restrain men from in-
> juring one another, shall leave them otherwise free to regulate their
> own pursuits of industry and improvement, and shall not take from
> the mouth of labor the bread it has earned. This is the sum of good
> government.... [25]

The key to effectuating this "good government" is, first of all, a
moral people. A society of moral people who practice self-restraint,
respect the rights and property of others, responsibly provide for
themselves and their families, and voluntarily practice charity toward the truly destitute, have no need for large government. But a
moral people must also be a wise people if they are not to fall victim
to the tyranny of good intentions. For, as Daniel Webster sagely remarked:

> Good intention will always be pleaded for every assumption of
> power.... It is hardly too strong to say that the Constitution was made
> to guard the people against the dangers of good intentions. There are
> men in all ages who mean to govern well, but they mean to govern.
> They promise to be good masters, but they mean to be masters. [26]

Always, the would-be masters promise to supply this benefit and
inaugurate that program, or to solve this problem and provide for
that need. But before they can "give" to one, they must first take
from another. To do so, they must assume more power. They say,
"trust me." Thomas Jefferson, who would have none of it, warned
that "confidence is everywhere the parent of despotism.... In questions of power let no more be heard of confidence in man, but bind
him down from mischief by the chains of the constitution." [27]
Are these "first principles" any less valid today than they were
two centuries ago? Has human nature so drastically changed for the
better that these warnings should no longer be heeded? Are the rulers of the nations that make up the United Nations saints and angels with whom we may confidently entrust unrestrained powers?
More than a hundred million voices of the victims of totalitarianism

in this century alone cry out from their graves with a thunderous "NO! NEVER!" The recent findings of Professor Rummel, together with all the recorded history of our world, echo that cry and solemnly warn those who would indulge such vain hopes and folly that they are inviting global tyranny and democide of a magnitude never seen before on this planet.

Answering UN Clichés

But we will place constitutional limits on the United Nations or any other world-state system.

This is the plea, for instance, of *Time* magazine's Editor-at-Large Strobe Talbott (CFR director, TC). His blatant appeal for world government, "The Birth of the Global Nation," appeared in the July 20, 1992 issue of *Time*. The global government he envisions, he claims, "is not an all-powerful Leviathan or centralized superstate, but a federation, a union of separate states that allocate certain powers to a central government while retaining many others for themselves." We hear these explanations and many others like them. Yet who but a fool believes that promises to limit world authority would be kept — even if such commitments were made in good faith by honorable men.

Addressing the Virginia Convention in 1788, Madison stated: "I believe there are more instances of the abridgement of the freedom of the people by gradual and silent encroachments of those in power than by violent and sudden usurpations."[28]

Jefferson, writing in 1800 about this same concern for our new government, expressed his belief that "a single consolidated government would become the most corrupt government on the earth."[29] Twenty-one years later he remarked, "Our government is now taking so steady a course as to show by what road it will pass to destruction, to wit: by consolidation first, and then corruption, its necessary consequence."[30]

If these men could entertain such pessimistic views of government and perceive the dangers in their day when government was remarkably smaller, the populace still vigilant, and the constitutional chains still firm, how is it possible that the far greater peril from our own ever-growing government and the incalculable dangers of global government under the UN create so little apprehension?

It is painfully obvious to anyone with eyes to see that abridgements of our freedom by gradual and silent encroachments have already proceeded to the point that the federal government has very nearly become our "fearful master." And the consolidation and corruption in Washington have indeed followed the grim course outlined by Jefferson, though he could not possibly have imagined the incredible depravity to which government has sunk in our day. Certainly there is nothing in our present predicament to contradict this warning expressed by Jefferson:

> When all government, domestic and foreign, in little as in great things, shall be drawn to Washington as the centre of all power, it will render powerless the checks provided of one government on another, and will become as venal and oppressive as the government from which we separated.[31]

If Jefferson's admonition was valid concerning our national government — and it was — it must apply infinitely more to a centralized global government. Considering the past and present makeup of the United Nations membership, the background of the communist criminals and conspirators who founded the organization, and the total lack of fundamental constitutional restraints in the UN Charter to protect against encroachment or usurpation, there can be no excuse whatsoever for any hope that, once vested with increased power, the UN will not abuse it. To restrain growing UN power we must contend against not only the natural tendency toward the accumulation of power in government but also a longstanding, organized conspiracy of powerful forces working to build, piece by piece, step by step, an omnipotent global government.

The Club of Rome asserts that "world policing will have to be provided under the authority of the United Nations,"[32] and virtually every day brings new proposals from official sources and private groups for UN policing and control of the environment, the economy, industry — essentially every part of the globe and every aspect of our lives. Strobe Talbott's assurances notwithstanding, UN conventions on ozone depletion, carbon dioxide and biodiversity, and the massive Agenda 21 program for global ecofascism have the potential all by themselves to turn the UN into "an all-powerful Leviathan or centralized superstate."

The UN is the world's last best hope for peace.

This cliché has achieved near universal acceptance because of sheer repetition; it has been repeated so often that people assume it must be true. However, only by some tortured application of Orwellian "Newspeak" can the UN be referred to as a "peace" organization.

During the summer of 1945, Ambassador J. Reuben Clark, Jr., one of America's foremost scholars in the field of international law, prepared an analysis of the UN Charter. His learned appraisal and cogent remarks fly in the face of popular platitudes and conventional "wisdom" concerning the "revered" document. Ambassador Clark's examination led him to conclude that the Charter "is a war document not a peace document," and that it "is built to prepare for war, not to promote peace." The Ambassador noted:

[T]here is no provision in the Charter itself that contemplates ending war. It is true the Charter provides for force to bring peace, but such use of force is itself war. [33]

Moreover, said Ambassador Clark,

Not only does the Charter Organization not prevent future wars, but it makes practically certain that we shall have future wars, and as to such wars it takes from us the power to declare them, to choose the side on which we shall fight, to determine what forces and military equipment we shall use in the war, and to control and command our sons who do the fighting. [34]

The Ambassador's predictions were soon borne out — first in Korea and then in Vietnam, the first two wars America fought with UN involvement and the only two which the United States has ever failed to win. [35]

Dr. J. B. Matthews, former chief investigator for the House Committee on Un-American Activities and one of America's outstanding scholars on Marxist-Leninist theory and practice, was but one of many leading Americans who exposed the UN-as-peace-dove myth. Dr. Matthews was not one to mince words. "I challenge the illusion that the UN is an instrument of peace," he said. "It could not be less of a cruel hoax if it had been organized in Hell for the sole purpose of aiding and abetting the destruction of the United States."[36] Senator William Langer (R-ND), one of only two senators with enough courage and foresight to vote against the UN Charter, said "I feel from the bottom of my heart that the adoption of the Charter ... will mean perpetuating war."[37]

The UN's monstrous war against the people of Katanga should forever lay to rest any reference to the UN as a peace organization. The UN and its supporters may persist in the charade of calling the UN's warmaking powers "peacemaking" or "peacekeeping," but no sensible person of goodwill should give the slightest credence to such patently deceitful abuse of language.

We cannot have peace as long as the world is divided into warring countries and armaments continue to proliferate. Only a disarmed world under some world authority offers an answer.

Observing that wars are most often between nations, many people mistakenly believe that nationhood itself is the cause of war and have thus fallen for the fallacious argument that an "end to nationhood" would mean an end to war. But what are the causes of war?

The Apostle James asked this same question, "From whence come wars and fightings among you?" And he answered, "Come they not here, even of your lusts that war in your members? Ye lust, and have not; ye kill and desire to have, and cannot obtain; ye fight and war...." (James 4:1-2). His answer points us back to the faults of our own human nature. Will forming a world government change man's basic nature? Obviously not. So how can we expect peace to come from transferring our weapons to a global authority? As Professor Rummel's research so clearly pointed out, our paramount political concern should be with *limiting and restraining* existing governments. Creating an unrestrained global bureaucratic behemoth goes in the opposite direction, violates every principle of sound government, and virtually guarantees global democide.

World government, unless it be led by the Prince of Peace, can offer our world no salvation from the troubles that beset us. Even such a New World Order luminary as Princeton professor Richard A. Falk (CFR), a leading "World Peace Through World Law" proponent and a member of the World Order Models Project, has admitted, "There is nothing intrinsic about the idea of world government that precludes elitism, mass poverty, ecological decay, or even large-scale violence."[38]

Writing in 1955, Frank Chodorov noted:

> Ten years ago the United Nations was ushered into the world as the guarantor of peace. It has failed. Despite that obvious fact, there are many whose faith in some sort of Superstate as an instrument of peace is unshaken, and who lay the failure of the UN to the limitations put upon it by the autonomy of its members. That is to say, they believe in peace through coercion; the more coercion, the more peace.
>
> History cannot give this faith the slightest support. The grandeur that was Rome did not prevent the parts of that empire from coming into conflict with one another nor from rising up against the central authority. Even our American coalition of commonwealths came near breaking up in war, and uprisings have all but disintegrated the British Empire.[39]

Still, the cult of statism has continued to grow, and, most unfortunately, has converted many believers in the Bible to its cause. They fail to appreciate that statism is not only politically unwise, but is actually an idolatrous, humanist doctrine completely at odds with Christianity. Concerning this basic and neglected truth, author Douglas R. Groothuis writes:

> Christian realism demands that no one political institution claim total power. Since all people are sinners and imperfect, political power should be counterbalanced between various institutions and nations. A centralization of power (statism) in a fallen world is even more dan-

gerous than current national diversity. To put one's hope for peace and prosperity into a world government and not God is the same idolatry committed by the builders of the tower of Babel (Gen. 11:1-9).

The Christian political conscience must reject idolatrous internationalism with as much enthusiasm as it rejects any idolatrous nationalism. [40]

The UN will be restricted to using its military forces for "collective security" and to supervise disarmament.

All the assurances of the UN and the CFR Establishment notwithstanding, the fact remains that once we have reached the stage "where no state would have the military power to challenge the progressively strengthened U.N. Peace Force," we will, by definition, have established a worldwide military dictatorship. At that point, so-called "restrictions" on its use of force will offer about as much protection as the paper on which they are written. As Lord Acton aptly observed: "Absolute power and restrictions on its exercise cannot exist together. It is but a new form of the old contest between the spirit of true freedom and despotism in its most dexterous disguise." [41]

"Every Communist must grasp the truth, 'Political power grows out of the barrel of a gun,' " preached Mao Tse-tung. "Our principle is that the Party commands the gun ... All things grow out of the barrel of a gun." [42] Following Mao's principle, the UN-new world order globalists intend to hold all power by commanding all the guns. If they should succeed, it is certain they would also follow Mao's program of terror and mass murder.

Nations, like individuals must be made accountable to the rule of law. It is not possible to have world peace without world law.

Such appeals are "dangerously misleading," counseled legal scholar Lyman A. Garber, because they convey "the thought that law has some self-enforcing quality. This is not so. No such thing as 'law' exists unless there is the combination of a court, plus adequate force." [43] Which, as former American Bar Association president Frank Holman so logically pointed out, "necessarily adds up to world government."⁴⁴ And again we are confronted with the dangerously insoluble problem of power.

Historian Rev. Frederick Copleston, S.J., has observed:

> History shows that there never has been a truly world-wide government. It does not exist, never did exist, and never could have existed. Suárez maintained as we have seen, that the existence of a single political community for all men is morally impossible and that, even if possible, it would be highly inexpedient. If Aristotle was right, as he was, in saying that it is difficult to govern a very large city properly, it would be far more difficult to govern a world-State.⁴⁵

Morally impossible, yes. And certainly impossible to govern properly. But the "world-State" as an immoral global dictatorship is rapidly being built. The new world order advocates can prattle all they want about "the rule of law," but the facts remain that the UN is a completely lawless organization; its charter and its actions are based not on law but on arbitrariness and caprice. And for the UN to become the basis for a fully-functioning world government, the "rule of law" in America (our constitutional system) and in every other nation must be destroyed.

What could we really expect from a world government? Cutting through the syrupy platitudes and deceitful propaganda that usually attend this topic, John F. McManus offered this realistic appraisal in 1979 in his book *The Insiders*:

> **One:** Rather than improve the standard of living for other nations, world government will mean a forced redistribution of all wealth and a sharp reduction in the standard of living for Americans.
> **Two:** Strict regimentation will become commonplace, and there will no longer be any freedom of movement, freedom of worship, private property rights, free speech, or the right to publish.
> **Three:** World government will mean that this once glorious land of opportunity will become another socialistic nightmare where no amount of effort will produce a just reward.
> **Four:** World order will be enforced by agents of the world government in the same way that agents of the Kremlin enforce their rule

throughout Soviet Russia today.[46]

For those who insist on the necessity of "world law," consider how the United Nations has repeatedly violated its own charter in opposition to the best interests of world peace. Congressman Philip Crane (R-IL) made these observations in 1976:

> According to Article Four of the Charter of the United Nations, "Membership in the UN is open to all peace-loving states which accept the obligations contained in the present Charter...." Many now seem willing to forget that communist China was condemned by the United Nations for its aggressive role in Korea. In fact, the UN went to war to protect South Korea against Communist aggression. Now, by stretching the definition found in Article Four to include Communist China, the UN has shown that its own Charter is irrelevant to its real operating procedures. It has now embraced the philosophy of "universality," a phrase not found in the Charter, rather than the concept of "peace-loving," which is specifically set forth. Yet "universality" does not cover Taiwan, which has been expelled; Rhodesia, against whom an embargo has been declared; or the Republic of South Africa.[47]

It is a cruel mockery even to speak of world law, world peace, and world government emanating from an organization that welcomes, honors, and treats as members-in-good-standing the world's premier criminals and greatest threats to peace.

World federalism merely means extending to the world arena the same federal principles that united American colonists. How could any American oppose that?
Concerning our own federation, leading federalist John Jay had this to say:

> Providence has been pleased to give this one connected country to one united people — a people descended from the same ancestors, speaking the same language, professing the same religion, attached to the same principles of government, very similar in their manners and customs....[48]

Can anything remotely similar be said of the United Nations? Do we have any common ground with practitioners of genocide, democide, and religious and political persecution? Should we unite with sponsors of international terrorism and revolution?

The President must have latitude to commit U.S. forces for collective security under the mandate of the UN Charter.

It is to defend the Constitution of the United States, not the UN Charter, that the President (and every other U.S. official) swears an oath when entering office. The Constitution, *not* the Charter, is still the "supreme law of the land." The Constitution specifies that Congress alone shall have the power to declare war. Yet, from Korea to Vietnam to the Persian Gulf, our nation has been on an increasingly slippery slope as a result of violating this constitutional provision.

In Essay No. 69 of *The Federalist Papers*, Hamilton carefully explained the executive war powers. He said:

> *First.* The President will have only the occasional command of such part of the militia of the nation as by legislative provision may be called into the actual service of the Union. The king of Great Britain and the governor of New York have at all times the entire command of all the militia within their several jurisdictions. In this article, therefore, the power of the President would be inferior to that of either the monarch or the governor. *Second.* The President is to be commander-in-chief of the army and the navy of the United States. In this respect his authority would be nominally the same with that of the king of Great Britain, but in substance much inferior to it. It would amount to nothing more than the supreme command and direction of the military and naval forces, as first general and admiral of the Confederacy; while that of the British king extends to the *declaring* of war and to the *raising* and *regulating* of fleets and armies — all which, by the Constitution under consideration, would appertain to the legislature. [49] [Emphasis in original]

This constitutional concept is not difficult to understand; the thinking behind it is marvelously simple. Abraham Lincoln summarized it this way:

> The provision of the Constitution giving the war-making power to Congress was dictated, as I understand it, by the following reasons.... Kings had always been involving and impoverishing their people in wars, pretending generally, if not always, that the good of the people was the object. This, our Convention understood to be the most oppressive of all Kingly oppressions; and they resolved to so frame the Constitution that *no one man* should hold the power of bringing this oppression upon us.[50] [Emphasis in original]

At least the UN provides a forum where the nations of the world can come together to talk and work out their differences.

If we had some means of assuring that the United Nations would never go beyond that function, it might be tolerable, but the effectiveness of such a forum would still be highly dubious. Author G. Edward Griffin offers the following analogy to illustrate the folly of expecting the UN to be a workable platform for dealing with world grievances:

> Consider what would happen if every time a small spat arose between a husband and wife they called the entire neighborhood together and took turns airing their complaints in front of the whole group. Gone would be any chance of reconciliation. Instead of working out their problems, the ugly necessity of saving face, proving points, and winning popular sympathy would likely drive them further apart. Likewise, public debates in the UN intensify international tensions. By shouting their grievances at each other, countries allow their differences to assume a magnitude they would otherwise never have reached. Quiet diplomacy is always more conducive to progress than diplomacy on the stage.[51]

At the UN, of course, bellicose "diplomacy on the stage" has always been the order of the day. "Not only has the United Nations become a travesty and farce as a unified system of political world government," noted William Henry Chamberlain long ago, "but its meetings and operations have contributed greatly to international disunity, hostility, and bellicosity. Its meetings provide an unprecedented platform and sounding board for denunciation, vituperation, and bitter accusations."[52]

Interdependence is a fact; a return to isolationism would be not only counterproductive, but dangerous.

Isolationism is a bogeyman internationalists trot out every time the American people begin to rebel against globalist, interventionist plotting. The truth is that America has never been "isolationist"; as a people we have always had a vigorous and extensive involvement with the peoples of other countries.

"The great rule of conduct for us in regard to foreign nations," wrote President Washington in his farewell address, "is, in extending our commercial relations to have with them as little *political* connection as possible. So far as we have already formed engagements let them be fulfilled with perfect good faith. Here let us stop."[53] (Emphasis in original) That wise counsel remains completely valid today.

"Why quit our own to stand upon foreign ground?" Washington asked. "Why, by interweaving our destiny with that of any part of Europe, entangle our peace and prosperity in the toils of European ambition, rivalship, interest, humor, or caprice?" Why indeed? Rather, he said, "Observe good faith and justice toward all nations. Cultivate peace and harmony with all. Religion and morality enjoin this conduct."[54] His is a true prescription for peace among nations. It was in this same spirit that the 19th century British statesman Richard Cobden declared: "Peace will come to this earth when her peoples have as much as possible to do with each other; their governments the least possible."[55]

In foreign relations as in all other areas of public affairs, government involvement beyond what is absolutely necessary was wisely viewed with suspicion and alarm during our republic's early history. Until the ascendancy of the CFR foreign policy elitists in our State Department, private citizens engaging in real people-to-people exchange — through commerce, tourism and educational, charitable and church contacts — were considered far better ambassadors of goodwill than were professional diplomats. And they provided far less opportunity for getting America involved in foreign quarrels and intrigues.

John Quincy Adams's "isolationist" position commends itself well to our era and offers a philosophical compass to guide us out of much of our current distress. Adams said:

America goes not abroad in search of monsters to destroy. She is the well-wisher to the freedom and independence of all. She is the champion and vindicator only of her own. She will recommend the general cause by the countenance of her voice, and the benignant sympathy of her example. She well knows that by once enlisting under other banners than her own, were they even the banners of foreign independence, she would involve herself beyond the power of extrication in all the wars of interest and intrigue, of individual avarice, envy and ambition, which assume the colors and usurp the standards of freedom. The fundamental maxims of her policy would insensibly change from liberty to force.[56]

From Liberty to Force

For failing to heed the wise counsel of these founding patriots and allowing conspiratorial internationalists to lead us into schemes of global conquest, we have already paid dearly in blood and treasure. However, a far higher price may soon be extracted. Unless sufficient numbers of Americans awaken shortly from their slumber, they will find they have joined the long list of this world's victims who have paid for their lethargy with their liberty, their property, their countries, and their lives.

While Americans exult at the "end of the Cold War" and the supposed triumph of capitalism over communism, America is being *transformed* (a favorite word of the Insider globalists) before our very eyes into *Amerika*. The globalists call this transformation *convergence*: an ex-USSR and soon-to-be ex-America will be merged with all nations into a new world order UN superstate.

Recognizing this phenomenon years ago, historians Will and Ariel Durant wrote in their 1968 philosophical retrospective, *The Lessons of History:*

Socialism in Russia is now restoring individualistic motives to give its system greater productive stimulus.... Meanwhile capitalism undergoes a correlative process of limiting individualistic acquisition by semi-socialistic legislation and the redistribution of wealth through the "welfare state." ... [I]f the Hegelian formula of thesis, antithesis, and synthesis is applied to the Industrial Revolution as thesis, and to capitalism versus socialism as antithesis, the third condition would be a *synthesis of capitalism and socialism; and to this reconciliation the Western world visibly moves. Year by year the role of Western governments in the economy rises, the share of the private sector declines.... East is West and West is East, and soon the twain will meet.*[57] [Emphasis added]

While the Durants fairly accurately described the *fact* of what has been occurring, they *inaccurately* gave the impression that the process results from disembodied Hegelian forces over which we have no control. And from their matter-of-fact description of the final "synthesis," one could be easily misled into thinking it is nothing to get alarmed about.

But it is time to get alarmed! Americans have already ignored far too many danger signals. Far too few paid heed in the 1950s and '60s when Norman Dodd warned of the U.S.-Soviet merger plan as it was told to him by one of the planners, Rowan Gaither. The East-West synthesis now underway is not the result of unstoppable, blind, historical forces, but the consequence of the purposeful, long-range planning and actions of evil men.

The nation should have come to full attention in December 1987 when Senator Jesse Helms, in a speech before the U.S. Senate, exposed and denounced the CFR-Trilateral plans for U.S.-USSR merger. "A careful examination of what is happening behind the scenes," he said, "reveals that all of these interests are working in concert with the masters of the Kremlin in order to create what some refer to as a new world order." Moreover, said Helms:

In the globalist point of view, nation-states and national boundaries do not count for anything. Political philosophies and political principles seem to become simply relative. Indeed, even constitutions are irrelevant to the exercise of power. Liberty and tyranny are viewed as neither necessarily good nor evil, and certainly not a component of policy. In this point of view, the activities of international financial and industrial forces should be oriented to bringing this one-world design — with a convergence of the Soviet and American systems as its centerpiece — into being.[58]

Americans should also have paid sharp notice nearly a decade earlier when Senator Barry Goldwater sounded a similar warning. In his 1979 personal and political memoir, *With No Apologies,* the Arizona senator wrote:

> In my view the Trilateral Commission represents a skillful, coordinated effort to seize control and consolidate the four centers of power — political, monetary, intellectual, and ecclesiastical....
>
> Freedom — spiritual, political, economic — is denied any importance in the Trilateral construction of the next century....
>
> What the Trilaterals truly intend is the creation of a worldwide economic power superior to the political governments of the nation-states involved.... As managers and creators of the system they will rule the future.[59]

What kind of future will that be? Almost a decade before Senator Goldwater's warning, in a speech entitled "Which World Will It Be?" Robert Welch outlined our current situation with remarkable prescience. Speaking in Atlanta, Georgia in August 1970, he warned:

> The United Nations hopes and plans — or, more accurately, the *Insiders,* the Conspiratorial bosses above it, hope and plan for it — to use population controls, ecological or environmental controls, controls over scientific and technological developments, control over the arms and military strength of individual nations, control over education, control over health, and all the controls it can gradually establish under all of the different excuses for *international* jurisdiction that it can devise. These variegated separate controls are to become components of the gradually materializing total control that it expects to achieve by pretense, deception, persuasion, beguilement, and falsehoods, while the

enforcement of such controls by brutal force and terror is also getting under way.[60]

To most Americans at that time, Welch's alarm probably would have sounded, well, "alarmist." It was too far ahead of the managed news they were accustomed to receiving from the Establishment media. That should not be the case today. The "news" is just as managed, but those who are not willfully blind can now see the prison walls rising about them on all sides. Many are finally beginning to recognize, as Senator Taft eventually did, that the UN is a trap. Even so, many are still reluctant to grasp consciously that the approaching world order will entail the use of "brutal force and terror" — right here in America.

Unless we face up to the whole, brutal truth, however, we are deceiving ourselves, and we run the terrible risk of contenting ourselves with ineffectual, half-hearted efforts at resistance.

Project Their Track Record

We are deceiving ourselves if we think that the Insider globalists who have consistently supported democidal totalitarian regimes all over this planet will spare Americans from the same gruesome fate already suffered by millions of victims of the New World Order.

Consider, for instance, David Rockefeller, current patriarch of the Rockefeller empire. For 15 years, he was chairman of the Council on Foreign Relations (of which he is still a member). He founded and remains honorary chairman of the Trilateral Commission. For many years, he was chairman of the board at Chase Manhattan Bank. As the recognized "Chairman of the Establishment," he is one of the foremost partisans for world government under the UN. Rockefeller had this to say after visiting mass murderer Mao Tse-tung in 1973:

> Whatever the price of the Chinese Revolution, it has obviously succeeded not only in producing more efficient and dedicated administration, but also in fostering high morale and community of purpose....
> The social experiment in China under Chairman Mao's leadership is one of the most important and successful in human history.[61]

Just one chairman to another, right? Equally at home in Moscow or Beijing, Rockefeller then sent these greetings to his Kremlin comrades in November 1977: "My congratulations on the occasion of the 60th anniversary of the October Revolution."[62] Congratulations? To the totalitarian monsters who are responsible for the heinous crimes cataloged by Professor Rummel? But Chairman David's support hasn't been limited merely to words. He and his banker friends have showered the communist world with billions of dollars in loans (guaranteed and subsidized by the American taxpayers).[63] More importantly, he and his CFR confreres directing American foreign policy opened the official U.S. aid spigots to the communist world, allowing the massive transfusions of capital, technology, and expertise that have saved the Marxist-Leninist totalitarians from collapse time after time and helped the communist butchers to consolidate control over much of the earth.[64]

For half a century, the CFR elitists have controlled or greatly influenced much of our government's foreign and domestic policies. They have betrayed us at every turn. Consider the following small sampling of betrayals leading to their new world order:

• In order to frighten Americans into world government through the ostensible threat of nuclear confrontation, they built the USSR into a nuclear superpower with transfusions of nuclear materials and technology for accurate missile guidance systems and mirving capabilities.[65]

• They initiated as the cornerstone of American strategic "defense" the indefensibly insane policy of "mutually assured destruction" (MAD), whereby the American people would be held permanently hostage by the threat of nuclear annihilation from a totalitarian, megalomaniacal enemy. Moreover, they frustrated nearly every effort at civil or anti-ballistic missile defense, even as the Soviet Union pushed forward with massive efforts in both areas.[66]

• Tens of thousands of our finest men — sons, fathers, brothers — have been killed or left captive in wars they were not allowed to win. CFR policy makers tied their hands with impossible restrictions. After abandoning our POW/MIAs to lasting captivity, they lied and covered up evidence of POW survival and thwarted all investigations.[67]

- They have bankrupted our nation with "foreign aid" that has been used for decades to fund communism, socialism, and one-worldism around the globe.[68]

- One anti-communist ally after another has been betrayed and destroyed by the CFR-controlled State Department and the CFR-controlled media. An abbreviated list of those betrayals would include Eastern Europe, China, Cuba, Iran, Nicaragua, Chile, Katanga, Rhodesia, the Philippines, and South Africa.[69]

- They have supported the most brutal terrorist groups and communist "liberation" movements worldwide.[70]

- They have sabotaged our constitutional process by capturing the party machinery of both major parties in order to control the selection of presidential candidates.[71]

- They have subverted our constitutional system by fastening on America Marxist programs like the graduated income tax and the Federal Reserve central banking system.[72]

- They are leading the call for a new constitutional convention in order to overthrow completely our constitutional order.[73]

Reversing the Course

Throughout the years since its founding in 1958, The John Birch Society carried forth a lonely crusade to warn the American public of the deadly peril to our nation and our liberty from the United Nations. With an ever-increasing arsenal of books, pamphlets, flyers, films, filmstrips, audio tapes, petitions, billboards and other educational materials, Society members continued to expose the corrupt, bloody record of the UN megalomaniacs and their sordid New World Order plans for global dictatorship.

Gradually, those educational efforts paid off. Public support for the UN declined dramatically. The non-CFR-controlled media became better informed and began to take a more critical look at UN activities. During the late 1970s, members of the Society collected over 11 million signatures on petitions urging Congress to *"Get US out!* of the United Nations."

In the mid 1980s, however, the Establishment media commenced an enormous pro-UN propaganda campaign playing off U.S.-Soviet arms treaties, Mikhail Gorbachev's glasnost, alleged global ecological crises, refugee and famine relief, Middle East peacekeeping, and other high-profile activities designed not only to rehabilitate the UN's tarnished image, but to make the global menagerie on New York's East River appear indispensable to mankind's survival. It worked. Opinion polls began to show increasing support for the United Nations. Then came the Persian Gulf War. President George Bush and his fellow globalists magnificently exploited the patriotic fervor it elicited to promote their the UN-New World Order plans. They are still riding high; but that could begin to change very rapidly, as the information in this book becomes more widely known.

America's pro-UN attitude *must* begin to change very rapidly if we are to have a realistic chance of averting global tyranny and worldwide democide. That will not happen unless significant numbers of Americans join the fight to *"Get US out!* of the United Nations," to stop the New World Order, and to preserve American independence. "If we wish to be free," declared Patrick Henry in a time of similar peril, "if we mean to preserve inviolate those inestimable privileges for which we have been so long contending ... we must fight! I repeat it, sir, we must fight!"[74]

President Hoover: "Unless the UN is completely reorganized without the Communist nations in it, we should get out of it."

Senator Robert Taft: "The UN has become a trap. Let's go it alone."

Far from being mankind's "last best hope for peace," the UN is rapidly being built into a global totalitarian regime. Senator Goldwater was correct in saying it should be moved to Moscow or Peking.

Charles Darwin was among the prophets who set modern man "free" from God — with horrific consequences.

Robert Welch clearly saw the tragedy of the "increasing quantity of government in all nations."

The principles of limited government and unalienable God-given rights embodied in the U.S. Constitution are completely at odds with the unrestrained structure and totalitarian designs of the UN. Americans must decide between the U.S. Constitution and the UN Charter.

In this century, notes Dr. R. J. Rummel, "governments probably have murdered 119,400,000 people — Marxist governments about 95,200,000 of them." Totalitarian government, he found, is "many times deadlier than war." An all-powerful UN government is a guarantee of global tyranny and unprecedented human holocaust.

The UN's role in Korea and Vietnam placed unconscionable restrictions on our armed forces, cost tens of thousands of American lives, and resulted in abandonment of thousands of American POWs and guaranteed U.S. defeat.

MAD "defense" policy devised by CFR strategists has placed the American people as hostages to threat of nuclear annihilation from a totalitarian enemy. The Insiders hoped to frighten Americans into accepting world government as an alternative to nuclear war.

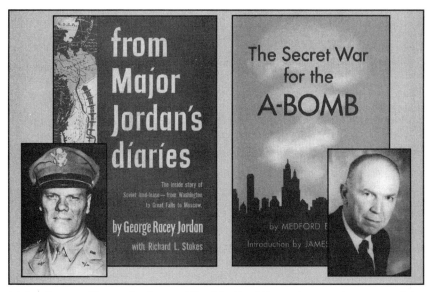

Major George Racey Jordan and Dr. Medford Evans have written two of the most important volumes documenting the betrayal at the highest levels of American government in providing the Soviets with technology, information, and materials for the atomic bomb.

Recognizing that the UN is a dire threat to world peace and American independence and freedom, The John Birch Society has for more than three decades led the fight to "*Get US out!* of the United Nations and get the United Nations out of the United States."

*When bad men combine, the good must associate;
else they will fall one by one, an unpitied sacrifice
in a contemptible struggle.*

— Edmund Burke (April 23, 1770)

Since 1958, members of The John Birch Society have been working to expose the drive for totalitarian world government. For more information about The John Birch Society's programs, write:

The John Birch Society
P. O. Box 8040
Appleton, WI 54913

Notes

Introduction

1. For factual information and perspective on developments in the USSR and Eastern Europe, see, for example, the following articles from *The New American*: John F. McManus interview with Russian chess grandmaster Lev Albert, "Lev Albert's Defense," March 30, 1987; Kirk Kidwell, "Has the Soviet Union Changed?" August 29, 1988; Robert W. Lee, "U.S.S.R. & Eastern Europe," January 29, 1991; James J. Drummey, "Nice Smile, Iron Teeth," March 12, 1991; Robert W. Lee, "The New, Improved USSR," November 19, 1991; William F. Jasper, "From the Atlantic to the Urals (and Beyond)," January 27, 1992; William F. Jasper, "Meeting Ground of East and West," February 24, 1992.

2. George J. Church, "A New World," *Time*, September 17, 1990, p. 23.

3. President Bush in a televised address before a Joint Session of Congress, September 11, 1990, *Weekly Compilation of Presidential Documents*, September 17, 1990, Vol. 26 — Number 37, pp. 1359-60.

4. Robert W. Lee, *The United Nations Conspiracy* (Appleton, WI: Western Islands, 1981), p. ix.

5. Ibid., p. xi.

6. Andrew Tully, "[Mayor] Koch Should Chase UN Out of Town," *San Gabriel Valley Tribune* (CA), March 3, 1982.

7. Author in telephone interview with Matthew Norzig, UN spokesman at UN information Office, Washington, DC on September 11, 1992: 40,000+ UN troops in 12 operations in 13 countries.

8. "American Support for United Nations Highest in 20 Years; Strong Support for Permanent Peacekeeping Force," *The Gallup Poll News Service*, Vol. 55, No. 23, October 24, 1990.

9. Ibid.

10. William H. McIlhany, II, *The Tax-Exempt Foundations* (Westport, CT: Arlington House, 1980), p. 63. See also Norman Dodd, videotaped interview of, *The Hidden Agenda: Merging America Into World Gov-*

ernment, Westlake Village, CA: American Media, one hour (VHS).

11. Walt Whitman Rostow, *The United States in the World Arena* (New York: Harper & Brothers, 1960), p. 549.

12. Senator Jesse Helms, *Congressional Record*, December 15, 1987, p. S 18146.

13. Hermann Rauschning, *Hitler m'a dit* (Paris: Coopération,1939), quoted by Jean-Michel Angebert, *The Occult and the Third Reich* (New York: Macmillan, 1974), p. 155.

Chapter 1 • The New World Army

1. *National Security Strategy of the United States* (The White House, August 1991).

2. The United Nations Security Council, "Provisional Verbatim Record of the Three Thousand and Forty-sixth Meeting" (New York: UN Headquarters, January 31, 1992), pp. 49, 54-55.

3. Ibid., p. 8.

4. Ibid., p. 42.

5. Ibid., p. 59-60.

6. Ibid., p. 61.

7. Thomas Jefferson, quoted by Lewis C. Henry (ed.), *Best Quotations for all Occasions* (Greenwich, CT: Fawcett Publications, 1964), p. 45.

8. The United Nations Security Council, "Provisional Verbatim Record of the Three Thousand and Forty-sixth Meeting," pp. 9-10.

9. Ibid., p. 18.

10. Ibid., p. 72.

11. Ibid., p. 44.

12. Ibid., p. 46.

13. Ibid., p. 91.

14. Jim Mann, "Chinese Premier gets chilly U.N. reception," *Los Angeles Times*, February 1, 1992, pp. A1, A6.

15. Joseph S. Nye Jr., "Create a U.N. Fire Brigade," *New York Times*, February 1, 1992.

16. Ibid.

17. Norman Kempster, "Army Could Give U.N. New Punch," *Los Angeles Times*, February 1, 1992.

18. Jim Sasser, quoted by Barbara Crossette, "Spending for U.N. Peacekeeping Getting a Hard Look in Congress," *New York Times*, March 6, 1992, p. A6.
19. Ibid.
20. "The New World Army," *New York Times* lead editorial, March 6, 1992.
21. Ibid.
22. Maurice F. Strong, quoted by Paul Raeburn, AP, "Ecology Remedy Costly," *Sacramento Bee* (CA), March 12, 1992.
23. President Bush's Pax Universalis speech at UN headquarters on September 23, 1991, *Weekly Compilaton of Presidential Documents*, Volume 27 — Number 39, pp. 1324-27.
24. Leslie H. Gelb, "Why the U.N. Dog Didn't Bark: Mr. Bush's incendiary theme," *New York Times*, September 25, 1991.
25. *Freedom From War: The United States Program for General and Complete Disarmament in a Peaceful World* (Department of State Publication 7277, Disarmament Series 5, Released September 1961, Office of Public Services, Bureau of Public Affairs).
26. Ibid., p. 18.
27. Ibid., pp. 18-19.
28. *Blueprint for the Peace Race: Outline of Basic Provisions of a Treaty on General and Complete Disarmament in a Peaceful World* (United States Arms Control and Disarmament Agency Publication 4, General Series 3, Released May 1962).
29. Ibid., p. 33.
30. Congressman Ted Weiss (D-NY), remarks in *Congressional Record*, May 25, 1982, pp. H 2840-49.
31. A. Richard Richstein, in letter dated May 11, 1982, quoted by Congressman Ted Weiss in Congressional Record, May 25,1982, p. H 2841.
32. William Nary, telephone interview by author, January 1991.
33. Grenville Clark and Louis B. Sohn, *World Peace Through World Law*, 2d ed. (Cambridge: Harvard Univ. Press, 1962).
34. Ibid., pp. xxix, 232-33, 246-257.
35. Trygve Lie, *In the Cause of Peace* (New York: Macmillan Company, 1954), p. 45.
36. Ibid., p. 45.
37. Ibid., p. 46.
38. Boutros, Boutros-Ghali, *An Agenda for Peace* (New York: United Nations, 1992)

39. Ibid., pp. 16, 25.
40. Ibid., p. 9.
41. Ibid., p. 1-2.
42. Ibid., p. 2.
43. Ibid., p. 6-7.
44. Ibid., p. 7.
45. President George Bush, "The United Nations: Forging a Genuine Global Community," address before the UN General Assembly on September 21, 1992, in *US Department of State Dispatch*, September 28, 1992, Vol. 3, No. 39, pp. 721-24.
46. Sam Francis, "New World Order's Call To Arms," *Los Angeles Daily News*, Tuesday, August 4, 1992.

Chapter 2 • In the Name of Peace

1. Smith Hempstone, *Rebels, Mercenaries, and Dividends* (New York: Frederic A. Praeger, 1962), p. 190.
2. Graham Hancock, *Lords of Poverty: The Power, Prestige, and Corruption of the International Aid Business* (New York: Atlantic Monthly Press, 1989), p. 108.
3. V. Orval Watts, *The United Nations: Planned Tyranny* (New York: Devin-Adair, 1955), pp. 7-8.
4. Adlai E. Stevenson, "Working Toward a World Without War" in *Disarmament: The New U.S. Initiative*, United States Arms Control and Disarmament Agency Publication 8, General Series 5, released September 1962 (Washington, DC: U.S. Government Printing Office), p. 19.
5. Lincoln P. Bloomfield, *A World Effectively Controlled by the United Nations*, Institute For Defense Analyses, March 10, 1962. Prepared for IDA in support of a study submitted to the Deparment of State under contract No. SCC 28270, February 24, 1961.
6. Ibid., p. iv.
7. Ibid., p. 1.
8. Ibid., p. 2.
9. Ibid., pp. 2-3.
10. Ibid., p. 3.
11. Ibid., p. 19.
12. Ibid., p. 23.
13. Ibid., p. 25.
14. Ibid.
15. See, for example, Philippa Schuyler, *Who Killed The Congo?* (New York: Devin-

Adair, 1962.)

16. See, for example, G. Edward Griffin, *The Fearful Master: A Second Look at the United Nations* (Appleton, WI: Western Islands, 1964), Part I, "Katanga: A Case History," Chapter 4, "The Moderates."

17. See, for example, Griffin, p. 11.

18. See, for example, Griffin, Chapter 3, "Seceding From Chaos."

19. Hempstone, p. 68.

20. UN document S/4347. See also: Griffin, p. 16; and Hempstone, pp. 110-111.

21. Hempstone, pp. 190-93.

22. The 46 Civilian Doctors of Elisabethville, *46 Angry Men* (Belmont, MA: American Opinion, 1962; originally published by Dr. T. Vleurinck, 96 Avenue de Broqueville, Bruxelles 15, 1962), pp. 60-63.

23. Congressman Donald L. Jackson (narrator), *Katanga: The Untold Story*, available on video (VHS, 59 minutes) from American Media, Westlake Village, CA.

24. See, for example: Richard N. Gardner, "The Case for Practical Internationalism," *Foreign Affairs*, Spring 1988, p. 837.

25. "Protest Over Berlin," *New York Times* editorial, August 16, 1961.

26. "The Political Control of An International Police Force," by Walter Millis. Published by the Peace Research Institute, Inc. April 1963 under U.S. Arms Control and Disarmament Agency Grant ACDA/IR-8, Volume II, p. A-14.

27. Bloomfield, p. 12.

28. See, for examples: Medford Evans, *The Secret War for the A-Bomb* (Chicago: Henry Regnery, 1953); Joseph Finder, *Red Carpet* (New York: Holt, Rinehart and Winston, 1983); George Racey Jordan, USAF (Ret.), *Major Jordan's Diaries* (New York: Harcourt, Brace, 1952); Charles Levinson, *Vodka Cola* (London and New York: Gordon & Cremonesi, 1978).

And see especially the following works by Antony C. Sutton: *Western Technology and Soviet Economic Development, 1917-1930* (Stanford University, Stanford, CA: Hoover Institution, 1968); *Western Technology and Soviet Economic Development, 1930-1945* (Stanford University, Stanford, CA: Hoover Institution, 1971); *Western Technology and Soviet Economic Development, 1945-1965* (Stanford University, Stanford, CA: Hoover Institution, 1973);

National Suicide: Military Aid to the Soviet Union (New Rochelle, NY: Arlington House, 1973); *The Best Enemy Money Can Buy* (Billings, MT: Liberty House Press, 1986).

29. See, for example, Glenard P. Lipscomb (R-CA), quoted in *Congressional Record — House*, February 10, 1964, pp. 2720-24.

30. See, for example, Vincent P. Rock, "Common Action for the Control of Conflict: An Approach to the Problem of International Tension and Arms Control," July 1963, summary document of a Project Phoenix Study performed by the Institute for Defense Analyses for the U.S. Arms Control and Disarmament Agency. Also see "Study Phoenix Paper, June 4, 1963," p. 33, quoted in *Congressional Record House*, May 13, 1964.

31. Ibid.

32. Bloomfield, p. 21.

33. Ibid., p. 22.

34. Ibid.

35. Douglas Waller and Margaret Garrard Warner, "Superpowers as Superpartners," *Newsweek*, September 17, 1990, p. 27.

36. *National Security Strategy of the United States*, The White House, August 1991, p. v.

37. *A Charter for American-Russian Partnership and Friendship*, signed by Presidents Bush and Yeltsin on June 17, 1992 (seven-page document released by the White House, Office of the Press Secretary, June 17, 1992), pp. 2, 4-5.

Chapter 3 • The UN's Founders

1. President Bush in televised address before a Joint Session of Congress, September 11, 1990, *Weekly Compilation of Presidential Documents*, Vol. 26 — Number 37, p. 1360.

2. Carnegie Endowment's National Commission on America, *Changing Our Ways: America and the New World* (Washington, DC: Brookings Institution, 1992), p. 2.

3. Clarence Carson, *A Basic History of the United States — Book V: The Welfare State, 1929 – 1985* (Wadley, AL: American Textbook Committee, 1986), p. 151.

4. James Perloff, *The Shadows of Power: The Council on Foreign Relations and the American Decline* (Appleton, WI: Western

Islands, 1988), p. 71.

5. Robert W. Lee, *The United Nations Conspiracy* (Appleton, WI: Western Islands, 1981), p. 243.

6. John W. Davis, *The Council On Foreign Relations: A Record of Twenty-Five Years, 1921 – 1946* (New York: Council on Foreign Relations, 1947), pp. 15-17, quoted by Lee, p. 7.

7. Lee, p. 7.

8. See "Rules, Guidelines, and Practices," in Council on Foreign Relations *Annual Report:* July 1, 1990 – June 30, 1991, p. 168.

9. Phyllis Schlafly and Chester Ward, Rear Admiral, USN (Ret.), *Kissinger on the Couch* (New Rochelle, NY: Arlington House, 1975), pp. 146, 149-50.

10. "President's Report," August 31, 1972, Council on Foreign Relations, quoted by Schlafly, Ward, p. 149.

11. Charles Seymour (ed.), *The Initimate Papers of Colonel House*, Vol. I, "Behind The Political Curtain: 1912 – 1915" (Boston: Hougton Mifflin, 1926), p. 114.

12. George Sylvester Viereck, *The Strangest Friendship in History: Woodrow Wilson and Colonel House* (New York: Liveright, 1932), p. 349.

13. Ibid., p. xi.

14. Ibid., p. 54.

15. Charles Seymour (ed.), *The Initimate Papers of Colonel House*, Vol. III, "Into the World War: April, 1917 – June, 1918" (Boston: Hougton Mifflin, 1928), p. 171. See also Alan Stang, *The Actor: The True Story of John Foster Dulles Secretary of State, 1953 – 1959* (Appleton, WI: Western Islands, 1968), p. 19.

16. Colonel Edward Mandell House, *Philip Dru: Administrator* (New York: B.W. Huebsch, 1912).

17. J. B. Matthews, "Philip Dru: Fascist Prototype," *American Mercury*, November 1954, p. 132.

18. Viereck, p. 28.

19. Matthews, p. 134.

20. Charles P. Howland, *Survey of American Foreign Relations 1928*, published for the Council on Foreign Relations (New Haven: Yale University Press, 1928), p. 236.

21. William P. Hoar, *Architects of Conspiracy: An Intriguing History* (Appleton, WI: Western Islands, 1984), pp. 91-92.

22. Howland, p. 237.

23. Ibid., pp. 237-38.

24. Ibid., p. 239.

25. Gary Allen with Larry Abraham, *None Dare Call It Conspiracy* (Rossmoor, CA: Concord Press, 1971), pp. 92-93.

26. Sarah Gertrude Millin, *Cecil Rhodes* (New York: Harper & Brothers, 1933), p. 8.

27. Allen, p. 93. See also Joseph Kraft, "School for Statesmen," *Harper's* July 1958, p. 64.

28. Robert D. Schulzinger, *The Wise Men of Foreign Affairs: The History of the Council on Foreign Relations* (New York: Columbia Unviersity Press, 1984), p. 6. See also Carroll Quigley *Tragedy and Hope: A History of the World in our Time* (New York: Macmillan, 1966), p. 952.

29. Perloff, p. 38.

30. Stitch-in subscription card in *Foreign Affairs*, Summer 1986. Also, letter to subscribers from David Kellogg, publisher, 1991 or 1992.

31. Letter to former subscribers from George Winchester, *Foreign Affairs* stationery, 1991 or 1992.

32. Schlafly, Ward, p. 151.

33. Charles W. Eliot, "The Next American Contribution to Civilization," *Foreign Affairs*, September 15, 1922, p. 65, quoted by Perloff, p. 37.

34. Howland, CFR Survey: 1928, p. 123.

35. Schlafly, Ward, p. 150.

36. William H. McIlhany, II, *The Tax-Exempt Foundations* (Westport, CT: Arlington House, 1980), pp. 60-61. See also videotaped interview of Norman Dodd, *The Hidden Agenda: Merging America Into World Government* (Westlake Village, CA: American Media), one hour (VHS).

37. McIlhany, p. 61.

38. Perloff, p. 51.

39. Arthur M. Schlesinger, *A Thousand Days* (Boston: Houghton Mifflin, 1965), quoted by Hoar, p. 78.

40. Alan Brinkley, "Minister Without Portfolio," *Harper's*, February 1983, p. 31.

41. John J. McCloy, quoted by J. Anthony Lukas, "The Council on Foreign Relations: Is It a Club? Seminar? Presidium? Invisible Government?" *New York Times Magazine*, November 21, 1971, pp. 125-26, quoted by Perloff, p. 8. See also Max Holland, "Citizen McCloy," *The Wilson Quarterly*, Autumn 1991, p. 35.

42. Richard J. Barnet, *Roots of War* (New

York: Atheneum, 1972), p. 49, quoted by Perloff, pp. 9-10.

43. Edith Kermit Roosevelt, "Elite Clique Holds Power in U.S.," *Indianapolis News*, December 23, 1961, p. 6, quoted by Perloff, p. 14.

44. Schlafly, Ward, p. 150.

Chapter 4 • Reds

1. *Activities of U.S. Citizens Employed by the UN*, hearings before the Senate Committee on the Judiciary, 1952, pp. 407-08, quoted by G. Edward Griffin, *The Fearful Master: A Second Look at the United Nations* (Appleton, WI: Western Islands, 1964), p. 98.

2. Gary Allen, with Larry Abraham, *None Dare Call It Conspiracy* (Rossmoor,CA: Concord Press, 1971), p. 138.

3. Official 1936 program of the Communist International, recorded in hearings before the Senate Committee on Foreign Relations, July 11, 1956, p. 196, quoted by Griffin, pp. 69-70.

4. *Pravda*, March 23, 1946, quoted by Robert W. Lee, *The United Nations Conspiracy* (Appleton, WI: Western Islands, 1981), p. 73.

5. William Z. Foster, *Toward Soviet America* (Balboa Island, CA: Elgin Publications, 1961), pp. 272, 326.

6. Earl Browder, *Victory — and after* (New York: International Publishers, 1942), p. 110.

7. Ibid., p. 160.

8. Ibid., p. 169.

9. G. Edward Griffin, *The Fearful Master: A Second Look at the United Nations* (Appleton, WI: Western Islands, 1964), p. 75.

10. Ibid., pp. 76-7.

11. Bella V. Dodd, *School of Darkness* (New York: Devin-Adair, 1954), p. 179.

12. Griffin, p. 120.

13. Executive Hearings before the House Committee on Un-American Activities, May 13 and 14, 1953, *Soviet Schedule For War — 1955* (Washington: United States Government Printing Office, 1953), p. 1721.

14. Griffin, p. 87-106.

15. Louis F. Budenz, *The Cry Is Peace* (Chicago: Henry Regnery Company, 1952),

Whittaker Chambers, *Witness* (New York: Random House, 1952), Hede Massing, *This Deception* (New York: Duell, Sloan and Pearce, 1951), and Allen Weinstein, *Perjury: The Hiss-Chambers Case* (New York: Vintage Books, 1978).

16. William H. McIlhany II, *The Tax-Exempt Foundations* (Westport, CT: Arlington House, 1980), p. 40.

17. Robert W. Lee, *The United Nations Conspiracy* (Appleton, WI: Western Islands, 1981), p. 20.

18. *Los Angeles Times*, April 7, 1970, quoted by Lee, p. 26-7.

19. John Barron, *KGB: The Secret Work Of Soviet Secret Agents* (New York: Reader's Digest Press, 1974), p. 19.

20. Hilaire du Berrier, "The Multi-colored Kurt Waldheim," *The New American*, June 2, 1986, p. 27.

21. John F. McManus, "Selective Blindness," *The Birch Log*, April 8, 1976, republished as "Ahead of the *Times*," *The New American*, April 7, 1986, p. 45.

22. Frederick Kempe, "Perez de Cuellar Wins U.N. New Respect," *Wall Street Journal*, September 26, 1988, p. 22.

23. Javier Perez de Cuellar, Foreword to Frank Barnaby, *Gaia Peace Atlas* (Garden City, NY: Doubleday, 1988).

24. William P. Hoar, "Review of the News," *The New American*, August 10, 1992, p. 11.

25. *Los Angeles Times*, May 4, 1963, quoted by Griffin, p. 73.

26. Chapman Pincher, *The Secret Offensive* (New York: St. Martin's Press, 1985), p. 129.

27. Ladislav Bittman, *The KGB and Soviet Disinformation: An Insider's View* (McLean, VA: Pergamon-Brassey's International Defense Publishers, 1985), pp. 56-7.

28. Pincher, p. 129.

29. Ibid., p. 204.

30. Ibid., p. 129-30.

31. Christopher Andrew and Oleg Gordievsky, *KGB: The Inside Story of Its Foreign Operations from Lenin to Gorbachev* (New York: HarperCollins, 1991), pp. 539-40.

32. Barron, *KGB: The Secret Work of Soviet Secret Agents*, p. 20.

33. John Barron, *KGB Today: The Hidden Hand* (New York: Reader's Digest Press, 1983), p. 243-44.

34. Trygve Lie, *In the Cause of Peace* (New York: Macmillan Company, 1954), p. 57.
35. Ibid., pp. 58-60.
36. Ibid., pp. 113-14.
37. Zdzislaw Rurarz, "Yeltsin's Police," *Washington Inquirer*, January 4, 1992, p. 4.
38. Albert L. Weeks, "KGB's Undiminished Power Haunts Russian Reform," *Washington Inquirer*, April 17, 1992, pp. 1, 7.
39. Bill Gertz, "KGB targets U.S. businessmen, scientists to recruit them as spies," *The Washington Times*, March 14, 1991.
40. Telephone interview with the author, October 19, 1992.
41. Anatoliy Golitsyn, *New Lies For Old* (New York: Dodd, Mead & Company, 1984). For further information and perspective on developments in the Soviet Union and Eastern Europe see: Edward J. Epstein, *Deception: The Invisible War Between the KGB and the CIA* (New York: Simon and Schuster, 1989). Also see the following articles from *The New American*: Thomas R. Eddlem interview with Charles Via, chairman of the Center for Intelligence Studies, "Soviet Goals Remain the Same," October 8, 1991; Thomas R. Eddlem, "Appearance Versus Reality," October 22, 1991; Bryan J. Ellison, "Behind the Facade," May 21, 1991; "Still the Masters of Deceit," December 4, 1989, p. 37.

Chapter 5 • The Drive for World Government

1. Philip Kerr, "From Empire to Commonwealth," *Foreign Affairs,* December 1922, pp. 97-98, quoted by James Perloff, *The Shadows of Power: The Council on Foreign Relations And The American Decline* (Appleton, WI: Western Islands, 1988), p. 11.
2. Allen W. Dulles and Beatrice Pitney Lamb, *The United Nations* (booklet), Headline Series, No. 59 (New York: The Foreign Policy Association, September-October, 1946), pp. 44, 86, quoted by Alan Stang, *The Actor: The True Story of John Foster Dulles Secretary of State, 1953 – 1959* (Appleton, WI: Western Islands, 1968), pp. 127, 180.
3. Saul H. Mendlovitz in Introduction, Saul H. Mendlovitz (ed.). *On the Creation of a Just World Order: Preferred Worlds for the*

1990's (New York: The Free Press, 1975), p. xvi.
4. Lincoln P. Bloomfield, *A World Effectively Controlled by the United Nations*, Institute For Defense Analyses, March 10, 1962. Prepared for the IDA in support of a study submitted to the Department of State under contract No. SCC 28270, February 24, 1961, p. 3.
5. H. G. Wells, *The New World Order* (New York: Alfred A. Knopf, 1940), p. 9.
6. Ibid., pp. 23-24.
7. Reinhold Niebuhr, Lewis Mumford, et al., *The City of Man: A Declaration on World Democracy* (New York: Viking Press, 1940), p. 25.
8. Ibid., p. 23.
9. Center for the Study of Democratic Institutions, *A Constitution for the World* (New York: The Fund for the Republic, 1965), p. 7.
10. Ibid., p. 8.
11. Ibid., p. 6, 8-9.
12. Senate Concurrent Resolution 66 first introduced in the Senate on September 13, 1949 by Senator Glen Taylor (D-ID), quoted by Dennis L. Cuddy, *The "New World Order": A Critique and Chronology*, a pamphlet (Milford, PA: America's Future, Inc., 1992), p. 10.
13. Cuddy, p. 10.
14. John Foster Dulles, *War or Peace* (New York: Macmillan, 1950), p. 40, quoted by Robert W. Lee, *The United Nations Conspiracy* (Appleton, WI: Western Islands, 1981), p. 141.
15. William H. McIlhany II, *The Tax-Exempt Foundations* (Westport, CT: Arlington House, 1980), p. 40. See also, Alan Stang, *The Actor: The True Story of John Foster Dulles Secretary of State, 1953 – 1959* (Appleton, WI: Western Islands, 1968), pp. 164-65.
16. Rev. Edmund A. Opitz, "Religious Propagandists for the UN," *The Freeman*, March 1955, p. 382.
17. Ibid.
18. Dulles, *War or Peace*, p. 204, quoted by Lee, p. 115.
19. Senate Report (Senate Foreign Relations Committee), *Revision of the United Nations Charter: Hearings Before a Subcommittee of the Committee on Foreign Relations, Eighty-First Congress* (Wash-

ington: United States Government Printing Office, 1950) p. 494.

20. Giuseppe Antonio Borgese, *Foundations of the World Republic* (Chicago: Univ. of Chicago Press, 1953), inside flap of dust jacket.

21. Editorial, "The Climate of Freedom," *The Saturday Review*, July 19, 1952, p. 22.

22. Lewis Mumford, *The Transformations of Man* (New York: Harper & Brothers, 1956), p. 184.

23. James P. Warburg, *The West in Crisis* (Garden City, NY: Doubleday & Company, Inc., 1959), p. 30.

24. Ibid., p. 171.

25. "The Goal is Government of All the World," " an address by Atlantic Union Committee treasurer Elmo Roper delivered in 1960, quoted by Dennis L. Cuddy, *Now Is the Dawning of the New Age New World Order* (Oklahoma City: Hearthstone Publishing, Ltd., 1991), p. 240.

26. Norman Cousins, abstracts from two addresses delivered on Earth Day, April 22, 1970 published as "Managing the Planet," in *Earth Day – The Beginning* (New York: Arno Press & The New York Times, 1970), p. 242.

27. Humanist Manifesto II first appeared in The Humanist, September/October 1973 (Vol. XXXIII, No.5). See also, Paul Kurtz (ed.), "Humanist Manifesto II" in *Humanist Manifestos I and II* (Buffalo, NY: Prometheus Books, 1973), p. 21.

28. *A Constitution for the World*, op. cit.

29. Sponsorship list from World Constitution and Parliament Association, 1480 Hoyt Street, Suite 31, Lakewood, CO 80215.

30. Kerr, pp. 97-98.

31. *American Public Opinion and Postwar Security Commitments* (New York: CFR, 1944), p. 4, quoted by Alang Stang, *The Actor* (Appleton, WI: Western Islands, 1968), p. 35.

32. Philip C. Jessup, *International Problems of Governing Mankind* (Claremont, CA: Claremont Colleges, 1947), p. 2.

33. Hans (Henry) Morgenthau, quoted by Lester R. Brown, *World Without Borders* (New York: Vintage Books, 1972), p. 353.

34. "Why We Need to Change the System, And How We Can Do It," *Transition*, a bimonthly publication of the Institute for World Order, Inc., Vol. 2., No.1, January

1975, p. 3.

35. Walt Whitman Rostow, *The United States in the World Arena* (New York: Harper & Brothers, 1960), p. 549.

36. J. William Fulbright, *Old Myths and New Realities* (New York: Random House, 1964), p. 87.

37. Ibid., p. 108.

38. Nelson A. Rockefeller, *The Future of Federalism: The Godkin Lectures at Harvard University, 1962* (Cambridge: Harvard University Press, 1964), p. 64.

39. Ibid., 67.

40. Ibid., p. 74.

41. Ibid., p. 79-80.

42. Brown, p. 353.

43. Ibid., p. 354.

44. Lester Brown, quoted by Cuddy, *Now is the Dawning*, p. 266.

45. Henry Steele Commager, "The Declaration of INTERdependence", October 24, 1975. World Affairs Council of Philadelphia, 1975.

46. John Ashbrook, quoted in *Congressional Record*, May 12, 1976, p. H 4312.

47. Harlan Cleveland, *The Third Try at World Order* (New York: Aspen Institute for Humanistic Studies, 1976), p. 2.

48. Ibid., pp. 8-9.

49. Harlan Cleveland in Introduction, Richard N. Gardner, *In Pursuit of World Order: U.S. Foreign Policy and International Organizations* (New York: Fredrick A. Praeger, 1964), p. xviii.

50. Richard N. Gardner, "The Hard Road to World Order," *Foreign Affairs*, April 1974, p. 558-59.

Chapter 6 • Treaties and Treason

1. Thomas Jefferson in letter to Wilson C. Nicholas, Monticello, September 1803, quoted by John P. Foley (ed.), *The Jeffersonian Cyclopedia* (New York: Funk & Wagnalls, 1900), p. 190.

2. Secretary of State John Foster Dulles, "Treatymaking and National Unity," an address delivered at the regional meeting of the American Bar Association, Louisville, KY, April 11, 1952, as recorded in *Treaties and Executive Agreements*, Hearings on S. J. Res. 1 & S. J. Res. 43; Feb., Mar., & Apr. 1953, Y4.J89/2:T71/2, p. 862.

3. George L. Sherry, *The United Nations Reborn: Conflict Control in the Post-Cold War World*, Council on Foreign Relations Critical Issues series (New York, 1990), p. 8.
4. Frank Chodorov, "One Worldism," *The Freeman*, March 1955, p. 335.
5. Ibid.
6. Thomas Jefferson, quoted by Lewis C. Henry (ed.), *Best Quotations for all Occasions* (Greenwich, CT: Fawcett Publications, 1964), p. 45.
7. Chodorov, p. 335.
8. John F. McManus,"Examining the Rule of Law," *The John Birch Society Bulletin* (Appleton, WI: June 1991), p. 4.
9. Charles P. Howland, *Survey of American Foreign Relations 1928*, published for the Council on Foreign Relations (New Haven: Yale University Press, 1928), p. 88.
10. Ibid., p.111.
11. Ibid., pp. 111-12.
12 Ibid., p. 286.
13. James MacGregor Burns, *The Power To Lead* (New York, Simon & Schuster, 1984), as reprinted in Donald L. Robinson (ed.), *Reforming American Government: The Bicentennial Papers of the Committee on the Constitutional System*, (Boulder, CO: Westview Press, 1985), p. 160.
14. See, for example: Don Fotheringham, "The Con-Con Network," *The New American*, February 10, 1992.
15. Charles Hardin, "Toward a New Constitution (1974)," in Donald L. Robinson (ed.), *Reforming American Government: The Bicentennial Papers of the Committee on the Constitutional System*, (Boulder, CO: Westview Press, Inc., 1985), p. 150.
16. Ibid., p. 149.
17. Ibid.
18. *Charter of the United Nations and Statute of the International Court of Justice* (Lake Success, NY: The United Nations, Department of Public Information, 1950), p. 5.
19. William G. Carr, *One World In the Making: The United Nations* (Boston: Ginn and Company, 1946), p.45, quoted by Robert W. Lee, *The United Nations Conspiracy* (Appleton, WI: Western Islands, 1981), p. 120.
20. Moses Moskowitz, "Is the U.N.'s Bill of Human Rights Dangerous? A Reply to President Holman," *American Bar Association Journal*, Vol. 35, April 1949, p. 285.

21. Foreword by President Truman, *Foreign Affairs Policy, Series 26*, Department of State publication #3972, September 1952, quoted by G. Edward Griffin, *The Fearful Master: A Second Look At The United Nations* (Appleton, WI: Western Islands, 1964), p. 186.
22. President Dwight Eisenhower, speech at St. John's College, Anapolis Maryland, May 22, 1959, quoted by Griffin, p. 186.
23. Dulles, loc. cit.
24. John F. McManus, "Treaties versus the Constitution," *The New American*, July 27, 1992, p. 44.
25. Frank E. Holman, *Story of the "Bricker" Amendment* (New York: Committe for Constitutional Government, Inc., 1954), p. 23.
26. James Madison, quoted by Jonathan Elliot, *The Debates in the Several State Conventions on the Adoption of the Federal Constitution* (originally published in 1830; republished 1937, J. B. Lippincott), Vol. 3, p. 514.
27. Thomas Jefferson, *A Manual of Parliamentary Practice* (New York: Clark & Maynard, 1873), p.110, quoted by Roger Lea MacBride, MacBride, *Treaties Versus the Constitution* (Caldwell, ID: The Caxton Printers, Ltd., 1956), pp. 37-38.
28. Thomas Jefferson in letter to Wilson C. Nicholas, Monticello, September 1803, quoted by John P. Foley (ed.), *The Jeffersonian Cyclopedia* (New York: Funk & Wagnalls, 1900), p. 190.
29. Richard B. Morris (ed.), *Alexander Hamilton and the Founding of the Nation* (New York: The Dial Press, 1957), p. 203.
30. *Hamilton's Works*, Volume 4, p. 342, quoted by Holman, *Story of the "Bricker" Amendment*, p. 28.
31. Supreme Court Justice Story, quoted by MacBride, p. 35.
32. Justice Stephen J. Field, quoted in J. C. Bancroft Davis (reporter), *United States Reports, Volume 133: Cases Adjudged in The Supreme Court at October Term, 1889* (New York and Albany: Banks & Brothers, 1890), pp. 266-67.
33. Stephen K. Williams, LLD. (ed.), *Cases Argued and Decided in the Supreme Court of the United States: 9, 10, 11, 12 Peters*, Book 9, Lawyers' Edition (Rochester, NY: The Lawyers Co-operative Publishing Co., 1888), p. 735 (Peters 10, p. 662).

34. Holman, p. 28.
35. MacBride, p. 51.
36. Senator Jesse Helms in "International Covenant on Civil and Political Rights," hearing before the Committee on Foreign Relations, United States Senate, November 21, 1991 (Washington: U.S. Government Printing Office, 1992), p. 2.
37. Ibid.
38. The International Covenant on Civil and Political Rights in *The International Bill of Human Rights: Fact Sheet No. 2* (United Nations, November 1989), p. 32.
39. Ibid., p. 33.
40. Ibid., p. 34.
41. *Congressional Record*, April 2, 1992, pp. S 4783-84.
42. Helms, p. 2.
43. Statement of International Human Rights Law Group in "International Covenant on Civil and Political Rights," Hearing before the Committee on Foreign Relations, United States Senate, November 21, 1991 (Washington: U.S. Government Printing Office, 1992), p. 130.
44. Statement of the U.S. Council for International Business, by Abraham Katz President, in "International Covenant on Civil and Political Rights," Hearing before the Committee on Foreign Relations, United States Senate, November 21, 1991 (Washington: U.S. Government Printing Office, 1992), p. 180.
45. See, for example: Robert W. Lee, "Restraining the World Court," *The New American*, September 7, 1992, pp. 17-18.
46. Griffin, p. 188.
47. Ibid. Note further: There are 15 justices on the World Court. In accordance with Article 25 of the *Statute of the International Court of Justice*, "A quorum of nine judges shall suffice to constitute the Court" to conduct business. Since a majority of the nine can render judgments, this means that five justices can decide a case. Article 26 states: "The Court may from time to time form one or more chambers, composed of three or more judges as the Court may determine, for dealing with particular categories of cases...." In such cases, decisions can be rendered by as few as two judges. See *Statute of the International Court of Justice* in *Review of the United Nations Charter: A Collection of Docu-*

ments by the Subcommittee on the United Nations Charter of the U.S. Senate Committee on Foreign Relations. (Washington: U.S. Government Printing Office, 1954).
48. *Digest of United States Practice in International Law 1973*, quoted by Ernest S. Easterly III, "The Rule of Law and the New World Order," pre-publication draft, p. 10.
49. "1990s declared UN Decade of International Law," *UN Chronicle*, March 1990, p. 77.

Chapter 7 • The Global Green Regime

1. Alexander King and Bertrand Schneider, *The First Global Revolution*, A Report by the Council of the Club of Rome (New York: Pantheon Books, 1991), p. 115.
2. See, for examples: Petr Beckman, *The Health Hazards of NOT Going Nuclear* (Boulder, CO: Golem Press, 1976); Sherwood B. Idso, Ph.D., *Carbon Dioxide and Global Change: Earth in Transition* (Tempe, AZ: IBR Press, 1989); Jay H. Lehr, *Rational Readings on Environmental Concerns* (New York: Van Nostrand Reinhold, 1992); Samuel McCracken, *The War Against the Atom* (New York: Basic Books, 1982); Dr. Dixy Lee Ray, *Trashing the Planet* (Chicago: Regnery Gateway, 1990); Julian L. Simon and Herman Kahn (eds.), *The Resourceful Earth: A Response to Global 2000* (New York: Basil Blackwell, Inc., 1984); and S. Fred Singer, *Global Climate Change* (New York: Paragon House, 1989).
3. See, for examples: Murray Feshback and Alfred Friendly, Jr., *Ecocide in USSR: Health and Nature Under Siege* (New York: Basic Books, 1992); and Jon Thompson, "Eastern Europe's Dark Dawn: The Iron Curtain Rises to Reveal a Land Tarnished by Pollution," *National Geographic*, June 1991.
4. Dr. Fred L. Smith, in speech delivered at an Earth Summit Alternatives conference held during the 1992 Earth Summit in Rio de Janeiro, recorded by author, portions of which appeared in his "Solution's from Rio," *The New American*, July 27, 1992, p. 16.
5. Maurice F. Strong, quoted by Paul

Raeburn, Associated Press, "Ecology Remedy Costly," *Sacramento Bee* (CA), March 12, 1992.

6. Maurice Strong, "The relationship between demographic trends, economic growth, unsustainable consumption patterns and environmental degradation," an UNCED PrepCom report, August 1991, quoted by GreenTrack International, Report 26 — August 15, 1991, Libertytown, MD, p. 3.

7. Ibid.

8. Maurice Strong, Introduction to Jim MacNeil, Pieter Winsemius, and Taizo Yakushiji, *Beyond Interdependence: The Meshing of the World's Economy and the Earth's Ecology.* (New York: Oxford University Press, 1991), p. ix.

9. Ibid., pp. ix-x.

10. Ibid., p. 128.

11. Roger D. Stone and Eve Hamilton, *Global Economics and the Environment: Toward Sustainable Rural Development in the Third World* (New York: Council on Foreign Relations Press, 1991).

12. Lester R. Brown, *World Without Borders.* New York: Vintage Books, 1972, p. 308.

13. Ibid.

14. Ibid., pp. 308-09.

15. Lester R. Brown.

16. Lester R. Brown, "The New World Order," in Lester R. Brown et al., *State of the World 1991: A Worldwatch Institute Report on Progress Toward a Sustainable Society* (New York: W.W. Norton, 1991), p. 3.

17. Ibid., p. 18.

18. Ibid.

19. George Kennan, "This Is No Time for Talk of German Reunification," *Washington Post*, November 12, 1989.

20. Mikhail Gorbachev addressing the 1990 Global Forum conference of spiritual and parliamentary leaders in Moscow in late January 1990, quoted in "We must 'ecologize' our society before it's too late," *Birmingham* [Alabama] *News*, April 22, 1990.

21. Ibid.

22. Flora Lewis, "Gorbachev Turns Green," *New York Times*, August 14, 1991.

23. John Lawrence Hargrove, quoted in "The United Nations: Back to the Future," *The Ford Foundation Letter*, February 1989, p. 3.

24. Richard N. Gardner, quoted in "The United Nations: Back to the Future," *The Ford Foundation Letter*, February 1989, p. 3.

25. See, for example: *Ford Foundation Letter*, February 1989, p. 3; or Thomas G. Weiss and Meyrl A. Kessler, "Moscow's U.N. Policy," *Foreign Policy*, Summer 1990, p. 100: "By reading recent Soviet literature and speeches on the United Nations, one could easily come away with the impression that Soviet leaders and their senior advisers have been converted to world federalism. For example ... Gorbachev adviser Georgi Shakhnazarov wrote a striking article optimistically appraising the possibility of 'world government.' Gorbachev and Foreign Minister Eduard Shevardnadze themselves liberally pepper their speeches with references to 'interdependence'...."

26. CFR membership lists and summaries appear in the Annual Reports of the Council on Foreign Relations (58 East 68th Street, New York, NY 10021). As examples, the August 31, 1972 edition reports 121 members in the journalism and communications professions out of a total of 1,476, whereas the 1992 edition claims 327 members in this category out of a total of 2,905.

27. See: Gary Allen, "Making Plans," American Opinion, April 1971; *Report From Iron Mountain on the Possibility and Desirability of Peace* (New York: Dial Press, 1967), pp. viii, x-xi, xix, 14.

28. *Report From Iron Mountain*, op cit.

29. John Kenneth Galbraith, quoted in *London Times* per Associated Press dispatch, January 5, 1968. See also: Gary Allen, "Making Plans," *American Opinion*, April 1971, p. 19.

30. *Report From Iron Mountain*, pp. 66-67.

31. Ibid., pp. 70-71.

32. Ibid., p. 71.

33. Ibid.

34. Ibid., pp. 66-67.

35. Ibid., p. 67.

36. Ibid., p. 58.

37. UNCED booklet, *In Our Hands: Earth Summit '92*, p. 23.

38. William K. Stevens, "Lessons of Rio: A New Prominence and an Effective Blandness," *New York Times*, June 14, 1992.

39. "Earth Summit: Press Summary of Agenda 21" prepared by Communications and Project Management Division, Depart-

ment of Public Information, as part of the United Nations information programme for the UN Conference on Environment and Development, Rio de Janeiro, Brazil, June 3-14, 1992.

40. "Parties to Earth Summit in Accord on Increasing Aid to Third World," *New York Times*, June 14, 1992, p. 6. See also, Daniel R. Abbasi, "'Development' commission almost up," *Earth Summit Times*, June 7, 1992, p. 1.

41. Ibid. (*New York Times* and Abbasi)

42. Jack Freeman, "Gorbachev: Red head for the Green Cross," *Earth Summit Times*, June 8, 1992.

43. President George Bush, address to the United Nations Conference on Environment and Development in Rio de Janeiro, Brazil, June 12, 1992. *Weekly Compilation of Presidential Documents*, June 22, 1992, Volume 28 — Number 25, pp. 1043-44.

44. President George Bush quoted by Michael Wines, "Bush Leaves Rio With Shots at Critics, U.S. and Foreign," *New York Times*, June 14, 1992.

45. Lester R. Brown (interview of), "A transition to a new era?" *Terraviva*, June 3, 1992, p. 10.

46. Ibid.

47. Ibid.

48. Ibid.

49. Hilary F. French, *After the Earth Summit: The Future of Environmental Governance*, Worldwatch Institute Paper 107, March 1992, p. 6.

50. Ibid., p. 23.

51. Ibid.

52. Ibid.

53. Stevens.

54. French, p. 38.

55. Dr. Fred L. Smith, quoted by author's on the scene report "Solution's from Rio," *The New American*, July 27, 1992, p. 16.

56. Ibid.

Chapter 8 • The UN Grab for Your Child

1. *Congressional Record*, September 17, 1990, p. H 7687.

2. "Suffer the Little Children," *Time*, October 8, 1990, p. 41.

3. Ibid.

4. "A Landmark for Children's Rights," in *The Rights of the Child: Fact Sheet No. 10* (United Nations, 1990), p. 1.

5. UNICEF director James Grant quoted by Senator Jesse Helms in *Congressional Record*, September 11, 1990, p. S 12788.

6. Thomas Bliley, *Congressional Record*, September 17, 1990, p. H 7687-88.

7. Bliley, "U.N. Playpen Politics: A Bid to Nanny," *Washington Times*, September 24, 1990, p. G3.

8. Bliley, *Congressional Record*, p. H 7687.

9. Ibid.

10. Ibid.

11. Bliley, *Washington Times*.

12. Andrei Vishinsky in UN General Assembly debate, quoted by Robert W. Lee, *The United Nations Conspiracy* (Appleton, WI: Western Islands, 1981), p. 100. See also John Foster Dulles, *War or Peace* (New York: Macmillan, 1950), p. 203.

13. Bliley, *Washington Times*.

14. Bliley, *Congressional Record*, p. H 7687.

15. Ibid.

16. Bliley, *Washington Times*.

17. Ibid.

Chapter 9 • The War on Population

1. Dr. Paul R. Ehrlich, *The Population Bomb*, 1st ed. (New York: Ballantine Books, 1968), Prologue.

2. Statement of Maurice Strong at opening of UNCED in Rio De Janeiro, Brazil, June 3, 1992, in release by UNCED, p. 3.

3. Claire Chambers, *The SIECUS Circle: A Humanist Revolution* (Appleton, WI: Western Islands, 1977), p. 3.

4. Rev. Paul Marx interview by author, August 12, 1992.

5. Paul R. Ehrlich and Anne H. Ehrlich, *The Population Explosion* (New York: Simon and Schuster, 1990).

6. Ehrlich, *The Population Bomb*, 1st ed., Prologue.

7. See, for example: Colin Clark, *Population Growth: The Advantages* (Santa Ana, CA: R. L. Sassone, 1972).

8. Ehrlich, *The Population Bomb*, pp. 88, 135.

9. Paul R. Ehrlich, "World Population: Is the Battle Lost?" *Stanford Today*, Winter 1968, quoted by Chambers, p. 9.

10. Chambers, p. 9.

11. Ibid.
12. Donnela H. and Dennis L. Meadows et al., *The Limits to Growth*, a report for the Club of Rome's Project on the Predicament of Mankind (New York: Universe Books, Publishers, 1972).
13. Gerald O. Barney (Study Director), *Global 2000: Report to the President of the United States: Entering the Twenty-First Century* (New York: Penguin Books, 1982).
14. Meadows, p. 196-7.
15. Julian L. Simon and Herman Kahn (eds.), *The Resourceful Earth: A Response to Global 2000* (New York: Basil Blackwell Inc., 1984), p. 34-5.
16. Christopher Freeman, "Malthus with a Computer," in H. S. D. Cole, et al. (eds.), *Models of Doom: A Critique of the Limits to Growth* (New York: Universe Books, 1975), p. 5.
17. Barney, *Global 2000*, Letter of transmittal from Thomas Pickering and Gus Speth.
18. Simon, p. 45.
19. Jacqueline Kasun, *The War Against Population* (San Francisco: Ignatius Press, 1988), p. 50.
20. Carnegie Endowment for International Peace National Commission on America and the New World, *Changing Our Ways: America and the New World* (Washington, DC: Brookings Institution, 1992), p. 41.
21. Ibid.
22. Ibid.
23. Kasun, pp. 90-91.
24. Steven W. Mosher, "A Mother's Ordeal," *Reader's Digest*, February 1987, p. 55.
25. Peking, New China News Agency, July 11, 1987, FBIS-CHI-87-133, July 13, 1987, p. A1, quoted by Stephen W. Mosher, "Chinese Officials Invade Family Life," *HLI Reports* (Human Life International, Gaithersburg, MD), October, 1987, p. 5.
26. Kasun, p. 90.
27. Ibid.
28. Chambers, p. 330.
29. Father Paul Marx, "World Bank puts bounty on lives of unborn children," news release of Human Life International, Gaithersburg, MD, March 30, 1992.
30. Chambers, p. 3.
31. Kasun, p. 79.
32. See, for example, Chambers, pp. 8, 239.
33. Julian Huxley, *UNESCO: Its Purpose and Its Philosophy* (Washington DC: Public Affairs Press, 1947), p. 21.
34. Chambers, p. 337.
35. Ibid., pp. 337-38.
36. Kasun, pp. 200-201.
37. Chambers, p. 338.
38. Ibid.
39. Ibid., p. 339.
40. Ibid.
41. Kasun, p. 167.
42. Statement of Maurice Strong at opening of UNCED in Rio De Janeiro, Brazil, June 3, 1992, in release by UNCED, p. 3.
43. Jacques Cousteau, quoted by Vivek Menezes, "Cousteau's warning: 'Demographic tsunami,'" *Earth Summit Times*, June 6, 1992, p. 3.
44. Statements by Gro Harlem Brundtland and Dr. Mostafa K. Tolba at the opening of UNCED in Rio de Janeiro, June 3, 1992 — text provided by UNCED at the Earth Summit in Rio.
45. Luis Cordova, "How to guarantee well-being for a population growing by the second?" *Terraviva* (Brazil), June 10, 1992, p. 9.
46. Lewis Preston, remarks at Earth Summit, June 1992.
47. Marx, HLI news release.
48. Jean M. Guilfoyle, "World Bank Safe Motherhood Initiative" *Population Research Institute Review*, May/June 1992, p.1.
49. Ibid.
50. Ibid.
51. Marx, HLI news release.
52. Guilfoyle, p. 3.
53. Marx, HLI news release.
54. Ibid.

Chapter 10 • NWO Money System

1. William D. Ruckelshaus, quoted by Larry B. Stammer, *Los Angeles Times*, May 26, 1992, p. H11.
2. Daniel Wood, "The Wizard of Baca Grande," *West*, May 1990, p. 35.
3. Colonel Edward Mandell House, *Philip Dru: Administrator: A Story of Tomorrow — 1920 – 1935* (New York: B. W. Huebsch, 1919).
4. Wood, p. 33.
5. Dr. Antony C. Sutton, *The War on Gold* (Seal Beach, CA: '76 Press, 1977), p. 99.

6. Dan Smoot, "The Dan Smoot Report: Pushed Into Bankruptcy," *The Review of the News*, February 14, 1979, p. 31.

7. James Perloff, *The Shadows of Power: The Council on Foreign Relations And The American Decline*. Appleton, WI: Western Islands, 1988, p. 72.

8. See: David Rees, *Harry Dexter White: A Study in Paradox* (New York: Coward, McCann & Geoghegan, 1973); Whittaker Chambers, *Witness* (New York: Random House, 1952); Allen Weinstein, *Perjury: The Hiss-Chambers Case* (New York: Vintage Books, 1978); James Burnham, *The Web of Subversion: Underground Networks in the U.S. Government* (New York: The John Day Co., 1954); Elizabeth Bentley, *Out of Bondage* (New York: Devin-Adair, 1951); and Christopher Andrew and Oleg Gordievsky, *KGB: The Inside Story: Of Its Foreign Operations from Lenin to Gorbachev* (New York: HarperCollins Publishers, 1991).

9. See: Louis F. Budenz, *The Techniques of Communism* (Chicago: Henry Regnery, 1954), p. 235-36; Burnham, pp. 37-39; and *Activities of United States Citizens Employed by the United Nations*, hearings before the Senate Subcommittee on Internal Security, December 1, 1952, pp. 227-56 and January 2, 1953, p. 7.

10. Henry (Hans) Morgenthau, quoted by Henry Hazlitt, *From Bretton Woods to World Inflation* (Chicago: Regnery Gateway, 1984), p. 88.

11. Smoot, pp. 32-33.

12. Hazlitt, p. 7.

13. Ibid., p. 14.

14. Ibid., p. 26-7.

15. Ibid., p. 19.

16. Miriam Camps and Catherine Gwin, *Collective Management: The Reform of Global Economic Organizations*, 21st volume in the CFR's 1980s Project series (New York: McGraw Hill, 1981).

17. Thomas G. Weiss and Meryl A. Kessler, "Moscow's U.N. Policy," *Foreign Policy*, Summer 1990, p. 112.

18. See, for examples, William F. Jasper "From the Atlantic to the Urals (and Beyond)," *The New American*, January 27, 1992; and the author's interviews with Yuri N. Maltsev and Llewellyn H. Rockwell reported in "Meeting Ground of East and West," *The New American*, February 24, 1992, pp. 23-24.

19. Boutros Boutros-Ghali, *An Agenda for Peace: Preventive Diplomacy, Peacemaking and Peace-Keeping* (New York: United Nations, 1992), pp. 41-43.

20. Carnegie Endowment for International Peace National Commission on America and the New World, *Changing Our Ways: America and the New World* (Washington, DC: Brookings Institution, 1992), p. 54.

21. Ibid., p. 5.

22. Ibid., p. 44.

23. Ibid., pp. 46, 38-39.

24. Stephan Schmidheiny with the Business Council for Sustainable Development, *Changing Course: A Global Business Perspective on Development and the Environment* (MA: MIT Press, 1992).

25. Ibid., p. xi.

26. William D. Ruckelshaus, quoted by Larry B. Stammer, *Los Angeles Times*, May 26, 1992, p. H11.

27. Alexander King & Bertrand Schneider, *The First Global Revolution*, a report by the Council of the Club of Rome (New York: Pantheon Books, 1991), p. 156.

28. Ibid., pp. 156-57.

29. Ibid., pp. 157-59.

30. Ibid., p. 198.

31. Ibid., p. 257.

32. An artist's drawing of the Fabian Window now displayed in Beatrice Webb House is provided in Zygmund Dobbs (Research Director), *The Great Deceit: Social Pseudo-Sciences* (West Sayville, NY: Veritas Foundation, 1964), p. viii.

Chapter 11 • The Compassion Con

1. Dr. Rony Brauman, "Famine Aid: Were We Duped?" *Reader's Digest*, October 1986, p. 71.

2. James Bovard, "The World Bank vs. the World's Poor," Cato Institute Policy Analysis, No. 92, September 28, 1987, p. 1.

3. Brauman, p. 72.

4. Robert W. Lee, "International Welfare," *The New American*, March 23, 1992, p. 26.

5. Robert W. Lee, "The Truth About the Communist Planned Famine in Ethiopia," *American Opinion*, April 1985.

6. Bovard, pp. 2, 5.

7. Ibid., p. 5.
8. Graham Hancock, *Lords of Poverty* (New York: Atlantic Monthly Press, 1989), p. 85.
9. Ibid., p. 104.
10. Paul Lewis, "U.N. Refugee Chief Quits Over His Use of Funds," *New York Times*, October 27, 1989.
11. Brauman, p. 70.
12. Ibid., p. 71.
13. Bovard, p. 3.
14. Ibid.
15. Ibid., p. 1.
16. Doug Bandow, "Why Waste Aid on Russia? Consider the I.M.F's dismal record," *New York Times*, March 26, 1992.
17. Ibid.
18. Senator Jesse Helms, *Congressional Record*, December 15, 1987, p. S 18148.
19. Official vita supplied to author by World Bank on September 1, 1992.
20. Hancock, p. 144.
21. Ibid.
22. Ibid., p. 145.
23. Ibid., pp. 122-23.
24. Ibid., p. 178.
25. Ibid.
26. Ibid., p. 180.
27. P.T. Bauer, *Reality and Rhetoric* (Cambridge, MA: Harvard University Press, 1984), pp. 43-44.
28. David Chilton, *Productive Chrisitans in an Age of Guilt-Manipulators* (Tyler, TX: Institute for Christian Economics, 1981), pp. 300-01.
29. Douglas Waller, "Foreign-Aid Follies," *Newsweek*, April 16, 1990, p. 23.
30. Hancock, p. 109.
31. Ibid., p. 190.

Chapter 12 • The New World Religion

1. Donald Keys, "Transformation of Self and Society," an address at a symposium, "Toward a Global Society," held in Asheville, NC on November 11, 1984, quoted by Dennis L. Cuddy, *Now Is the Dawning of the New Age New World Order* (Oklahoma City: Hearthstone Publishing, Ltd., 1991), pp. 268-69.
2. *Golden Book of the Theosophical Society* (1925), pp. 28-29, quoted by Constance Cumby, *The Hidden Dangers of the Rainbow: The New Age Movement and Our Coming Age of Barbarism* (Shreveport, LA: Huntington House, 1983), p. 44.
3. From a Theosophical Society brochure, quoted by Cumby, p. 45.
4. *Golden Book*, pp. 63-64, quoted by Cumby, pp. 45-46.
5. Tal Brooke, *When the World Will Be As One* (Eugene, OR: Harvest House Publishers, 1989) pp. 175-76.
6. Ibid.
7. Ibid.
8. Ibid., pp. 175-76.
9. From "The Lucis Trust," a pamphlet distributed by the Lucis Trust.
10. *The New Group of World Servers*, a pamphlet distributed by World Goodwill, an activity of Lucis Trust, p. 3.
11. Ibid., pp. 2, 8-10.
12. Ibid., pp. 6-7.
13. Ibid., p. 7.
14. Ibid., p. 10.
15. Troy Lawrence, *New Age Messiah Identified: Who Is Lord Maitreya?* (Lafayette, LA: Huntington House, 1991), pp. 7-11.
16. Benjamin Creme, *The Reappearance of the Christ and the Masters of Wisdom* (London: Tara Press, 1980), p. 69, quoted by Lawrence, pp. 60-61.
17. Benjamin Creme, quoted by Lawrence, pp. 60.
18. Ibid., p. 123, 178.
19. Tara Center's *Network News*, Tony Townsend editor, October 1987, p. 1.
20. Statement of Maurice Strong at opening of UNCED in Rio De Janeiro, Brazil, June 3, 1992, UNCED release, pp. 11-12.
21. "The Declaration of the Sacred Earth Gathering, Rio 92," *Earth Summit Times*, June 3, 1992.
22. "Ten Commandments on Environment and Development," extracts from an address presented to UNCED by Dr. Uri Marinov, June 3, 1992 — text provided by UNCED at Earth Summit in Rio.
23. *World Goodwill Newsletter*, 1992, No. 3, p. 7.
24. Jose Lutzenberger at Rio Earth Summit, *The '92 Global Forum*, Release #115, June 5, 1992.
25. Bob Baker, "Hayden on Earth," *Los Angeles Times*, October 16, 1991, pp. B1, B4.
26. Ibid., B4.
27. William Irwin Thompson, *Quest*, Spring

1991, quoted by Cuddy, p. 311-12.
28. Ibid.
29. From a pamphlet distributed by the Lindsfarne Center.
30. David Spangler, *Reflections on the Christ*, 3rd. ed. (Scotland: Findhorn Publications, 1981), p. 41.
31. Donald Keys, quoted by Douglas R. Groothuis, *Unmasking the New Age* (Downers Grove, IL: InterVarsity Press, 1986), p. 118.
32. "Planetary Citizens," a pamphlet from Planetary Citizens.
33. Alexander King and Bertrand Schneider, *The First Global Revolution*, a report by the Council of The Club of Rome (New York: Pantheon Books, 1991), p. 218.
34. Ibid., p. 154.
35. Ibid., p. 244.
36. Ibid., p. 237.
37. Ibid., p. 245.
38. Robert Muller, quoted by Brooke, p. 207.
39. Robert Muller, *New Genesis: Shaping a Global Spirituality*, Image Books ed. (Garden City, NY: Doubleday, 1984), p. 167.
40. Daniel Wood, "The Wizard of Baca Grande", *West*, May 1990.
41. UN report *The New International Economic Order: A Spiritual Imperative*, quoted by Cuddy, pp. 255-56.
42. Rev. Clarence Kelly, *Conspiracy Against God and Man* (Appleton, WI: Western Islands, 1974) p. 179.
43. Ibid.
44. See, for example, Chapter 8 "The Secret Origins of Nazism" in Jean-Michel Angebert, *The Occult and the Third Reich* (New York: Macmillan, 1974).

Chapter 13 • UN Regionalism — The European Community

1. M. Peter McPherson, "The European Community's Internal Market Program: An American Perspective," an address before the Institute for International Economics, August 4, 1988, *Treasury News*, B-1505, p. 2.
2. Merry and Serge Bromberger, *Jean Monnet and the United States of Europe* (New York: Coward-McCann Publishers, 1969), p. 19.
3. Ibid.
4. Arnold J. Zurcher, *The Struggle to Unite Europe 1940-1958* (New York: New York Univ. Press, 1958), pp. 4-5.
5. Hans F. Sennholz, *How Can Europe Survive?* (New York: D. Van Nostrand Company, 1955), p. 70.
6. Ibid., pp. 29, 137.
7. Zurcher, p. 14.
8. Ibid., p. 15.
9. Ibid., p. 13.
10. Bromberger, p. 33.
11. Ibid.
12. Ibid.
13. George Racey Jordan, *From Major Jordan's Diaries* (New York: International Graphics, 1952).
14. Clarence Streit, *Union Now* (New York: Harper & Brothers, 1940).
15. Dan Smoot, *The Invisible Government* (Appleton, WI: Western Islands, 1965), p. 94.
16. Hans Heymann, *Plan for Permanent Peace* (New York: Harper and Brothers, 1941), p. 78.
17. Ibid., pp. 263-64 and Chapters V, VI, VII, and X.
18. James Perloff, *The Shadows of Power* (Appleton, WI: Western Islands, 1988), p. 127.
19. *European Movement and the Council of Europe* with Forewords by Winston S. Churchill and Paul-Henri Spaak, published on behalf of the European Movement. (London, New York: Hutchinson & Co, 1958), pp. 33-34, 36.
20. Ibid, p. 34. See also *HduB Reports*, April 1972, p. 2.
21. Michael J. Hogan, *The Marshall Plan* (New York: Cambridge University Press, 1987), p. 43.
22. Bromberger, p. 62.
23. Laurence Shoup and William Minter, *Imperial Brain Trust: The Council on Foreign Relations and United States Foreign Policy* (New York: Monthly Review Press, 1977), p 35.
24. Hogan, pp. 97-98.
25. Ibid., pp. 99, 98.
26. Ibid., p. 98.
27. Walter Isaacson and Evan Thomas, *The Wise Men* (New York: Simon and Schuster, 1986), p. 289.
28. William P. Hoar, "The Amazing John J. McCloy," *American Opinion*, March, 1983,

pp. 25-40.

29. Max Holland, "Citizen McCloy," *The Wilson Quarterly*, Autumn 1991, p. 37.
30. Hoar, p. 39. See also Gar Alperovitz and Kai Bird, "Dream of Total Disarmament Could Become Reality," *Los Angeles Times*, January 5, 1992, p. M6.
31. Isaacson and Thomas, p. 397.
32. Sennholz, p. 185.
33. Hogan, p. 429.
34. Ibid., p. 40.
35. Ernst H. van der Beugel, *From Marshall Aid to Atlantic Partnership* (Amsterdam, New York: Elsevier Publishing Co., 1966), pp. 101-02.
36. *H. du B. Reports*, November-December 1972, p. 6.
37. *H. du B. Reports*, September 1972, p. 2.
38. Carroll Quigley, *Tragedy and Hope: A History of the World in Our Time* (New York: Macmillan, 1966), page 1284.
39. Ibid.
40. *H. du B. Reports*, May, 1972, pp. 1-2. See also Don Cook, "Monnet: Europe's Gentle Guiding Hand." *Los Angeles Times*, October 8, 1976, pp. 8-9, and "Monnet, Key to European Unity, Dead at Age 90," *Los Angeles Times*, March 17, 1979, pp. 1, 15.
41. Hogan, p. 367.
42. Ibid.
43. Ibid.
44. *H.du B. Reports*, May 1972, p. 1.
45. Joseph Alsop, July 9, 1964, quoted ibid., p. 6.
46. Bromberger, p. 123.
47. Ibid.
48. Quigley, pp. 1284-85. See also *H. du B. Reports*, September 1972, pp. 1-2.
49. Ibid., p. 1285.
50. Richard N. Gardner, "The Hard Road To World Order," *Foreign Affairs*, April 1974, p. 558.
51. Quigley, p. 1286.
52. van der Beugel, p. 245.
53. Ibid., p. 323.
54. Ibid., p. 246. See also: Hogan, pp. 153-63; and *H. du B. Report*, July/August 1979, pp. 4-5.
55. "1992: The Great European Market?" address by Willy De Clercq at the Eurug Conference, Ghent, 25 October 1987, text provided by EC Office of Press & Public Affairs, Washington, DC.
56. Anatoliy Golitsyn, *New Lies For Old* (New

York: Dodd, Mead, & Co., 1984), pp. 341-42.
57. William Wallace, *The Transformation of Western Europe* (London: Royal Institute of International Affairs, 1990), p. 94.
58. *Program of the Communist International* (New York: Workers Library Publishers, 1936), p. 36.
59. Hans-Dietrich Genscher, "The Future of Europe," speech delivered in Lisbon on July 12, 1991, *Statements & Speeches*, Vol. XIV, No. 8, German Information Center, New York.

Chapter 14 • Get US out!

1. U.S. Senator Robert Taft, quoted by Representative James B. Utt, *Congressional Record House*, January 15, 1962.
2. U.S. Senator Patrick McCarran, quoted by G. Edward Griffin, *The Fearful Master: A Second Look at the United Nations* (Appleton, WI: Western Islands, 1964), p. 158.
3. U.S. Senator Barry Goldwater, *Congressional Record*, October 26, 1971, p. S 16764, quoted by Robert W. Lee, *The United Nations Conspiracy* (Appleton, WI: Western Islands, 1981), p. 194.
4. Herbert Hoover, quoted by Representative James B. Utt, *Congressional Record*, January 15, 1962.
5. Robert Welch, *The Blue Book of The John Birch Society* (Appleton, WI: Western Islands, 1959), p. 125.
6. Jane H. Ingraham, "The Consequence of Error," *The New American* November 24, 1986.
7. R. J. Rummel, *Lethal Politics: Soviet Genocide and Mass Murder since 1917* (New Brunswick, NJ: Transaction Publishers, 1990), p. xi.
8. Ibid., pp. 191, 217, 3-4. Professor Rummel places the number of victims killed during the "Postwar and Stalin's twilight period, 1945-1953," at 15,613,000. For the "Post-Stalin period, 1954-1987, his research indicated a toll of around 6,872,000 victims.
9. Ibid., p. 5.
10. R. J. Rummel, "War Isn't This Century's Biggest Killer," *Wall Street Journal*, July 7, 1986.
11. Ibid.
12. The following books recount the human

cost of Communism: *The Gulag Archipelago* by Aleksandr Solzhenitsyn; *The Great Terror* by Robert Conquest; *The Harvest of Sorrow* by Robert Conquest; *Kolyma* by Robert Conquest; *Execution by Hunger* by Miron Dolot; *Utopia in Power* by Mikhail Heller; *The Ordeal of the Captive Nations* by Hawthorne Daniel; *The Uses of Terror* by Boris Lewytzkyj; *Chekisty* by John J. Dziak; *Murder of a Gentle Land* by John Barron and Anthony Paul.

13. Rummel, *Lethal Politics*, p. 9.
14. Ibid., pp. 11-12.
15. G. Edward Griffin, "More Deadly Than War," transcript of a filmed lecture (Thousand Oaks, CA: American Media, 1968).
16. Rummel, *Wall Street Journal*.
17. Ibid.
18. Pitirim A. Sorokin quoted in Welch, p. 119.
19. Welch, pp. 119-20.
20. John Adams, quoted by Philip M. Crane, *The Sum of Good Government* (Ottawa, IL: Green Hill, 1976.), p. 3.
21. James Madison, Essay No. 51, in Alexander Hamilton, James Madison, and John Jay, *The Federalist Papers* (New York: Mentor, 1961), p. 322.
22. Aldous Huxley, *The Perennial Philosophy* (London: Collins, 1958), pp. 133-34.
23. John Adams, quoted by Crane, p. 3.
24. George Washington, quoted by Griffin, *The Fearful Master* (Appleton, WI: Western Islands, 1964), p. 196.
25. Thomas Jefferson, First Inaugural Address, 1801, quoted in *A Compilation of the Messages and Papers of the Presidents*, Vol. I (New York: Bureau of National Literature, 1897), p. 311.
26. Daniel Webster, quoted by Lyman A. Garber, *Of Men and Not of Law: How the Courts are Usurping the Political Function* (New York: Devin-Adair, 1966), p. 170.
27. Thomas Jefferson, *Kentucky Resolutions*.
28. James Madison, speech in the Virginia Convention, June 16, 1788, quoted by John Bartlett, *Bartlett's Familiar Quotations* (Boston: Little, Brown, and Company, 1980), p. 398.
29. Thomas Jefferson in a letter to Gideon Granger, Monticello, August 1800, quoted by John P. Foley (ed.), *The Jeffersonian Cyclopedia* (New York: Funk & Wagnalls, 1900), p. 130.
30. Thomas Jefferson in a letter to Nathaniel Macon, Monticello, 1821, quoted by Foley (ed.), p. 130.
31. Thomas Jefferson in a letter to C. Hammond, Monticello, 1821, quoted by Foley (ed.), p. 133.
32. Alexander King & Bertrand Schneider, *The First Global Revolution*, a report by the Council of The Club of Rome (NewYork: Pantheon Books, 1991), p. 149.
33. J. Reuben Clark, Jr., quote by Lee, p. 35.
34. Ibid.
35. Both the Korean War and Vietnam War were fought under the auspices of SEATO (the Southeast Asia Treaty Organization) a regional alliance under the authority of the United Nations. SEATO was formed in 1954 under the guiding hand of John Foster Dulles for the purpose of involving the U.S. militarily in Southeast Asia. The SEATO treaty states:

Article 1. The parties undertake, as set forth in the Charter of the United Nations ... and to refrain in their international relations from the threat or use of force in any manner inconsistent with the purposes of the United Nations.

Article 4. ... [Military] Measures taken under this paragraph shall be immediately reported to the Security Council of the United Nations....

In Korea, CFR Insiders allowed the UN to dictate the "no-win" policies that guaranteed heavy losses of our soldiers and, ultimately, defeat. Secretary of Defense George Marshall admitted that the U.S. "hot pursuit" policy allowing our pilots to pursue attacking enemy aircraft back into their own territory was abandoned because the policy had failed to win UN support. Secretary of State Dean Acheson stated: "There have been resolutions of the General Assembly which make clear the course that the General Assembly thinks wise; and the United States is endeavoring to follow the course which has tremendous international support and is not contemplating taking unilateral steps of its own."

General Douglas MacArthur, in explaining the unprecedented and unconscionable restrictions placed on his military options said: "I realized for the first time that I had actually been denied the use of my full military power to safeguard the lives of my

GLOBAL TYRANNY ... STEP BY STEP

soldiers and the safety of my army. To me, it clearly foreshadowed a future tragic situation in Korea, and left me with a sense of inexpressible shock."

Through the UN, the Communist forces were kept informed of "allied" military plans and operations. General MacArthur stated: "That there was some leak in intelligence was evident to everyone. [Brigadier General Walton] Walker continually complained to me that his operations were known to the enemy in advance through sources in Washington." General Mark Clark said: "I could not help wondering and worrying whether we were faced with open enemies across the conference table and hidden enemieswho sat with us in our most secret councils."

Red Chinese General Lin Piao made this shocking admission: "I would never have made the attack and risked my men and military reputation if I had not been assured that Washington would restrain General MacArthur from taking adequate retaliatory measures against my lines of supply and communication." He knew the fix was in in Washington.

For more in-depth coverage of the Korean and Vietnam betrayals, see especially: Robert W. Lee, *The United Nations Conspiracy* (Appleton, WI: Western Islands, 1981), Chap. 5, "Korea," pp. 51-60; G. Edward Griffin, *The Fearful Master: A Second Look at the United Nations* (Appleton, WI: Western Islands, 1964), Chapter 14, "A Substitute for Victory," pp. 169-83; James Perloff, *The Shadows of Power: The Council on Foreign Relations And The American Decline* (Appleton, WI: Western Islands, 1988), Chap. 6, "The Truman Era," pp. 81-83, and Chap. 8, "The Establishment's War in Vietnam," pp. 120-35; Douglas MacArthur, *Reminiscences* (New York: McGraw-Hill Book Company, 1964); Mark Clark, *From the Danube to the Yalu* (New York: Harper & Brothers, 1954); and Hilaire du Berrier, *Background to Betrayal: The Tragedy of Vietnam* (Appleton, WI: Western Islands, 1965).

36. J. B. Matthews, quoted by Griffin, *The Fearful Master*, p. 158.
37. Griffin, *The Fearful Master*, p. 158.
38. Richard A. Falk, quoted by Mark Satin, *New Age Politics: Healing Self and Society*

(West Vancouver, B.C.: Whitecap Books, 1978), p. 127.
39. Frank Chodorov, "One Worldism," *The Freeman*, March 1955, p. 334.
40. Douglas R. Groothuis, *Unmasking the New Age* (Downers Grove, IL: InterVarsity Press, 1986), p. 128.
41. Lord Acton, quoted in *The Freeman*, March 1955, p. 373.
42. Mao Tse-tung, "Problems of War and Strategy" (November 6, 1938), *Selected Works*, Vol II, (Peking).
43. Lyman A. Garber, *Of Men and Not of Law: How the Courts are Usurping the Political Function* (New York: Devin-Adair, 1966), p. 7.
44. Frank E. Holman, "The Problems of the World Court and the Connally Reservation," a pamphlet (Seattle, WA: Frayn Printing Co., Seattle, July 25, 1960), quoted in Garber, p. 8.
45. Frederick Copleston, S.J., *A History of Philosophy, Volume III: Ockham to Suarez* (New York: Doubleday, 1963), p. 397.
46. John F. McManus, *The Insiders: Architects of the New World Order*, (3rd ed.) (Appleton, WI: The John Birch Society, 1992), p. 20.
47. Crane, p. 63.
48. John Jay, Essay No. 2 in *The Federalist Papers*, p. 38.
49. Alexander Hamilton, Essay No. 69 in *The Federalist Papers*, p. 417-18.
50. Abraham Lincoln to William H. Hendon, quoted by John F. McManus, "Sins of Our Fathers," *The New American*, April 9, 1991, p. 25.
51. Griffin, p. 229.
52. William Henry Chamberlain, "The Bankruptcy of a Policy," in Harry Elmer Barnes (ed.), *Perpetual War for Perpetual Peace* (Caldwell, ID: Caxton Printers, 1953), p. 523.
53. George Washington, Farewell Address, September 17, 1796, quoted in *A Compilation of the Messages and Papers of the Presidents*, Vol. I, p. 214.
54. Ibid., pp. 213-15.
55. Richard Cobden, quoted by Welch, p. 150.
56. John Quincy Adams, quoted by Barnes (ed.), frontpiece.
57. Will and Ariel Durant, *The Lessons of History* (New York: Simon and Schuster, 1968), pp. 66-67.

312

NOTES

58. Senator Jesse Helms, *Congressional Record*, December 15, 1987, p. S 18146.
59. Barry M. Goldwater, *With No Apologies* (New York: William Morrow & Co., 1979), pp. 284-85.
60. Robert Welch, "Which World Will It Be?," *American Opinion* Reprint Series (Appleton, WI: The John Birch Society, 1970), p. 23.
61. David Rockefeller, "From A China Traveler," *New York Times*, August 10, 1973.
62. David Rockefeller, quoted in the Soviet *New Times*, November, 1977, reported by *The Review Of The News*, January 18, 1978, p.59.
63. See volumes on Western aid to the Soviet Union by Evans, Finder, Sutton, et al. listed in Chapter 2, endnote 27. Also see: Werner Keller, *East Minus West = Zero* (New York: G. P. Putnam's Sons, 1962); Sol Sanders, *Living Off the West* (New York: Madison Books, 1990); Jane H. Ingraham, "The Great Wealth Transfer: Establishing the New International Economic Order," *The New American*, May 8, 1989.
64. Ibid. See also: *Aid and Trade Documents: A Compilation* (Appleton, WI: Larry McDonald Crusade, revised and updated July 1987); Testimony of Lawrence J. Brady, Acting Director of Export Administration, before House Committee on Armed Services Subcommittee on Research and Development, May 24, 1979; Richard E. Band, "The Traders: Selling Rope for the Hanging," *American Opinion*, January 1974.
   See also the following articles from *The New American*: John W. Robbins, "Birds of a Feather: American and Soviet traders are flocking together," April 27, 1987; Kirk Kidwell, "Bolsheviks Bankrupt at 70," October 26, 1987; James J. Drummey, "Building the Evil Empire," July 20, 1987; Drummey, "By Trade Betrayed," February 12, 1990; Drummey, "Defenseless: Our Patriot and Other High-Tech Giveaways," April 9, 1991.
65. See for examples: George Racey Jordan USAF (Ret.), *Major Jordan's Diaries* (New York: Harcourt, Brace, 1952); Medford Evans, *The Secret War for the A-Bomb* (Chicago: Henry Regnery, 1953); Antony C. Sutton, *The Best Enemy Money Can Buy* (Billings, MT: Liberty House Press, 1986); John Barron, *KGB Today: The Hidden Hand* (New York: Reader's Digest Press, 1983).
66. See for examples: Gregory A. Fossedal and Daniel O. Graham, *A Defense That Defends,* (Old Greenwich, CT: The Devin-Adair Company, 1983); Daniel O. Graham, *High Frontier* (New York: Thomas Doherty Associates, 1983); Quentin Crommelin, Jr. and David S. Sullivan, *Soviet Military Supremacy: The Untold Facts* (Los Angeles: Defense and Strategic Studies Program, University of Southern California, 1985); Brian D. Dailey and Patrick J. Parker, editors, *Soviet Strategic Deception* (Lexington, Massachusetts: D.C. Heath and Company, 1987); M. Stanton Evans, *The Politics of Surrender* (New York: The Devin-Adair Company, 1966); Joseph D. Douglas and Neil C. Livingston, *America the Vulnerable: The Threat of Chemical/Biological Warfare* (Lexington, Massachusetts: Lexington Books, 1987).
67. The following book and reports provide extensive evidence of intentional abandonment of known POWs to lasting captivity: U.S. Senate Committee on Foreign Relations Republican Staff, *An Examination of U.S. Policy Toward POW/MIAs* (Washington, DC: U.S. Senate Foreign Relations Committee Republican Staff, May 23, 1991); Monika Jensen-Stevenson and William Stevenson, *Kiss the Boys Goodbye* (New York: Dutton, 1990); *POW/MIA Policy and Process*, hearings before the Select Committee on POW/MIA Affairs, United States Senate, two volumes (Washington, DC: U.S. Government Printing Office, 1992).
   The following selection from *The New American* represent a sampling of the many articles on the POW/MIA issue that have appeared in that magazine over the years and will provide the reader with a good overview of the coverups, the betrayals, and the facts concerning our missing soldiers from World Wars I and II, Korea and Vietnam: John M. G. Brown and Thomas V. Ashworth, "Mikhail Gorbachev, Let Our People Go," a two-part series, May 21, 1990 and June 4, 1990; William F. Jasper, "Official Policy: Abandon POWs," February 12, 1991; Jasper, "They Deserve to

Come Home," September 10, 1991; Sarah E. Foster, "Pentagon Flim-Flam Masters," and Jasper, "Bring Them Home!" September 24, 1991; Jasper, "Betrayed in Action," November 19, 1991; William P. Hoar, "President Bush to POW/MIA Families: 'Shut Up and Sit Down,'" August 24, 1992.
68. See for examples: Herman H. Dinsmore, *The Bleeding of America* (Appleton, WI: Western Islands, 1974); James J. Drummey, "Building the Evil Empire," *The New American*, July 20, 1987; Robert W. Lee, "International Welfare," *The New American*, March 23, 1992.
69. See the following: Arthur Bliss Lane (U. S. Ambassador to Poland, 1944-1947), *I Saw Poland Betrayed* (Bobb-Merrill Company, 1948); John T. Flynn, *While You Slept: Our Tragedy in Asia and Who Made It* (New York: Devin-Adair, 1951); Robert Welch, *May God Forgive Us* (Chicago: Henry Regnery, 1952); Earl E. T. Smith, U.S. Ambassador to Cuba, 1957-59, *The Fourth Floor: An Account of the Castro Communist Revolution* (New York: Random House, 1962); William J. Gill, *The Ordeal of Otto Otepka* (New Rochelle, NY: Arlington House, 1969).
   For evidence of more recent betrayals see: Anastasio Somosa and Jack Cox, *Nicaragua Betrayed* (Appleton, WI: Western Islands, 1980); Henry R. Pike, *A History of Communism in South Africa*, (Primrose Hill, Germiston, South Africa: Christian Mission International of South Africa, 1985); Warren L. McFerran, *The Betrayal of Southern Africa* (Winter Park, FL: Garfield Publishing Corp., 1985); David B. Funderburk, *Pinstripes and Reds: An American Ambassador Caught Between the State Department and the Romanian Communists, 1981-1985* (Washington, DC: Selous Foundation Press, 1987).
   See also the following articles from *The New American*: James J. Drummey "The Captive Nations: How they were captured and why they are still enslaved," July 14, 1986; Robert W. Lee, "No Accident: The continuing betrayal of American interests is a matter of policy," March 30, 1987, Warren F. McFerran, "[South Africa] On the Edge," October 22, 1990.
70. See for examples: Pike, op. cit.; McFerran, op. cit.; and William P. Hoar "Making of a

Monster," *The New American*, September 7, 1992, which shows how Insiders Kissinger, Bush, Baker, Eagleburger provided critical weapons technology to Saddam Hussein even while he was known as a primary sponsor of international terrorism.
   See also the annual reports of the Council on Foreign Relations, which include a roster of the speakers who have addressed CFR programs. These have traditionally included many foreign communist leaders, even those heading terrorist organizations. Besides Nelson Mandela, officials of the communist/terrorist ANC (African National Congress) who have graced the CFR dais include Thabo Mbeki, John Samuel and Chris Hani. Other terrorist leaders and supporters who have enjoyed honored slots on the CFR's Meetings Program include Joe Slovo, General-Secretary of South African Communist Party; Sam Nujoma and Andimba Toivo ja Toivo of SWAPO (Southwest Africa Peoples Organization); Robert Mugabe of ZANU (Zimbabwe African National Union); Joshua Nkomo of ZAPU (Zimbabwe African People's Union); Guillermo Ungo of the National Revolutionary Movement of El Salvador; Daniel Ortega of Nicaragua.
71. See for examples: Gary Allen, *None Dare Call It Conspiracy* (Rossmoor, CA: Concord Press, 1971); Allen, *The Rockefeller File* (Seal Beach, CA: '76 Press, 1976); James Perloff, *The Shadows of Power*; and Robert W. Lee, "The Power Behind the Throne," *The New American*, September 21, 1992.
72. See for examples: Allen, *None Dare Call It Conspiracy*; Perloff, *The Shadows of Power*; and Robert Adelmann, "The Federal Reserve System," *The New American*, October 27, 1986.
73. See for examples: Donald L. Robinson (ed.), *Reforming American Government*; James MacGregor Burns, *The Power to Lead* (New York, Simon & Schuster, 1984); Perloff, *The Shadows of Power*, Chap. 14, "On the Threshold of a New World Order," pp. 199-208; Don Fotheringham, "The Con-Con Network," *The New American*, February 10, 1992.
74. Patrick Henry, speech in Virginia Convention, March 23, 1775, quoted by *Bartlett's*, p. 383.

Bibliography

— Books —

Allen, Gary with Larry Abraham. *None Dare Call It Conspiracy*. Rossmoor, CA: Concord Press, 1971.

Allen, Gary. *The Rockefeller File*. Seal Beach, CA: '76 Press, 1976.

Andrew, Christopher and Oleg Gordievsky. *KGB: The Inside Story of Its Foreign Operations from Lenin to Gorbachev*. New York: HarperCollins Publishers, 1991.

Angebert, Jean-Michel. *The Occult and the Third Reich*. New York: Macmillan, 1974.

Barnaby, Frank. *Gaia Peace Atlas*. New York: Doubleday, 1988.

Barnet, Richard J. *Roots of War*. New York: Atheneum, 1972.

Barney, Gerald O. (Study Director). *Global 2000: Report to the President of the United States: Entering the Twenty-First Century*. New York: Penguin Books, 1982.

Barron, John. *KGB: The Secret Work Of Soviet Secret Agents*. New York: Reader's Digest Press, 1974.

— *KGB Today: The Hidden Hand*. New York: Reader's Digest Press, 1983.

— and Anthony Paul. *Murder of a Gentle Land: The Untold Story of Communist Genocide in Cambodia*. New York: Reader's Digest Press, 1977.

Bauer, Peter T. *Reality and Rhetoric: Studies in the Economics of Development*. Cambridge: Harvard Univ. Press, 1984.

Beckman, Petr. *The Health Hazards of NOT Going Nuclear*. Boulder, CO: Golem Press, 1976.

Bentley, Elizabeth. *Out of Bondage*. New York: Devin-Adair, 1951.

Bittman, Ladislav. *The KGB and Soviet Disinformation: An Insider's View*. McLean, VA: Pergamon-Brassey's International Defense Publishers, 1985.

Borgese, Giuseppe Antonio. *Foundations of the World Republic*. Chicago: Univ. of Chicago Press, 1953.

Bromberger, Merry and Serge. *Jean Monnet and the United States of Europe*. New York: Coward-McCann Publishers, 1969.

Brooke, Tal. *When the World Will Be As One*. Eugene, OR: Harvest House Publishers, 1989.

Browder, Earl. *Victory — and after*. New York: International Publishers, 1942.

Brown, Lester R. *World Without Borders*. New York: Vintage Books, 1972.

— et al. *State of the World 1991: A Worldwatch Institute Report on Progress Toward a Sustainable Society*. New York: W.W. Norton, 1991.

Budenz, Louis F. *The Cry Is Peace*. Chicago: Henry Regnery, 1952.

— *The Techniques of Communism*. Chicago: Henry Regnery, 1954.

Burnham, James. *The Web of Subversion: Underground Networks in the U.S. Government*. New York: The John Day Co., 1954.

Burns, James MacGregor. *The Power To Lead*. New York: Simon & Schuster, 1984.

Camps, Miriam with Catherine Gwin. *Collective Management: The Reform of Global Economic Organizations*. New York: McGraw Hill, 1981.

Carr, William G. *One World in the Mak-*

ing: The United Nations. Boston: Ginn and Company, 1946.

Carson, Clarence. *A Basic History of the United States — Book V: The Welfare State, 1929 – 1985.* Wadley, AL: American Textbook Committee, 1986.

Center for the Study of Democratic Institutions. *A Constitution for the World.* New York: The Fund for the Republic, 1965.

Chamberlain, William Henry. "The Bankruptcy of a Policy." In Harry Elmer Barnes (ed.). *Perpetual War for Perpetual Peace.* Caldwell, ID: Caxton Printers, 1953.

Chambers, Claire. *The SIECUS Circle: A Humanist Revolution.* Appleton, WI: Western Islands, 1977.

Chambers, Whittaker. *Witness.* New York: Random House, 1952.

Chilton, David. *Productive Christians in an Age of Guilt-Manipulators: A Biblical Response to Ronald Sider.* Tyler, TX: Institute for Christian Economics, 1981.

Clark, Colin. *Population Growth: The Advantages.* Santa Ana, CA: R. L. Sassone, 1972.

Clark, Grenville and Louis B. Sohn. *World Peace Through World Law,* 2d ed. Cambridge: Harvard Univ. Press, 1962.

Clark, Mark. *From the Danube to the Yalu.* New York: Harper & Brothers, 1954.

Cleveland, Harlan. *The Third Try at World Order.* New York: Aspen Institute for Humanistic Studies, 1976.

Committee to Frame a World Constitution. *Preliminary Draft of a World Constitution.* Chicago: Univ. of Chicago Press, 1948.

A Compilation of the Messages and Papers of the Presidents, Vol. I. New York: Bureau of National Literature, 1897.

Conquest, Robert. *The Great Terror.* Rev. ed. New York: Macmillan, 1973.

— *Kolyma: The Arctic Death Camps.* New York: Viking Press, 1978.

— *The Harvest of Sorrow: Soviet Collec-*

tivization and the Terror — Famine. New York: Oxford Univ. Press, 1986.

Cole, H. S. D., et al. (eds.). *Models of Doom: A Critique of the Limits to Growth.* New York: Universe Books, 1975.

Copleston, Frederick, S. J. *A History of Philosophy, Volume III: Ockham to Suarez.* New York: Doubleday, 1963.

Crane, Philip M. *The Sum of Good Government.* Ottawa, IL: Green Hill, 1976.

Creme, Benjamin. *The Reappearance of the Christ and the Masters of Wisdom.* London: Tara Press, 1980.

Crommelin, Quentin, Jr. and David S. Sullivan. *Soviet Military Supremacy: The Untold Facts.* Los Angeles: Defense and Strategic Studies Program, University of Southern California, 1985.

Cuddy, Dennis L. *Now is the Dawning of the New Age New World Order.* Oklahoma City: Hearthstone Publishing, Ltd., 1991.

Cumby, Constance. *The Hidden Dangers of the Rainbow: The New Age Movement and Our Coming Age of Barbarism.* Shreveport, LA: Huntington House, 1983.

Dailey, Brian D. and Patrick J. Parker, (eds.). *Soviet Strategic Deception.* Lexington, Massachusetts: D.C. Heath and Company, 1987.

Daniel, Hawthorne. *The Ordeal of the Captive Nations.* Garden City, NY: Doubleday, 1958.

Davis, John W. *The Council On Foreign Relations: A Record of Twenty-Five Years, 1921-1946.* New York: Council on Foreign Relations, 1947.

Dinsmore, Herman H. *The Bleeding of America.* Appleton, WI: Western Islands, 1974.

Dobbs, Zygmund (Research Director). *The Great Deceit: Social Pseudo-Sciences.* West Sayville, NY: Veritas Foundation, 1964.

Dodd, Bella V. *School of Darkness.* New York: Devin-Adair, 1954.

Dolot, Miron. *Execution by Hunger: The*

Hidden Holocaust. New York: W. W. Norton, 1985.

Douglas, Joseph D. and Neil C. Livingston. *America the Vulnerable: The Threat of Chemical/Biological Warfare*. Lexington, Massachusetts: Lexington Books, 1987.

du Berrier, Hilaire. *Background to Betrayal: The Tragedy of Vietnam*. Appleton, WI: Western Islands, 1965.

Dulles, Allen W. and Beatrice Pitney Lamb. *The United Nations* (booklet), Headline Series, No. 59. New York: The Foreign Policy Association, September-October, 1946.

Dulles, John Foster. *War or Peace*. New York: Macmillan, 1950.

Durant, Will and Ariel. *The Lessons of History*. New York: Simon and Schuster, 1968.

Dziak, John J. *Chekisty: A History of the KGB*. Lexington, MA: D. C. Heath, 1988.

Earth Day — The Beginning. New York: Arno Press & *The New York Times*, 1970.

Ehrlich, Dr. Paul R. *The Population Bomb*. New York: Ballantine Books, 1968, 1971.

— and Anne H. *The Population Explosion*. New York: Simon and Schuster, 1990.

Elliot, Jonathan. *The Debates in the Several State Conventions on the Adoption of the Federal Constitution*. Originally published in 1830; republished 1937, J. B. Lippincott.

Environmental Action (ed.). *Earth Day — The Beginning*. New York: Arno Press & *The New York Times*, 1970.

Epstein, Edward J. *Deception: The Invisible War Between the KGB and the CIA*. New York: Simon and Schuster, 1989.

European Movement and the Council of Europe with Forewords by Winston S. Churchill and Paul-Henri Spaak, published on behalf of the European Movement. London, New York: Hutchinson & Co, 1958.

Evans, M. Stanton. *The Politics of Surrender*. New York: Devin-Adair, 1966.

Evans, Medford. *The Secret War for the A-Bomb*. Chicago: Henry Regnery, 1953.

Feshback, Murray and Alfred Friendly, Jr. *Ecocide in USSR: Health and Nature Under Siege*. New York: Basic Books, 1992.

Finder, Joseph. *Red Carpet*. New York: Holt, Rinehart and Winston, 1983.

Flynn, John T. *While You Slept: Our Tragedy in Asia and Who Made It*. New York: Devin-Adair, 1951.

Fossedal, Gregory A. and Daniel O. Graham. *A Defense That Defends*. Old Greenwich, CT: The Devin-Adair Company, 1983.

Foster, William Z. *Toward Soviet America*. Balboa Island, CA: Elgin Publications, 1961.

Fulbright, J. William. *Old Myths and New Realities*. New York: Random House, 1964.

Funderburk, David B. *Pinstripes and Reds: An American Ambassador Caught Between the State Department and the Romanian Communists, 1981-1985*. Washington, DC: Selous Foundation Press, 1987.

Gannon, Dr. Francis X. *Biographical Dictionary of the Left*. Appleton, WI: Western Islands, 1969.

Garber, Lyman A. *Of Men and Not of Law: How the Courts are Usurping the Political Function*. New York: Devin-Adair, 1966.

Gardner, Richard N. *In Pursuit of World Order: U.S. Foreign Policy and International Organizations*. New York: Frederick A. Praeger, 1964.

Gill, William J. *The Ordeal of Otto Otepka*. New Rochelle, NY: Arlington House, 1969.

Goldwater, Barry M. *With No Apologies*. New York: William Morrow and Company, 1979.

Golitsyn, Anatoliy. *New Lies For Old*. New York: Dodd, Mead, & Co., 1984.

Graham, Daniel O. *High Frontier*. New York: Thomas Doherty Associates, 1983.

Griffin, G. Edward. *The Fearful Master: A Second Look at the United Nations*. Appleton, WI: Western Islands, 1964.

Groothuis, Douglas R. *Unmasking the New Age*. Downers Grove, IL: InterVarsity Press, 1986.

Hamilton, Alexander, James Madison, and John Jay. *The Federalist Papers*. New York: Mentor, 1961.

Hancock, Graham. *Lords of Poverty: The Power, Prestige, and Corruption of the International Aid Business*. New York: Atlantic Monthly Press, 1989.

Hazlitt, Henry. *From Bretton Woods to World Inflation*. Chicago: Regnery Gateway, 1984.

Heller, Mikhail and Aleksandr M. Nekrich. *Utopia in Power: The History of the Soviet Union from 1917 to the Present*. New York: Summit Books, 1986.

Hempstone, Smith. *Rebels, Mercenaries, and Dividends: The Katanga Story*. New York: Frederick A. Praeger, 1962.

Heymann, Hans. *Plan for Permanent Peace*. New York: Harper and Brothers, 1941.

Hoar, William P. *Architects of Conspiracy: An Intriguing History*. Appleton, WI: Western Islands, 1984.

Hogan, Michael J. *The Marshall Plan*. New York: Cambridge University Press, 1987.

Holman, Frank E. *Story of the "Bricker" Amendment*. New York: Committee for Constitutional Government, Inc., 1954.

House, Colonel Edward Mandell. *Philip Dru: Administrator: A Story of Tomorrow — 1920-1935*. New York: B. W. Huebsch, 1912.

Howell, Wilbur Samuel (ed.). Thomas Jefferson's parliamentary writings: *A Manual of Parliamentary Practice*. Princeton, NJ: Princeton Univ. Press, 1988.

Howland, Charles P. *Survey of American Foreign Relations: 1928*, Published for the Council on Foreign Relations. New Haven: Yale University Press, 1928.

— (prepared under the direction of). *Survey of American Foreign Relations*, Published for the Council on Foreign Relations. New Haven: Yale University Press, 1929.

Huxley, Aldous. *The Perennial Philosophy*. London: Collins, 1958.

Huxley, Julian. *UNESCO: Its Purpose and Its Philosophy*. Washington DC: Public Affairs Press, 1947.

Idso, Sherwood B., Ph.D. *Carbon Dioxide and Global Change: Earth in Transition*. Tempe, AZ: IBR Press, 1989.

Institute for Defense Analyses. *Study Phoenix Paper*, June 4, 1963. Prepared for the U.S. Arms Control and Disarmament Agency.

Isaacson, Walter and Evan Thomas. *The Wise Men*. New York: Simon and Schuster, 1986.

Jensen-Stevenson, Monika and William Stevenson. *Kiss the Boys Goodbye*. New York: Dutton, 1990.

Jessup, Philip C. *International Problem of Governing Mankind*. Claremont, CA: Claremont Colleges, 1947.

Jordan, George Racey, USAF (Ret.). *Major Jordan's Diaries*. New York: Harcourt, Brace, 1952.

Kasun, Jacqueline. *The War Against Population*. San Francisco: Ignatius Press, 1988.

Keller, Werner. *East Minus West = Zero: Russia's Debt to the Western World, 862 – 1962*. New York: G. P. Putnam's Sons, 1962.

Kelly, Rev. Clarence. *Conspiracy Against God and Man*. Appleton, WI: Western Islands, 1974.

King, Alexander and Bertrand Schneider. *The First Global Revolution*. A Report by the Council of The Club of Rome. New York: Pantheon Books, 1991.

Kurtz, Paul (ed.). "Humanist Manifesto II" in *Humanist Manifestos I and II*. Buffalo, NY: Prometheus Books, 1973.

Lane, Arthur Bliss (U. S. Ambassador to Poland, 1944-1947). *I Saw Poland Betrayed*. Bobb-Merrill Company, 1948.

Lawrence, Troy. *New Age Messiah Iden-*

tified: Who is Lord Maitreya? Lafayette, LA: Huntington House, 1991.

Lee, Robert W. *The United Nations Conspiracy*. Appleton, WI: Western Islands, 1981.

Lehr, Jay H. *Rational Readings on Environmental Concerns*. New York: Van Nostrand Reinhold, 1992.

Levinson, Charles. *Vodka Cola*. London and New York: Gordon & Cremonesi, 1978.

Lewytzkyj, Boris. *The Uses of Terror: The Soviet Secret Police, 1917 – 1970*. New York: Coward, McCann & Geoghegan, 1972.

Lie, Trygve. *In the Cause of Peace*. New York: Macmillan Company, 1954.

MacArthur, Douglas. *Reminiscences*. New York: McGraw-Hill, 1964.

MacBride, Roger Lea. *Treaties Versus the Constitution*. Caldwell, ID: The Caxton Printers, Ltd., 1956.

MacNeil, Jim, Pieter Winsemius, and Taizo Yakushij, Foreword by David Rockefeller, Introduction by Maurice Strong. *Beyond Interdependence: The Meshing of the World's Economy and the Earth's Ecology*. New York: Oxford University Press, 1991.

Mao Tse-tung. *Selected Works*, Vol II. Peking.

Massing, Hede. *This Deception*. New York: Duell, Sloan, and Pearce, 1951.

McCracken, Samuel. *The War Against the Atom*. New York: Basic Books, 1982.

McFerran, Warren L. *The Betrayal of Southern Africa*. Winter Park, FL: Garfield Publishing Corp., 1985.

McIlhany, William H., II. *The Tax-Exempt Foundations*. Westport, CT: Arlington House, 1980.

McManus, John F. *The Insiders: Architects of the New World Order*, 3rd ed. Appleton, WI: The John Birch Society, 1992.

Meadows, Donnela H. and Dennis L. *The Limits to Growth*. New York: Universe Books, Publishers, 1972.

Mendlovitz, Saul H. (ed.). *On the Creation of a Just World Order: Preferred Worlds for the 1990's*. New York: Free Press, 1975.

Millin, Sarah Gertrude. *Cecil Rhodes*. New York: Harper & Brothers, 1933.

Morris, Richard B. (ed.). *Alexander Hamilton and the Founding of the Nation*. New York: The Dial Press, 1957.

Muller, Robert. *New Genesis: Shaping a Global Spirituality*. Garden City, NY: Doubleday, 1984.

Mumford, Lewis. *The Transformations of Man*. New York: Harper & Brothers, 1956.

Niehbuhr, Reinhold, Lewis Mumford, et al. *The City of Man: A Declaration On World Democracy*. New York: Viking Press, 1940.

Perloff, James. *The Shadows of Power: The Council on Foreign Relations And The American Decline*. Appleton, WI: Western Islands, 1988.

Pike, Henry R. *A History of Communism in South Africa*. Primrose Hill, Germiston, South Africa: Christian Mission International of South Africa, 1985.

Pincher, Chapman. *The Secret Offensive*. New York: St. Martin's Press, 1985.

Program of the Communist International. New York: Workers Library Publishers, 1936.

Quigley, Carroll. *Tragedy and Hope: A History of the World in Our Time*. New York: Macmillan, 1966.

Ray, Dr. Dixie Lee. *Trashing the Planet*. Chicago: Regnery Gateway, 1990.

Rees, David. *Harry Dexter White: A Study in Paradox*. New York: Coward, McCann & Geoghegan, 1973.

Report From Iron Mountain on the Possibility and Desirability of Peace. New York: Dial Press, 1967.

Robinson, Donald L. (ed.). *Reforming American Government: The Bicentennial Papers of the Committee on the Constitutional System*. Boulder, CO: Westview Press, Inc., 1985.

Rockefeller, Nelson A. *The Future of Federalism: The Godkin Lectures at Harvard University, 1962*. Cambridge:

Harvard University Press, 1964.

Rostow, Walt Whitman. *The United States in the World Arena.* New York: Harper & Brothers, 1960.

Rummel, Dr. R. J. *Lethal Politics: Soviet Genocide and Mass Murder Since 1917.* New Brunswick, NY: Transaction Publishers, 1990.

Rushdoony, Rousas J. *The Myth of Overpopulation.* Fairfax, VA: Thoburn Press, 1974.

Sanders, Sol. *Living Off the West: Gorbachev's Secret Agenda and Why It Will Fail.* New York: Madison Books, 1990.

Sassone, Robert. *Handbook on Population.* Santa Ana, CA: R. L. Sassone, 1978.

Satin, Mark. *New Age Politics: Healing Self and Society.* West Vancouver, B.C.: Whitecap Books, 1978.

Schlafly, Phyllis and Chester Ward, Rear Admiral, USN (Ret.). *Kissinger on the Couch.* New Rochelle, NY: Arlington House, 1975.

Schlesinger, Arthur M. *A Thousand Days.* Boston: Houghton Mifflin, 1965.

Schmidheiny, Stephan with the Business Council for Sustainable Development. *Changing Course: A Global Business Perspective on Development and the Environment.* MA: MIT Press, 1992.

Schulzinger, Robert D. *The Wise Men of Foreign Affairs: The History of the Council on Foreign Relations.* New York: Columbia University Press, 1984.

Schuyler, Philippa. *Who Killed The Congo?* New York: Devin-Adair, 1962.

Sennholz, Hans F. *How Can Europe Survive?* New York: D. Van Nostrand Company, 1955.

Seymour, Charles (ed.). *The Intimate Papers of Colonel House*, Vol. I, "Behind The Political Curtain: 1912-1915." Boston: Hougton Mifflin, 1926.

— *The Intimate Papers of Colonel House*, Vol. III, "Into the World War: April, 1917 — June, 1918." Boston: Hougton Mifflin, 1928.

Sherry, George L. *The United Nations Reborn: Conflict Control in the Post-Cold War World*, Council on Foreign Relations Critical Issues series. New York, 1990.

Shoup, Laurence and William Minter. *Imperial Brain Trust: The Council on Foreign Relations and United States Foreign Policy.* New York: Monthly Review Press, 1977.

Simon, Julian L. *The Ultimate Resource.* Princeton: Princeton Univ. Press, 1981.

— and Herman Kahn (eds.). *The Resourceful Earth: A Response to Global 2000.* New York: Basil Blackwell, Inc., 1984.

Singer, S. Fred. *Global Climate Change.* New York: Paragon House, 1989.

Smith, Earl E. T. (U.S. Ambassador to Cuba, 1957-59). *The Fourth Floor: An Account of the Castro Communist Revolution.* New York: Random House, 1962.

Smoot, Dan. *The Invisible Government.* Appleton, WI: Western Islands, 1965.

Solzhenitsyn, Aleksandr I. *The Gulag Archipelago: 1918 – 1956.* New York: Harper & Row, 1973.

Somosa, Anastasio and Jack Cox. *Nicaragua Betrayed.* Appleton, WI: Western Islands, 1980.

Spangler, David. *Reflections on the Christ*, 3rd. ed. Scotland: Findhorn Publications, 1981.

Stang, Alan. *The Actor: The True Story of John Foster Dulles Secretary of State, 1953 – 1959.* Appleton, WI: Western Islands, 1968.

Stone, Roger D. and Eve Hamilton. *Global Economics and the Environment: Toward Sustainable Rural Development in the Third World.* New York: Council on Foreign Relations Press, 1991.

Streit, Clarence. *Union Now.* New York: Harper & Brothers, 1940.

Sutton, Antony C. *Western Technology and Soviet Economic Development, 1917-1930.* Stanford University, Stanford, CA: Hoover Institution, 1968.

— *Western Technology and Soviet Eco-*

nomic Development, 1930-1945. Stanford University, Stanford, CA: Hoover Institution, 1971.

— *Western Technology and Soviet Economic Development, 1945-1965.* Stanford University, Stanford, CA: Hoover Institution, 1973.

— *National Suicide: Military Aid to the Soviet Union.* New Rochelle, NY: Arlington House, 1973.

— *The War on Gold.* Seal Beach, CA: '76 Press, 1977.

— *The Best Enemy Money Can Buy.* Billings, MT: Liberty House Press, 1986.

van der Beugel, Ernst H. *From Marshall Aid to Atlantic Partnership.* Amsterdam, New York: Elsevier Publishing Co., 1966.

Viereck, George Sylvester. *The Strangest Friendship in History: Woodrow Wilson and Colonel House.* New York: Liveright, 1932.

Wallace, William. *The Transformation of Western Europe.* London: Royal Institute of International Affairs, 1990.

Warburg, James P. *The West in Crisis.* Garden City, NY: Doubleday & Company, Inc., 1959.

Wattenberg, Ben. *The Birth Dearth.* New York: St. Martin's Press, 1981.

Watts, V. Orval. *The United Nations: Planned Tyranny.* New York: Devin-Adair, 1955.

Weber, James A. *Grow or Die.* New Rochelle, NY: Arlington House, 1977.

Weinstein, Allen. *Perjury: The Hiss-Chambers Case.* New York: Vintage Books, 1978.

Welch, Robert. *May God Forgive Us.* Chicago: Henry Regnery, 1952.

— *The Blue Book of The John Birch Society.* Appleton, WI: Western Islands, 1959.

Wells, H. G. *The New World Order.* New York: A. A. Knopf, 1940.

Zurcher, Arnold J. *The Struggle to Unite Europe 1940-1958.* New York: New York Univ. Press, 1958.

— REPORTS AND DOCUMENTS —

The 46 Civilian Doctors of Elisabethville. *46 Angry Men: The 46 Civilian Doctors of Elisabethville Denounce U.N.O. Violations in Katanga.* Belmont, MA: American Opinion, 1962; originally published by Dr. T. Vleurinck, 96 Avenue de Broqueville, Bruxelles 15, 1962.

Activities of United States Citizens Employed by the United Nations. Hearings before the Senate Subcommittee on Internal Security, December 1, 1952.

Activities of United States Citizens Employed by the United Nations. Hearings before the Senate Subcommittee on Internal Security, January 2, 1953.

Aid and Trade Documents: A Compilation. Appleton, WI: Larry McDonald Crusade, revised and updated July 1987.

Agenda 21. United Nations Conference on Environment and Development, Rio de Janeiro, June 3-14, 1992.

Ashbrook, Representative John (R-OH). *Congressional Record*, May 12, 1976, p. H 4312.

Bliley, Representative Thomas J. (R-VA). *Congressional Record*, September 17, 1990, p. H 7687-88.

Bloomfield, Lincoln P. *A World Effectively Controlled by the United Nations.* Institute For Defense Analyses, March 10, 1962. Prepared for IDA in support of a study submitted to the Department of State under contract No. SCC 28270, dated February 24, 1961.

Blueprint for the Peace Race: Outline of Basic Provisions of a Treaty on General and Complete Disarmament in a Peaceful World (United States Arms

Control and Disarmament Agency Publication 4, General Series 3, Released May 1962).

Boutros, Boutros-Ghali. *An Agenda for Peace: Preventive Diplomacy, Peace-making and Peace-keeping.* Report of the Secretary-General pursuant to the statement adopted by the Summit Meeting of the Security Council on 31 January 1992. New York: United Nations, 1992.

Bovard, James. "The World Bank vs. the World's Poor." Cato Institute Policy Analysis, No. 92, September 28, 1987.

Brady, Lawrence J., Acting Director of Export Administration. Testimony before House Committee on Armed Services Subcommittee on Research and Development, May 24, 1979.

Brundtland, Gro Harlem. Statement provided at opening of UNCED in Rio de Janeiro, June 3, 1992. Text provided by UNCED at Earth Summit in Rio.

Burdick, Usher L. *Congressional Record — House*, April 28, 1954.

Bush, President George. Televised address before a Joint Session of Congress, September 11, 1990, *Weekly Compilation of Presidential Documents*, Vol. 26 — Number 37, pp. 1359-60.

— *Pax Universalis* speech at UN headquarters on September 23, 1991. *Weekly Compilation of Presidential Documents*, Volume 27 — Number 39, pp. 1324-27.

— Address to the United Nations Conference on Environment and Development in Rio de Janeiro, Brazil, June 12, 1992. *Weekly Compilation of Presidential Documents*, Volume 28 — Number 25, pp. 1043-44.

— "The United Nations: Forging a Genuine Global Community," an address before the UN General Assembly on September 21, 1992. *US Department of State Dispatch*, September 28, 1992, Vol. 3, No. 39, pp. 722-23.

Carnegie Endowment for International Peace National Commission on America and the New World. *Chang-ing Our Ways: America and the New World.* Washington, DC: Brookings Institution, 1992.

A *Charter for American-Russian Partnership and Friendship* signed by Presidents Bush and Yeltsin on June 17, 1992 (seven-page document released by the White House, Office of the Press Secretary, June 17, 1992).

Commager, Henry Steele. "The Declaration of INTERdependence", October 24, 1975. World Affairs Council of Philadelphia, 1975.

Communist International, official 1936 program of. Hearings before the Senate Committee on Foreign Relations, July 11, 1956, p. 196.

Council on Foreign Relations, *American Public Opinion and Postwar Security Commitments*, 1944.

De Clercq, Willy. "1992: The Great European Market?" an address delivered at the Eurug Conference, Ghent, 25 October 1987. EC Office of Press & Public Affairs, Washington, DC.

"The Declaration of the Sacred Earth Gathering, Rio 92." Quoted in *Earth Summit Times*, June 3, 1992.

Digest of United States Practice in International Law 1973.

Disarmament: The New U.S. Initiative, United States Arms Control and Disarmament Agency Publication 8, General Series 5, released September 1962. Washington, DC: U.S. Government Printing Office.

Dodd, Norman (video interview of). *The Hidden Agenda: Merging America Into World Government.* Westlake Village, CA: American Media, (VHS) one hour.

"Earth Summit Press Summary of Agenda 21." Prepared by Communications and Project Management Division, Department of Public Information, as part of the United Nations information programme for the UN Conference on Environment and Development, Rio de Janeiro, Brazil, June 3-14, 1992.

Earth Summit Times. The official newspaper of record for the United Nations Conference on Environment and Development published by Theodore W. Kheel and Katsuhiko Yazaki with the Kyoto Forum and EcoFund '92 in cooperation with *The New York Times* Fax and *Jornal Do Brasil*.

An Examination of U.S. Policy Toward POW/MIAs. Washington, DC: U.S. Senate Foreign Relations Committee Republican Staff, May 23, 1991.

Foreign Affairs Policy, Series 26, Foreword by President Truman. Department of State Publication 3972, September 1952.

Freedom From War: The United States Program for General and Complete Disarmament in a Peaceful World. Department of State Publication 7277, Disarmament Series 5, Released September 1961, Office of Public Services, Bureau of Public Affairs.

French, Hilary F. *After the Earth Summit: The Future of Environmental Governance*. Worldwatch Institute Paper 107, March 1992.

Genscher, Hans-Dietrich. "The Future of Europe," a speech delivered in Lisbon on July 12, 1991. *Statements & Speeches*, Vol. XIV, No. 8, German Information Center, New York.

The Global 2000 Report to the President: Entering the Twenty-First Century, A Report Prepared by the Council on Environmental Quality and the Department of State. New York: Penguin Books, 1982.

Goldwater, Senator Barry. *Congressional Record*, October 26, 1971, p. S 16764.

Helms, Senator Jesse. *Congressional Record*, December 15, 1987, p. S 18146-48.

— *Congressional Record*, September 11, 1990, pp. S 12787-88.

House of Representatives Report (Executive Hearings before the Committee on Un-American Activities, May 13 and 14, 1953). *Soviet Schedule for War — 1955*. Washington: United States Government Printing Office, 1953.

In Our Hands: Earth Summit '92, a booklet. UNCED.

Institute for Defense Analyses. *Study Phoenix Paper*, June 4, 1963. Prepared for the U.S. Arms Control and Disarmament Agency.

The International Covenant on Civil and Political Rights in *The International Bill of Human Rights: Fact Sheet No. 2*. United Nations, November 1989.

"International Covenant on Civil and Political Rights," hearings before the Committee on Foreign Relations, United States Senate, November 21, 1991. Washington: U.S. Government Printing Office, 1992.

Jackson, Congressman Donald L. (narrator), *Katanga: The Untold Story*, available on video (VHS, 59 minutes) from American Media, Westlake Village, CA.

"A Landmark for Children's Rights," in *The Rights of the Child: Fact Sheet No. 10*. United Nations, 1990.

Lipscomb, Representative Glenard P. (R-CA). *Congressional Record*, February 10, 1964, pp. 2720-24.

Lucis Trust. "The Lucis Trust," a pamphlet.

Lutzenberger, Jose. Statement at opening of Rio Earth Summit. *The '92 Global Forum*, Release #115, June 5, 1992.

Marinov, Dr. Uri. "Ten Commandments on Environment and Development," extracts from an address presented to UNCED, June 3, 1992. UNCED at Earth Summit in Rio.

Marx, Father Paul. "World Bank puts bounty on lives of unborn children." News release of Human Life International, Gaithersburg, MD, March 30, 1992.

McPherson, M. Peter. "The European Community's Internal Market Program: An American Perspective," an address before the Institute for International Economics, August 4, 1988. *Treasury News*, B-1505.

Millis, Walter, "The Political Control of An International Police Force." Published by the Peace Research Insti-

tute, Inc. April 1963 under U.S. Arms Control and Disarmament Agency Grant ACDA/IR-8, Volume II.
National Security Strategy of the United States. The White House, August 1991.
The New International Economic Order: A Spiritual Imperative, a UN report.
POW/MIA Policy and Process, Hearings before the Select Committee on POW/MIA Affairs, United States Senate, two volumes. Washington, DC: U.S. Government Printing Office, 1992.
"President's Report." Council on Foreign Relations. New York: August 31, 1972.
Rock, Vincent P. "Common Action for the Control of Conflict: An Approach to the Problem of International Tension and Arms Control," July 1963. Summary document of a Project Phoenix Study performed by the Institute for Defense Analyses for the U.S. Arms Control and Disarmament Agency.
Senate Report (Senate Foreign Relations Committee). *Revisions of the United Nations Charter: Hearings Before a Subcommittee of the Committee on Foreign Relations, Eighty-First Congress.* Washington: United States Government Printing Office, 1950.
State Department Security 1963-65: The Otepka Case. Senate Internal Security Subcommittee Hearings, 1963-65
Strong, Maurice. "The relationship between demographic trends, economic growth, unsustainable consumption patterns and environmental degradation." An UNCED PrepCom report, August 1991.
— Statement at opening of UNCED in Rio de Janeiro, Brazil, June 3, 1992. UNCED release.
Subcommittee on the United Nations Charter of the U.S. Senate Committee on Foreign Relations. "Statute of the International Court of Justice" in *Review of the United Nations Charter: A Collection of Documents.* Washington: U.S. Government Printing Office, 1954.

Tolba, Dr. Mostafa K. "The Way Ahead," statement provided at opening of UNCED in Rio de Janeiro, June 3, 1992. Text provided by UNCED at Earth Summit in Rio.
Treaties and Executive Agreements. Hearings on S. J. Res. 1 & S. J. Res. 43; Feb., Mar., & Apr. 1953, Y4.J89/2:T71/2.
"United Nations Security Council Provisional Verbatim Record of 3046th Meeting Held at Headquarters, New York on 31 January, 1992." (Final text to be printed in the *Official Records of the Security Council.*)
UN resolution on sending troops to the former Belgium Congo. UN document S/4387.
U.S. Senate ratification of International Covenant on Civil and Political Rights. *Congressional Record,* April 2, 1992, pp. S 4783-84.
Utt, Representative James B. *Congressional Record,* January 15, 1962.
Weiss, Representative Ted. *Congressional Record,* May 25, 1982, pp. H 2840-41.
The World Commission on Environment and Development (Gro Harlem Brundtland, Chairman), report of. *Our Common Future.* New York: Oxford University Press, 1987.
World Goodwill (an activity of Lucis Trust). *The New Group of World Servers,* a pamphlet.

— ARTICLES —

"1990s declared UN Decade of International Law." *UN Chronicle*, March 1990, p. 77.

Abbasi, Daniel R. " 'Development' commission almost up." *Earth Summit Times*, June 7, 1992.

Adelmann, Robert. "The Federal Reserve System." *The New American*, October 27, 1986.

Allen, Gary. "Making Plans." *American Opinion*, April 1971.

Alperovitz, Gar and Kai Bird. "Dream of Total Disarmament Could Become Reality." *Los Angeles Times*, January 5, 1992.

"American Support for United Nations Highest in 20 Years; Strong Support for Permanent Peacekeeping Force." *The Gallup Poll News Service*, Vol. 55, No. 23, October 24, 1990.

Baker, Bob. "Hayden on Earth." *Los Angeles Times*, October 16, 1991, pp. B1, B4.

Band, Richard E. "The Traders: Selling Rope for the Hanging." *American Opinion*, January 1974.

Bandow, Doug. "Why Waste Aid on Russia? Consider the I.M.F's dismal record." *New York Times*, March 26, 1992, p. A23.

Bliley, Thomas. "U.N. Playpen Politics: A Bid to Nanny." *Washington Times*, September 24, 1990, p. G3.

Brauman, Dr. Rony. "Famine Aid: Were We Duped?" *Readers Digest*, October 1986.

Brinkley, Alan. "Minister Without Portfolio." *Harper's*, February, 1983.

Brown, John M. G. "Mikhail Gorbachev, Let Our People Go," a two-part series. *The New American*, May 21, 1990 and June 4, 1990.

Brown, Lester R. (interview of). "A transition to a new era?" *Terraviva*, June 3, 1992.

Capell, Frank A. *The Review of The News*, August 21, 1974.

Chodorov, Frank. "One Worldism." *The Freeman*, March, 1955.

Church, George J. "A New World." *Time*, September 17, 1990.

"The Climate of Freedom." *The Saturday Review* editorial, July 19, 1952.

Cook, Don. "Europe's Gentle Guiding Hand." *Los Angeles Times*, October 8, 1976, pp. 8-9.

Cooper, Richard N. "A Monetary System for the Future." *Foreign Affairs*, Fall 1984.

Cordova, Luis. "How to guarantee well-being for a population growing by the second?" *Terraviva* (Brazil), June 10, 1992.

Cousins, Norman. "Managing the Planet," in *Earth Day — The Beginning*. New York: Arno Press & *The New York Times*, 1970.

Crossette, Barbara. "Spending for U.N. Peacekeeping Getting a Hard Look in Congress." *New York Times*, March 6, 1992, pp. A1, A6.

Cuddy, Dennis L. *The "New World Order": A Critique and Chronology*, a pamphlet. Milford, PA: America's Future, Inc., 1992.

Drummey, James J. "The Captive Nations: How they were captured and why they are still enslaved." *The New American*, July 14, 1986.

— "Building the Evil Empire." *The New American*, July 20, 1987.

— "By Trade Betrayed." *The New American*, February 12, 1990

— "Nice Smile, Iron Teeth." *The New American*, March 12, 1991.

— "Defenseless: Our Patriot and Other High-Tech Giveaways." *The New American*, April 9, 1991.

Krauthammer, Charles. "Let It Sink: The Overdue Demise of the United Nations." *The New Republic*, August 24, 1987.

du Berrier, Hilaire. *H. du B. Reports*, April 1972.

— A six-part series on the Common Market in *H. du B. Reports*, May 1972 through January 1973.

— "The Multi-colored Kurt Waldheim." *The New American*, June 2, 1986, p. 27.

Dunleavy, Steve. "Rip Down This Shocking Tower of Shame." *Star*, November 3, 1991.

Easterly, Ernest S., III. "The Rule of Law and the New World Order." Pre-publication draft.

Eddlem, Thomas R. "Soviet Goals Remain the Same," an interview with Charles Via. *The New American*, October 8, 1991.

— Appearance Versus Reality. *The New American*, October 22, 1991.

Ehrlich, Paul R. "World Population: Is the Battle Lost?" *Stanford Today*, Winter 1968.

Eliot, Charles W. "The Next American Contribution to Civilization." *Foreign Affairs*, September 15, 1922.

Foster, Sarah E. "Pentagon Flim-Flam Masters." *The New American*, September 24, 1991.

Fotheringham, Don. "The Con-Con Network." *The New American*, February 10, 1992.

Francis, Sam. "New World Order's Call To Arms." *Los Angeles Daily News*, Tuesday, August 4, 1992.

Freeman, Jack. "Gorbachev: Red head for the Green Cross." *Earth Summit Times*, June 8, 1992.

Gardner, Richard N. "The Hard Road To World Order." *Foreign Affairs*, April 1974.

— "The Case for Practical Internationalism." *Foreign Affairs*, Spring 1988.

Gelb, Leslie H. "Why the U.N. Dog Didn't Bark: Mr. Bush's incendiary theme." *New York Times*, September 25, 1991.

Gertz, Bill. "KGB targets U.S. businessmen, scientists to recruit them as spies." *Washington Times*, March 14, 1991.

Gorbachev, Mikhail. "We must 'ecologize' our society before it's too late." *Birmingham* [Alabama] *News*, April 22, 1990. Adapted from an address to the 1990 Global Forum conference of spiritual and parliamentary leaders in Moscow in late January 1990.

Griffin, G. Edward. "More Deadly Than War," transcript of a filmed lecture. Thousand Oaks, CA: American Media, 1968.

Guilfoyle, Jean M. "World Bank Safe Motherhood Initiative." *Population Research Institute Review*, Volume 2, Number 3, May/June 1992.

Hamilton, Lee H. "A Democrat Looks at Foreign Policy." *Foreign Policy*, Summer 1992.

Hoar, William P. "The Review of the News." *The New American*, August 10, 1992.

— "The Amazing John J. McCloy." *American Opinion*, March, 1983, pp. 25-40.

— "President Bush to POW/MIA Families: 'Shut Up and Sit Down.'" *The New American*, August 24, 1992.

— "Making of a Monster." *The New American*, September 7, 1992.

Holland, Max. "Citizen McCloy." *The Wilson Quarterly*, Autumn 1991.

Holman, Frank E. *The Problems of the World Court and the Connally Reservation*, a pamphlet. Seattle, WA: Frayn Printing Co., July 1960.

Impact of Science on Society, UNESCO's quarterly journal, Fall 1968.

Ingraham, Jane H. "The Consequence of Error." *The New American*, November 24, 1986.

— "The Great Wealth Transfer: Establishing the New International Economic Order." *The New American*, May 8, 1989.

Jasper, William F. "Official Policy: Abandon POWs." *The New American*, February 12, 1991.

— "They Deserve to Come Home." *The New American*, September 10, 1991.

— "Bring Them Home!" *The New American*. September 24, 1991.

— "Betrayed in Action." *The New American*. November 19, 1991.

— "From the Atlantic to the Urals (and Beyond)." *The New American*, January 27, 1992.

— "Meeting Ground of East and West." *The New American*, February 24, 1992.

— "Solution's from Rio." *The New American*, July 27, 1992.

Kempe, Frederick. "Perez de Cuellar Wins U.N. New Respect." *Wall Street Journal*, September 26, 1988, p. 22.

Kempster, Norman. "Army Could Give U.N. New Punch." *Los Angeles Times*, February 1, 1992.

Kennan, George. "This Is No Time for Talk of German Reunification." *Washington Post*, November 12, 1989.

Kerr, Philip. "From Empire to Commonwealth." *Foreign Affairs*, December 1922.

Kidwell, Kirk. "Bolsheviks Bankrupt at 70." *The New American*, October 26, 1987.

— "Has the Soviet Union Changed?" *The New American*, August 29, 1988.

Kraft, Joseph. "School for Statesmen." *Harper's*, July 1958.

Leach, James A. "A Republican Looks at Foreign Policy." *Foreign Affairs*, Summer 1992.

Lee, Robert W. "The Truth About the Communist Planned Famine in Ethiopia." *American Opinion*, April 1985.

— "No Accident: The continuing betrayal of American interests is a matter of policy." *The New American*, March 30, 1987.

— "U.S.S.R. & Eastern Europe." *The New American*, January 29, 1991.

— "The New, Improved USSR." *The New American*, November 19, 1991.

— "International Welfare." *The New American*, March 23, 1992.

— "Restraining the World Court." *The New American*, September 7, 1992.

— "The Power Behind the Throne." *The New American*, September 21, 1992.

Lewis, Flora. "Gorbachev Turns Green." *New York Times*, August 14, 1991.

Lewis, Paul. "U.N. Refugee Chief Quits Over His Use of Funds." *New York Times*, October 27, 1989.

Lukas, J. Anthony. "The Council on Foreign Relations: Is It a Club? Seminar? Presidium, Invisible Government?" *New York Times Magazine*, November 21, 1971.

Mann, Jim. "Chinese Premier gets chilly U.N. reception." *Los Angeles Times*, February 1, 1992, p. A1,6.

Masko, TSgt. David P. "The Russians Have Landed." *Airman*, July 1992.

Mathews, Jessica Tuchman. "... Two Views." *EPA Journal*, July/August 1990.

Matthews, J. B. "Philip Dru: Fascist Prototype." *American Mercury* November, 1954.

McFerran, Warren F. "[South Africa] On the Edge," *The New American*, October 22, 1990.

McManus, John F. "Selective Blindness." *The Birch Log*, April 8, 1976.

— "Ahead of the *Times*." *The New American*, April 7, 1986., p. 45.

— "Lev Albert's Defense." *The New American*, March 30, 1987.

— "Sins of Our Fathers." *The New American*, April 9, 1991.

— "Examining the Rule of Law." *The John Birch Society Bulletin*, June 1991.

— "Treaties versus the Constitution." *The New American*, July 27, 1992.

"Monnet, Key to European Unity, Dead at Age 90." *Los Angeles Times*, March 17, 1979, pp. 1, 15.

Morin, Richard. "U.N. Real Winner After Gulf War." *Salt Lake Tribune*, January 24, 1992.

Mosher, Steven W. "A Mother's Ordeal." *Reader's Digest*, February 1987.

— "Chinese Officials Invade Family Life." *HLI Reports* (Human Life International), October, 1987, p. 5.

Moskowitz, Moses. "Is the U.N.'s Bill of Human Rights Dangerous? A Reply to President Holman." *American Bar Association Journal*, Vol. 35, April 1949.

New Times (Soviet), November, 1977.

"The New World Army." *New York Times* lead editorial, March 6, 1992.

"Next Target for World's Conscience: Myanmar — An apocalyptic 'killing field' for the former Burma?" *Los An-*

geles Times lead editorial, March 16, 1992.

Nye, Joseph S., Jr., "Create A U.N. Fire Brigade." *New York Times*, February 1, 1992.

Oppenheimer, Michael. "From Red Menace to Green Threat." *New York Times*, March 27, 1990.

Opitz, Rev. Edmund A. "Religious Propagandists for the UN." *The Freeman*, March 1955.

Political Affairs, April 1945.

"Protest Over Berlin." *New York Times* editorial, August 16, 1961.

Raeburn, Paul, Associated Press. "Ecology Remedy Costly." *Sacramento Bee* (CA), March 12, 1992.

Robbins, John W. "Birds of a Feather: American and Soviet traders are flocking together." *The New American*, April 27, 1987.

Rockefeller, David. "From A China Traveler." *New York Times*, August 10, 1973.

Roosevelt, Edith Kermit. "Elite Clique Holds Power in U.S." *Indianapolis News*, December 23, 1961, p. 6.

Rosicrucian Digest, June 1941.

Rummel, R. J. "War Isn't This Century's Biggest Killer." *Wall Street Journal*, July 7, 1986.

Rurarz, Zdzislaw. "Yeltsin's Police." *Washington Inquirer*, January 4, 1992, p. 4.

Russett, Bruce and James S. Sutherlin. "The U.N. in a New World Order." *Foreign Affairs*, Spring 1991.

Schwenninger, Sherle R. "The United States in the New World Order." *World Policy Journal*, Summer 1992.

Smoot, Dan. "The Dan Smoot Report: Pushed Into Bankruptcy." *The Review of the News*, February 14, 1979, p. 31.

Spiers, Ronald I. "Keep the U.N. on a Roll." *New York Times*, March 13, 1992, p. A31.

Stammer, Larry B. Interview with William D. Ruckelshaus. *Los Angeles Times*, May 26, 1992, p. H11.

Stevens, William K. "Lessons of Rio: A New Prominence and an Effective Blandness." *New York Times*, June 14, 1992.

"Still the Masters of Deceit." *The New American*, December 4, 1989, p. 37.

"Suffer the Little Children." *Time*, October 8, 1990.

Talbott, Strobe. "The Birth of the Global Nation." *Time*, July 20, 1992, p. 70.

Thompson, Jon. "Eastern Europe's Dark Dawn: The Iron Curtain Rises to Reveal a Land Tarnished by Pollution." *National Geographic*, June 1991.

Thompson, William Irwin. *Quest*, Spring 1991.

Townsend, Tony (ed.), Tara Center's *Network News*, October 1987.

Tully, Andrew. "[Mayor] Koch Should Chase UN Out of Town." *San Gabriel Valley Tribune* (CA), March 3, 1982.

"The United Nations: Back to the Future." *The Ford Foundation Letter*, February 1989.

"The Unsung World Army." *New York Times* lead editorial, May 11, 1992, p. A14.

"UNsurpassed." *Our Sunday Visitor* editorial, January 19, 1992.

Waller, Douglas. "Foreign-Aid Follies." *Newsweek*, April 16, 1990.

— and Margaret Garrard Warner. "Superpowers as Superpartners." *Newsweek*, September 17, 1990.

Weeks, Albert L. "KGB's Undiminished Power Haunts Russian Reform." *Washington Inquirer*, April 17, 1992, pp. 1, 7.

Weiss, Thomas G. and Meryl A. Kessler. "Moscow's U.N. Policy." *Foreign Policy*, Summer 1990.

Welch, Robert. "Which World Will It Be?" American Opinion Reprint Series. Appleton, WI: The John Birch Society, 1970.

"Why We Need to Change the System, And How We Can Do It." *Transition*, a bi-monthly publication of the Institute for World Order, Inc., Vol. 2., No.1, January 1975.

Wines, Michael. "Bush Leave Rio With Shots at Critics, Foreign and Domestic." *New York Times*, June 14, 1992.

Index

Personal Acknowledgments

This book has been, in many respects, an ensemble effort. Heartfelt acknowledgments are therefore due to all who assisted and supported me in so many ways. For editorial labors above and beyond the usual call of duty, John McManus, Tom Gow, and Gary Benoit have my highest regard.

For research assistance in many areas, I am especially indebted to Tom Gow, Donna Glunn, Tom Eddlem, and John McManus. Myril Creer, Gary Benoit, Bernadine Smith, Dennis Cuddy, Patrick Mahoney, Steve Dapra, and Dave Chance also contributed valuable research aid.

When I was beset with computer problems, John Burns, Dave Wright and Larry Solesbee came to my rescue and helped me avert some major disasters. For providing excellent typing service under trying circumstances I will always be beholden to Sarah Foster, Christine Schuemperli, Dave Burns and Trina Solesbee.

For extraordinary efforts to help me with facilities to work on the manuscript while I was traveling on a speaking tour, I owe particular thanks to Dan and Tara McBride, Mark Walsh, and Herb and Janice Hartman. Agustina Farris, Kris Solesbee, Irma Blecker, Leticia Saucedo, Lois Conkle, Don Fotheringham, David Bohon, Scott Alberts, Steve DuBord, and David Martin also deserve special mention for their efforts which made completion of this volume possible.

For both inspiration and for the work they did in plowing the ground before me, acknowledgment is respectfully due to Robert Welch, V. Orval Watts, Frank Chodorov, John T. Flynn, Frank Holman, G. Edward Griffin, Robert W. Lee, Hilaire du Berrier, and many others. Above all, for herculean efforts in all aspects and stages of the production of this volume, for many sleepless nights and marathon editing sessions, Tom Gow will always have my appreciation.

Lastly, to my wife Carmen and my sons Jonathan and Christopher, who were widowed and orphaned the greater part of 1992, during my travels and periods of seclusion for writing, I am especially indebted for love, encouragement, and understanding.

About the Author

William F. Jasper is senior editor of *The New American* magazine and was a contributing editor to its predecessor, *The Review of the News.* He has written extensively on a wide array of topics, including the European Community, the United Nations, Central America, terrorism, espionage, Soviet disinformation, the new world order, subversive organizations, and abortion.

Mr. Jasper is a widely respected authority on education, immigration, and environmental issues. His articles from the UN Earth Summit in Rio de Janeiro provided some of the most informative and incisive reporting on that event available to American readers. He is in high demand as a speaker on many subjects and is a regular guest on radio and television programs across America.

A native of Idaho and a graduate of the University of Idaho, William Jasper joined The John Birch Society staff in 1976 and served as Director of Research for the West Coast office. He lives in California with his wife Carmen and two sons.